U0081107

抄這本就對了，
關鍵句型實際應用，
參考學測大考例題範文，
英文作文不再困難！

看到英文作文就一個頭兩個大，不知道該怎麼下筆嗎？但先別放棄，英文作文是有訣竅的，掌握寫作重點、使用實用句型，再參照範文練習，就能在英文作文拿高分！

拿高分 Step 1.
掌握各個題型的寫作重點

歷屆試題常見「**經驗敘述類**」、「**人物與物品描述類**」、「**圖表分析類**」、「**連環圖片類**」、「**單張照片類**」、「**書信類**」、「**假設與論述類**」與「**二選一類**」這八大題型，本書帶你一一釐清寫作重點，並提供讓作文更加豐富的簡單方法與練習技巧。

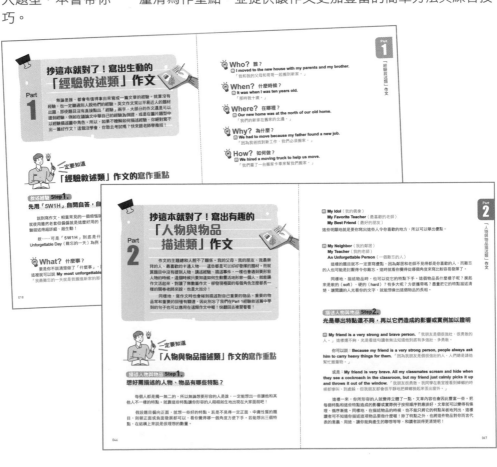

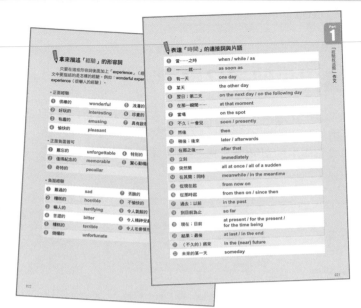
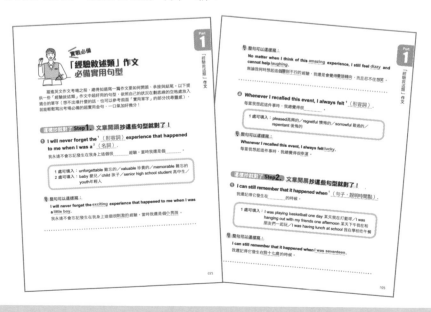

拿高分 Step**4.**

實戰運用這麼做，實用句型超好用

把實用句型背起來還不夠，能實際運用才是真的學會了！因此本書每個題目類型都會提供四篇範文，在範文中使用前面列出的實用句型，成為你寫作時的參考。在參考的時候，也要注意作文開展方式和使用的單字喔！這些單字其實都不難，但還是能夠明確地表達論點。相信你也可以！

大考臨危不亂，
學測指考歷屆試題
實戰驗證

能在考場上把學會的知識發揮出來，才能真的拿高分，因此本書蒐集約十年的學測、指考歷屆試題，再實際套用句型進行示範，並附上貼心叮嚀與說明，幫助大家寫出清楚明確又有個人特色的高分作文。

看國內更要看國外，
特別收錄美國SAT全真模擬試題

本書特別收錄美國高中升大學要考的 SAT 英文作文考題，SAT 的考題多半需要深度思考並闡述論點，對我們來說是更難的挑戰。如果寫不出來也沒關係，可以參考範文是如何在作文中使用實用句型，以及如何用各種方式來表達論點。

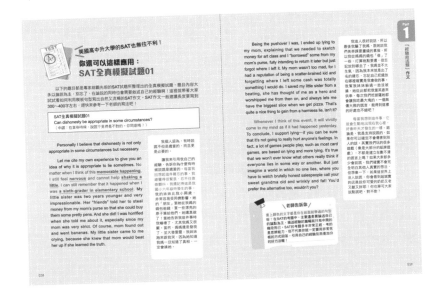

多年來在補習班中教課的經驗中，台灣的學生們在背誦與文意理解方面表現都不差，面對作文時卻經常手足無措，一方面需要釐清想法讓文章結構與論述完整，又要精準運用非母語的語言組織語句，可能會因為一時之間要處理的事情太多而慌了手腳。在這個資訊爆炸、四處充斥著各種意見的時代，擁有屬於自己的清晰思辨能力，並能夠明確地表達是很重要的，而考試的目的正是給予指定情境讓我們加以發揮，如果將每次考試都當成練習的大好機會，那麼學習就不會止步於校園與考試，而是能持續應用、精進，從中訓練起的資訊整合與表達能力，無論是在生活中的意見表達或是上台報告都能有所幫助。同時，結合思辨與文字組織能力的英文寫作，也會在許多不同情境中派上用場。

學好英文寫作絕不只是為了應付考試，以了解國際趨勢為例，舉凡期刊資料、新聞報導甚至是娛樂消息，擁有一定程度的英語閱聽能力，就能讓你掌握最即時的第一手資料；也能直接與國際上的朋友們交流，認識不同文化背景的人看待同一事件的角度，讓你開闊國際視野；現今的職場上外語能力也是不可或缺的硬實力，比起很會答題，聯繫外國客戶、電子郵件往來、撰寫英文介紹以拓展海外市場等等實際應用，才能在工作中真正派上用場。而這些都是具備英語能力才能接觸到的不同可能性，也能為自己未來的職場履歷與人生豐富程度大加分！

因此，本書選擇以最深入淺出的方式，為大家指出英文寫作的一條明路。假如面對英文作文你的試題紙總是一片空白，只要跟隨書中的引導，也能靠著簡單的模板句型，寫出一篇有著起承轉合、言之有物的作文，有了文章的基本架構，在上頭延伸發揮就會輕鬆許多，同時也能確保行文一直與主題緊密貼合，不用再害怕寫出支離破碎、千篇一律的死板文章。對於想要精進自我的

同學們，這本書能夠讓你的作文結構更加紮實，也能使用模板句型為文章帶來畫龍點睛的效果，梳理行文的整體脈絡與用字細節，讓你的作文更接近道地母語使用者！更進一步，本書也提供SAT作文題目與範本，讓你直接挑戰同齡美國高中生所要面對的題目，在長篇論述作文的寫作中，用字精確、文思邏輯的清晰程度與文章結構的完整度都益發重要，也更能檢視自己在寫作時還有哪些細節能夠精益求精！

　　希望同學們能夠將這本書作為一個管道，循序漸進地建構起屬於自己的寫作思維，別擔心起先不上手，語言能力最為有效且唯一的學習方式就是不斷練習，相信在實際操作的過程中，跟著老師一起面對不同題型、使用句型累積多樣內容的寫作經驗，寫作技巧一定會漸漸地變得更加純熟。期許同學們抱持著開放的心持續學習，磨練英語文字溝通能力是相當實用的自我投資，相信這一路上的努力都會在未來有所收穫的！

James

Contents 目錄

Part 4

抄這本就對了！寫出連貫的
「連環圖片類」作文

Part 7

抄這本就對了！寫出有想像力的 「假設與論述類」作文

Part

1

抄這本就對了！
寫出生動的

「經驗敘述類」
作文

抄這本就對了！寫出生動的「經驗敘述類」作文

　　無論是誰，都會有值得拿出來寫成一篇文章的經驗。就算沒有經驗，也一定聽過別人說他們的經驗。英文作文常以平易近人的題材出題，即使題目沒有直接點出「經驗」兩字，大部分的作文還是可以提到經驗，例如在議論文中舉自己的經驗為例證，或是在圖片題型中以經驗描述圖中角色。所以，如果不瞭解如何描述經驗，你絕對寫不出一篇好作文！這個沒學會，你敢去考試嗎？快來跟老師學幾招！

一定要知道

「經驗敘述類」作文的寫作重點

敘述經驗 Step 1.
先用「5W1H」自問自答，自然能回想起經驗中的所有細節

　　說到寫作文，相當常見的一個煩惱就是字數不夠多。沒關係！讓老師來告訴你，就使用雖然老套但偏偏就是這麼好用的「5W1H」，來充實文章的字數，並把這個經驗描述得超詳細、超生動！

　　欸……可是「5W1H」到底是什麼？這樣說很含糊對吧，老師以題目An Unforgettable Day（難忘的一天）為例，教大家怎麼利用「5W1H」進行聯想。

What? 什麼事？
　　要是你不說清楚做了「什麼事」，讀者可搞不清楚你難忘的一天到底在幹嘛。在這裡就可以說 **My most unforgettable day is the day I moved to a new house.**「我最難忘的一天就是我搬進新家的那一天。」

Who? 誰？
例 **I moved to the new house with my parents and my brother.**
「我和我的父母和哥哥一起搬到新家。」

 # When? 什麼時候？
例 **It was when I was ten years old.**
「那時我十歲。」

 # Where? 在哪裡？
例 **Our new home was at the north of our old home.**
「我們的新家在舊家的北邊。」

 # Why? 為什麼？
例 **We had to move because my father found a new job.**
「因為我爸找到新工作，我們必須搬家。」

 # How? 如何做？
例 **We hired a moving truck to help us move.**
「我們雇了一台搬家卡車來幫我們搬家。」

敘述經驗 Step 2. 讓畫面活起來

　　光是只有「什麼時候、做了什麼」等等的事實，只會讓文章看起來像課本一樣都是艱深難記的年代、人名。不想要讀者看作文像看課本一樣痛苦吧？這時候就要回想發生這個經驗時的情形：有什麼特別的地方？為什麼這件事比其他事值得一寫？為什麼這件事會讓你記得這麼久？

　　例如，你可以說 **Because we were moving to another city, I had to say goodbye to my friends. I thought I would never see them again, and it made me very sad. It was raining very hard that day, and we hugged and cried in the rain.** 「因為我們要搬去另一個城市，我得跟我的朋友說再見。我覺得我再也見不到他們了，這讓我很傷心。當天雨下得很大，我們在雨中相擁而泣。」

　　這麼一來，讀者便可以感覺到這件事對你有多重要，甚至感受到冰冷的雨點彷彿就打在身上。有了這樣清楚的畫面，在讀者心中一定會加分。

敘述經驗 Step**3.** 再加上感想

講完發生了什麼事之後就直接結束會太突然，也沒有一個結論。這時就可以加上你的心得感想：這件事讓你感覺如何？發生了這件事後，你的人生有什麼改變？有讓你從此對某些事情改觀嗎？同樣的經驗你還會想要再體驗一次嗎？

例如，你可以說**After this experience, I learned to cherish my friends even more. No matter old friends or new ones, I enjoyed every moment with them, because I can never know when they might be taken from me.**「經過這次經驗，我學會更珍惜我的朋友。無論是舊朋友還是新朋友，我享受和他們在一起的每一刻，因為我永遠不會知道他們何時會與我分開。」

就算題目只叫你描述事情，閱卷老師看到只有敘事而沒有感情的文章，還是會覺得有些機械化、好像少了什麼，而且無法感同身受。用自己的感想收尾，可以讓文章更完整也更生動。

實戰必備

「經驗敘述類」作文必備單字片語

經驗敘述類的作文，多少都一定有以下這些共同點：

> ❶ 講的是「過去已經發生」的事。
> ❷ 需要用一些形容詞來描述這個經驗發生時，帶給你的感覺。

要是不知道如何描述「過去的時間」、或不曉得怎麼描述自己的心情，背了再多句型，作文也是一樣寫不出來。右頁起為大家列出一些寫「經驗敘述類」作文必備的單字與片語！

表達「時間」的連接詞與片語

❶	當……之時	when / while / as
❷	一……就……	as soon as
❸	有一天	one day
❹	某天	the other day
❺	翌日；第二天	on the next day / on the following day
❻	在那一瞬間……	at that moment
❼	當場	on the spot
❽	不久；一會兒	soon / presently
❾	然後	then
❿	稍後；後來	later / afterwards
⓫	在那之後……	after that
⓬	立刻	immediately
⓭	突然間	all at once / all of a sudden
⓮	在其間；同時	meanwhile / in the meantime
⓯	從現在起	from now on
⓰	從那時起	from then on / since then
⓱	過去；以前	in the past
⓲	到目前為止	so far
⓳	現在；目前	at present / for the present / for the time being
⓴	結果；最後	at last / in the end
㉑	（不久的）將來	in the (near) future
㉒	未來的某一天	someday

拿來描述「經驗」的形容詞

　　只要在這些形容詞後面加上「experience」（經驗）這個單字，即可清楚表達作文中要描述的是怎樣的經驗。例如：wonderful experience（很棒的經驗）、terrifying experience（很嚇人的經驗）。

• 正面經驗

❶	很棒的	**wonderful**	❺	浪漫的	**romantic**
❷	好玩的	**interesting**	❻	珍貴的	**valuable**
❸	有趣的	**amusing**	❼	具有啟發性的	**inspiring**
❹	愉快的	**pleasant**			

• 正面負面皆可

❶	難忘的	**unforgettable**	❹	特別的	**unusual**
❷	值得紀念的	**memorable**	❺	驚心動魄的	**thrilling**
❸	奇特的	**peculiar**			

• 負面經驗

❶	難過的	**sad**	❼	丟臉的	**embarrassing**
❷	糟糕的	**horrible**	❽	不愉快的	**unpleasant**
❸	嚇人的	**terrifying**	❾	令人氣餒的	**discouraging**
❹	苦澀的	**bitter**	❿	令人精神受創的	**traumatic**
❺	糟糕的	**terrible**	⓫	令人毛骨悚然的	**hair-raising**
❻	倒楣的	**unfortunate**			

實戰必備

「經驗敘述類」作文
必備實用句型

　　踏進英文作文考場之前，總得知道寫一篇作文要如何開頭、承接與結尾。以下提供一些「經驗敘述類」作文中超好用的句型，依照自己的狀況在劃底線的空格處放入適合的單字（想不出填什麼的話，也可以參考前面「實用單字」的部分找尋靈感），就能輕鬆寫出考場必備的超實用金句，一口氣加好幾分！

這樣抄就對了 Step 1. 文章開頭抄這些句型就對了！

❶ **I will never forget the** [1]（形容詞）**experience that happened to me when I was a** [2]（名詞）**.**

我永遠不會忘記發生在我身上這個很_____經驗。當時我還是個_____。

> **1 處可填入**：unforgettable 難忘的／valuable 珍貴的／memorable 難忘的
> **2 處可填入**：baby 嬰兒／child 孩子／senior high school student 高中生／youth 年輕人

✍ **整句可以這樣寫：**

I will never forget the <u>exciting</u> experience that happened to me when I was a <u>little boy</u>.

我永遠不會忘記發生在我身上這個很**刺激的**經驗。當時我還是個**小男孩**。

❷ I am fond of recalling my past experiences, despite the fact that some of them are delightful or sorrowful. It is an undeniable fact that in the journey of life, we may come across many events, which may be hard to figure out. One of my unforgettable experiences happened in my [1] （名詞）.

我喜歡回想我過去的經驗，無論它們可能會讓我感到開心或難過。不能否認，在人生的旅程中，我們會遇到很多難解的事件。其中有個難忘的經驗發生在我_____的時候。

> **1 處可填入：** childhood 孩童時期／high school days 高中時期

🖐 **整句可以這樣寫：**

I am fond of recalling my past experiences, despite the fact that some of them are delightful or sorrowful. It is an undeniable fact that in the journey of life, we may come across many events, which may be hard to figure out. One of my unforgettable experiences happened in my junior high school days.

我喜歡回想我過去的經驗，無論它們可能會讓我感到開心或難過。不能否認，在人生的旅程中，我們會遇到很多難解的事件。其中有個難忘的經驗發生在我國中時期的時候。

· ·

❸ No matter when I think of this [1] （形容詞） experience, I still feel [2] （形容詞） and cannot help [3] （動詞+ing）.

無論我何時想起這個____經驗，我還是會覺得____，而且忍不住想____。

> **1 處可填入：** horrible 糟糕的／terrible 糟糕的／touching 感人的／sad 難過的
> **2 處可填入：** excited 興奮的／embarrassed 丟臉的／frightened 害怕的
> **3 處可填入：** crying 哭泣／laughing 笑

🖐 **整句可以這樣寫：**

No matter when I think of this <u>amazing</u> experience, I still feel <u>dizzy</u> and cannot help <u>laughing</u>.

無論我何時想起這個<u>讚到不行</u>的經驗，我還是會覺得<u>暈頭轉向</u>，而且忍不住<u>想笑</u>。

· ·

❹ Whenever I recalled this event, I always felt [1] （形容詞）.

每當我想起這件事時，我總覺得很_____。

> **1 處可填入：** pleased 高興的／regretful 懊悔的／sorrowful 難過的／
> repentant 後悔的

🖐 **整句可以這樣寫：**

Whenever I recalled this event, I always felt <u>lucky</u>.

每當我想起這件事時，我總覺得很<u>幸運</u>。

這樣抄就對了 Step 2. 文章開展抄這些句型就對了！

❶ I can still remember that it happened when [1] （句子，說明時間點）.

我還記得它發生在_____的時候。

> **1 處可填入：** I was playing basketball one day 某天我在打籃球／I was
> hanging out with my friends one afternoon 某天下午我在和
> 朋友們一起玩／I was having lunch at school 我在學校吃午餐

🖐 **整句可以這樣寫：**

I can still remember that it happened when <u>I was seventeen</u>.

我還記得它發生在<u>我十七歲</u>的時候。

· ·

❷ The ¹ **（名詞或名詞片語） has always remained crystal clear in my mind.**

這個＿＿＿＿一直清楚地印在我的腦海。

> **1 處可填入：** scene 畫面／image 畫面／memory of that day 那天的記憶

✋ **整句可以這樣寫：**

The <u>look on his face</u> has always remained crystal clear in my mind.
<u>他臉上的表情</u>一直清楚地印在我的腦海。

- -

❸ Whenever I think of this event, it will vividly come to my mind as if it just happened yesterday.

每當我想到這件事，它就會生動地出現在我心裡，好像昨天才發生的一樣。

這樣抄就對了 Step**3.** 結論收尾抄這些句型就對了！

❶ This precious experience has a(n) [1] （形容詞） impact on my life.

這個珍貴的經驗對我的人生有很_____影響。

> **1 處可填入**：great 很大的／everlasting 永久的／strong 強烈的

✋ **整句可以這樣寫：**

The precious experience has a <u>profound</u> impact on my life.

這個珍貴的經驗對我的人生有很**深遠的**影響。

• •

❷ This precious experience has changed my [1] （名詞+介系詞） [2] （名詞）.

這個珍貴的經驗改變了我對_____的_____。

> **1 處可填入**：view on 對……的看法／belief in 對……的信念／
> attitude towards 對……的態度
> **2 處可填入**：life 人生／studying 讀書

✋ **整句可以這樣寫：**

This precious experience has changed my <u>opinion on</u> <u>humans</u>.

這個珍貴的經驗改變了我對**人類**的**看法**。

• •

❸ **From this** [1] （形容詞） **experience, I learned how to** [2] （動詞或動詞片語）. 從這次_____經驗，我學會如何_____。

> 1 處可填入：precious珍貴的／valuable 珍貴的／strange奇怪的
> 2 處可填入：strive for the best 全力求好／focus on my goals 專注追求目標／face the harsh reality 面對殘酷的現實

✋ **整句可以這樣寫：**

From this terrible experience, I learned how to overcome difficulties.
從這次糟糕的經驗，我學會如何解決困難。

⋯⋯⋯⋯⋯⋯⋯⋯⋯⋯⋯⋯⋯⋯⋯⋯⋯⋯⋯⋯⋯⋯⋯⋯⋯⋯

❹ **This is the reason why I will always remember the experience.**
就是因為這樣，我永遠都會記得這個經驗。

⋯⋯⋯⋯⋯⋯⋯⋯⋯⋯⋯⋯⋯⋯⋯⋯⋯⋯⋯⋯⋯⋯⋯⋯⋯⋯

❺ **Would that this had never** [1] （講述「發生」的動詞）**, I would have become a(n)** [2] （形容詞）**person.**
如果這件事沒有_____的話，我可能已經變成一個_____人了。

> 1 處可填入：happened 發生／occurred 發生／taken place 發生
> 2 處可填入：completely different 完全不同的／lazy 懶惰的／
> less happy 沒那麼快樂的

✋ **整句可以這樣寫：**

Would that this had never happened, I would have become a selfish person.
如果這件事沒有發生的話，我可能已經變成一個自私的人了。

⋯⋯⋯⋯⋯⋯⋯⋯⋯⋯⋯⋯⋯⋯⋯⋯⋯⋯⋯⋯⋯⋯⋯⋯⋯⋯

⑥ I would like to ¹ （動詞或動詞片語）**something like this again.**

我想要再次_____像這樣的事情。

> **1 處可填入：** enjoy 享受／witness 目睹／participate in參與

✋ **整句可以這樣寫：**

I would like to underline{experience} **something like this again.**

我想要再次經歷像這樣的事情。

• •

⑦ After that experience, I learned that I should ¹ （動詞片語），
and started paying closer attention to ² （名詞片語）.

經過那次經驗後，我瞭解到我應該要_____，並開始對_____更加留意。

> **1 處可填入：** be a good son當個好兒子／stop being arrogant 不再驕傲／
> take care of myself 照顧自己
> **2 處可填入：** the little details小細節／other people's needs 其他人的需求
> ／my parents' words父母的話

✋ **整句可以這樣寫：**

After that experience, I learned that I should think before I act**, and started
paying closer attention to** people's feelings**.**

經過那次經驗後，我瞭解到我應該要三思而後行，並開始對其他人的感受更加留意。

這樣抄就對了！

示範一：丟臉的經驗

前面我們已經看過了「經驗敘述」題型中超實用的單字片語和句型了！現在就把這些單字與句型組合起來，一篇完整的文章就完成囉！一起來看看幾個例子，都是老師精心為你寫成的高分參考作文喔！注意，裡面套色的地方都是你在前面已經學過的句型。你看，會了這些句型是不是整篇文章就可以完成八成了呢？真的夠實用吧！

An Embarrassing Experience

I will never forget the **embarrassing** experience that happened to me when I was a **junior high school student**. No matter when I think of this **memorable** experience, I still feel **mortified** and cannot help **blushing**.

I can still remember that it happened when **I was in a school play**, and I got a very important role: Romeo in *Romeo and Juliet*. The whole school came to watch our performance. I thought I was very handsome, and tried hard to show off. I tried so hard that I fell off the stage. The crowd burst out laughing. The **sound of their laughter that day** has always remained crystal clear in my mind.

This precious experience has changed my **attitude towards life**. Would that this had never **happened**, I would have become an **arrogant** person. This is the reason why I will always remember the experience.

一次丟臉的經驗

我永遠不會忘記我還是國中生時發生在我身上的丟臉經驗。無論我什麼時候想起這個難忘的經驗，我總是覺得很丟臉，忍不住臉紅。

我還記得這件事是在我演出一齣學校的戲劇時發生的，我拿到一個很重要的角色：《羅密歐與茱麗葉》裡的羅密歐。全校都來看我們的表演。我覺得我超帥，一直拚命表現。我演得太過頭，結果摔下舞台。全場哄堂大笑。他們的笑聲永遠清晰地留在我心中。

這個珍貴的經驗改變了我對人生的看法。如果它沒有發生，我會變成一個驕傲的人。所以，我永遠不會忘記這個經驗。

這樣抄就對了！

★別忘了劃底線處可以依自己的
狀況套入別的單字或片語喔！

示範二：傷心的經驗

　　接下來嘗試寫寫看「傷心的經驗」吧！注意，裡面套色的地方都是你在前面已經學過的句型。你看，會了這些句型是不是整篇文章就可以完成八成了呢？真的夠實用吧！

My Most Unforgettable Experience

I am fond of recalling my past experiences, despite the fact that some of them are delightful or sorrowful. It is an undeniable fact that in the journey of life, we may come across many events, which may be hard to figure out. One of my unforgettable experiences happened in my **junior high school days**. I was on my way to school when I saw it happen. A van lost control and collided with a motorcycle. The female on the motorbike died right away.

Whenever I think of this event, it will vividly come to my mind as if it just happened yesterday. The lady was so young, maybe in her twenties. I could not imagine how her parents, siblings and friends must have felt. This **terrible** experience has an **everlasting** impact on my life. After that experience, I learned that I should **cherish every second**, and started paying closer attention to **where I'm walking**. After all, at any moment, life could end.

我最難忘的一次經驗

　　我喜歡回想我過去的經驗，無論它們可能會讓我感到開心或難過。不能否認的，在人生的旅程中，我們會遇到很多難解的事件。其中有個難忘的經驗發生在我國中的時候。我在去上學的路上看到這件事發生。一輛廂型車失控撞上了一台機車。機車上的女性當場死亡。

　　每當我想到這件事，它就會生動地出現在我心裡，好像昨天才發生的一樣。那位女性還很年輕，大概二十幾歲而已。我很難想像她的父母、兄弟姊妹與朋友的感受。這次可怕的經驗對我的人生有永久的影響。經過那次經驗後，我瞭解到我應該珍惜每一刻，並開始對用路安全更注意。畢竟，人生隨時都有可能結束。

這樣抄就對了！

★別忘了劃底線處可以依自己的狀況套入別的單字或片語喔！

示範三：快樂的經驗

接下來嘗試寫寫看「快樂的經驗」吧！注意，裡面套色的地方都是你在前面已經學過的句型。你看，會了這些句型是不是整篇文章就可以完成一大部分了呢？真的夠實用吧！

An Experience of Helping Others

I always feel very grateful when other people give me a hand. However, a recent experience taught me that helping others can make me very happy too. I can still remember that it happened when **I was walking home from school**. I saw an old lady looking at her phone, frustrated. I walked up to ask her what the matter was. It turned out that the phone was new, and she didn't know how to pick up a call with it.

I quickly helped her pick up her call, and after she finished talking, she turned to me with a huge smile and said I was a sweet girl. **Her genuine smile** has always remained crystal clear in my mind. Whenever I recalled this event, I always felt **warm inside**. I came to understand that happiness consisted in helping people, and I know that in the future I won't hesitate to help someone if I can.

一次幫助別人的經驗

每當其他人幫助我，我總是很感激。不過，最近的一次經驗告訴我，幫助別人也能讓我很開心。我還記得這件事發生在我正在從學校走回家的時候。我看到一位老太太正沮喪地看著自己的手機。我走上前，問她怎麼了。原來她的手機是新的，她不知道怎麼用它來接電話。

我馬上幫她接起了電話，而在她講完電話後，她轉過來給了我一個大大的笑容，説我是個貼心的女孩。她真誠的笑容一直清楚地印在我的腦海。每當我回想起這件事時，我總覺得心裡暖暖的。我瞭解到快樂來自於幫助別人，也知道未來如果有機會，我一定毫不猶豫地上前幫忙。

★別忘了劃底線處可以依自己的
狀況套入別的單字或片語喔！

這樣抄就對了！

示範四：生氣的經驗

接下來嘗試寫寫看「生氣的經驗」吧！注意，裡面套色的地方都是你在前面已經
學過的句型。你看，會了這些句型是不是整篇文章就可以完成一大部分了呢？真的夠
實用吧！

A Fight I've been in

I'm not usually the one to fight. I'm peaceful and gentle, and it takes a lot to make me angry. But last week, I had a fight with my aunt. No matter when I think of this **unforgettable** experience, I still feel **a bit mad** and cannot help **being unhappy**.

What happened was that I came home from school to find my aunt shouting at my grandfather, who was very old and forgetful. And why was she shouting? Because my grandpa didn't remember to pick up a package for her! I was seething. I told my aunt that she had no right to be mad at my grandpa for forgetting such a trivial thing, and her packages were her own responsibility. My aunt, on the other hand, told me that I had no right to talk to her like this, because she was an adult and I was not.

Whenever I think of this event, it will vividly come to my mind as if it just happened yesterday. I believe my aunt is still angry at me, and I don't care. This precious experience has changed my **view on the world**. I used to be an obedient child, but I now know that adults are not always right! If something similar came up again, I would do the same with no regrets.

一次吵架的經驗

我平常不是個愛吵架的人。我為人平靜又溫和，很不容易生氣。但上禮拜我和我的阿姨吵了一架。無論我何時想起這個難忘的經驗，我還是會覺得有點生氣，而且忍不住覺得不開心。

事情是這樣的，我從學校回到家，發現我阿姨正在對我又老又健忘的爺爺大吼大叫。為什麼她要大吼大叫呢？因為我爺爺忘記幫她去拿包裹了！我很火大。我告訴我阿姨，她沒有權利因為這種小事生我爺爺的氣，而且她的包裹是她自己的責任。我阿姨則說我沒有權利這樣說她，因為她是大人，我不是。

每當我想起這次事件，它就會生動地出現在我腦海中，好像昨天才發生的一樣。我阿姨好像還在生我的氣，而我可不在意。這個珍貴的經驗改變了我的世界觀。我以前是個乖小孩，但我現在知道大人不見得永遠都是對的！如果發生什麼類似的事，我還是會做出一樣的回應，絕不後悔。

自我挑戰試試看：
2015年指考作文題目

有了完整的句型模板，現在的你寫起作文絕對無往不利，大考的題目也難不倒你了！現在我們就來使用模板當武器，挑戰歷屆指考與學測中出現過的「經驗敘述」類題型。

2015年指定科目考試英文作文試題

提示：指導別人學習讓他學會一件事物，或是得到別人的指導而自己學會一件事物，都是很好的經驗。請根據你過去幫助別人學習，或得到別人的指導而學會某件事的經驗，寫一篇至少120個單詞的英文作文。文分兩段，第一段說明該次經驗的緣由、內容和過程，第二段說明你對該次經驗的感想。

The apartment complex with an atrium I grew up in used to have lots of kids playing together. Being an introvert, I never dare to think about getting involved in the group. Just when I thought the situation would last forever, things changed. I can still remember that it happened when **a neighbor, Jay, brought his snake board and showcased his well-versed skills.** As I dreamt of trying it out the first time I knew of this sport, I finally plucked up the courage to ask if I could join them. Surprisingly, they'd welcome me with warm greetings. Jay taught me to groove with the snake board and followed the lead of my body. With countless falls and adjustments, I let go of Jay's hands gradually, and the snake board seemed to become part of me. After that day, whenever I was playing snake board, Jay would say I was his most excellent pupil proudly.

我住的那個社區大樓以前有很多小孩會在中庭玩。身為一個內向的人，我從來不敢設想有天能加入他們。正當我以為這樣的狀態會永遠持續下去，事情有了轉機。我還記得那天是其中一個鄰居，阿傑，帶來了他的蛇板並大秀他熟練的技術。因為打從第一次知道這項運動我就很想嘗試看看，我終於鼓起勇氣問了能不能跟他們一起玩。出乎意料地，他們很熱情地歡迎我。阿傑教我要跟隨蛇板的擺動節奏，並順著身體的引領動作。歷經了數不清的跌倒和調整後，我漸漸放開了阿傑的手，而蛇板好像成為了我的一部分。那天

This experience was marvelous, starting with becoming friends with neighbors, requesting a tutorial of a sport I was inexperienced with until I finally mastered it. Would that this had never **occurred**, I would have become a **timid** person. The enormous fears possessed us were being amplified by our mind most of the time. The only way to break it is to face it directly, disassembling them piece by piece and you will find there will always be some solutions. Also, how huge the fulfillments are is way beyond our imagination, for the learners and the instructors both! After this experience, I learned that I should **step out of my comfort zone more often**, and started paying closer attention to **every possible chance**.

以後，每當我在滑蛇板，阿傑總會說我是他的得意門生。

這個經驗棒透了，從和鄰居們成為朋友開始、拜託別人教我一項自己不會的運動，到真正學會它。要是這一切沒有發生，我可能會成為一個膽小的人。大部分時候盤據我們心頭的龐大恐懼都是被自己放大的。唯有直接面對並將它們逐一拆解，你會發現永遠都會有解方的。同時，學會一件事情的成就感遠超我們的想像，對學習者和指導者來說都是！有了這個經驗，我學到了我應該要多多踏出舒適圈，並留意所有可能的機會。

\ 老師告訴你 /

套上顏色的文字都是你在前面就學過的句型喔！這篇題目的主題相對開放，可以選擇自己擅長或是有興趣的領域書寫，也別忘了放入學習過程的具體細節，或是加入有把握的相關專有名詞，讓閱卷老師對你留下深刻印象！

自我挑戰試試看：
2016年學測作文題目

2016年大學學科能力測驗英文作文試題
提示：你認為家裡生活環境的維持應該是誰的責任？請寫一篇短文說明你的看法。文分兩段，第一段說明你對家事該如何分工的看法及理由，第二段舉例說明你家中家事分工的情形，並描述你自己做家事的經驗及感想。

Speaking of housework allocation, while people may declare that it should be a responsibility of the whole family, the truth is it is still carried by the mothers often, even when they also have their own work to do. I believed the chores should be done not only by one member as we all live under the same roof. To be a responsible person, each household member can find some housework they are adept in to handle, or the one that they're not repulsive to, at least. Some may prefer folding the clothes to swiping the floor, and the chores can be shared by cooperation. Furthermore, through teamwork with close communication and interaction, relationships between family members can also be enhanced.

My mom stays at home as a full-time homemaker, taking care of the housework of all kinds. Even though my father and I help with doing the laundry, doing the dishes and taking out the trash, most of her time is occupied by the daily houseworks. But an incident happened on Chinese

談到家事分工，很多人可能會說這該是全家人的責任，但事實上這個負擔還是常常落在媽媽身上，即便她們也有自己的工作要做。我相信當我們都同住在一個屋簷下，家事就不應該都由同一個人完成。作為一個有責任心的人，每個家庭成員都能找些他們擅長、或是至少不那麼討厭的家事來做。比起掃地，有些人可能更喜歡洗碗，家事就能透過分工合作解決。另外，有良好溝通和互動的團隊合作，也能讓家人間的關係變得更好。

我媽是一個全職家庭主婦，打理著家裡大大小小的家事。即便我爸和我會幫忙洗衣服、洗碗和倒垃圾，她大部分的時間還是被日常家事佔滿。但過

New Year changed the circumstances. Whenever I recall this event, I always feel **complicated**. I can still remember that it happened when **I was reuniting with my family at my grandparents'**. "It's so kind of you for helping with these." my aunt said, while I was simply cleaning the plates after the reunion dinner. Suddenly it came to me that mothers like her do all of the chores everyday without any payback, some even suffer from the pressure of society or their in-laws. The only time people wouldn't take these for granted is on Mother's day! The short talk made a great impact on the way I think about housework allocation. After having a discussion with my parents, we formed a consensus: apart from the original responsibilities, my father and I will do all the housework on weekends together, to let my mom have some days off. From this experience, I learned how to **cherish things that may be taken for granted, and express gratitudes by taking actions**.

年時發生的一件事讓情況有了變化。無論何時我想起這件事，我的心情總是很複雜。我還記得它發生在大家回到阿嬤家團聚的時候。「你願意來幫忙真的是太好了。」我的嬸嬸說，而我只是在年夜飯後幫忙洗了碗盤。我忽然意識到媽媽們每天不求任何回報地包辦所有家務，有些人甚至還會受到來自社會或是岳父母的壓力。而人們只有在母親節時才不會認為這一切理所當然！這段短暫的對話對我在家事分配上的想法影響很深。和父母討論過後，我們達成了以下的共識：在原先的責任範圍外，我和我爸會一起負責週末所有的家事，讓我媽好好放假。透過這個經驗，我學到了如何珍惜我們容易忽略的事物，並且透過行動表達感謝。

＼老師告訴你／

套上顏色的文字都是你在前面就學過的句型喔！因為這份考題題目中有規定第一段必須論述對於家事分工的看法，第二段才開始以自身的經驗舉例，所以到了第二段才使用了好用的模板句。想知道像第一段這種屬於「論說」類的作文該怎麼寫的話，就請翻到 Part 7（p.206）看看吧！

美國高中升大學的SAT也無往不利！
你還可以這樣應用：
SAT全真模擬試題01

以下的題目都是專家綜觀先前的SAT試題所整理出的全真模擬試題，題目內容大多以論說為主，別忘了，在論說的同時也會需要敘述自己的經驗啊！這裡就帶著大家試試看如何利用模板句型寫出自然又流暢的SAT作文。SAT作文一般建議長度要寫到300～400字左右，趕快來參考一下老師的寫法吧！

> **SAT全真模擬試題01**
> Can dishonesty be appropriate in some circumstances?
> （中譯：在某些時候，說謊不見得是不對的。你同意嗎？）

Personally I believe that dishonesty is not only appropriate in some circumstances but necessary.

Let me cite my own experience to give you an idea of why it is appropriate to lie sometimes. No matter when I think of this **memorable happening**, I still feel **nervous** and cannot help **shaking a little**. I can still remember that it happened when I was **a sixth-grader in elementary school**. My little sister was two years younger and very impressionable. Her "friends" told her to steal money from my mom's purse so that she could buy them some pretty pens. And she did! I was horrified when she told me about it, especially since my mom was very strict. Of course, mom found out and went bananas. My little sister came to me crying, because she knew that mom would beat her up if she learned the truth.

我個人認為，有時說謊不但是適當的，而且更是必要的。

讓我來引用我自己的經驗，告訴你為什麼有時候說謊是適當的。每當我回想起這件難忘的事，我總覺得很緊張，忍不住微微顫抖。我還記得這是我國小六年級時發生的事。我的妹妹比我小兩歲，非常容易受同儕影響。她的「朋友」要她從我媽的錢包偷錢，買一些漂亮的原子筆給他們。她還真做了！當她告訴我這件事時我嚇壞了，尤其我媽又很嚴。當然，媽媽還是發現了，並大發雷霆。我妹妹跑來跟我哭，因為她知道我媽一旦知道了真相，一定會揍她。

Being the pushover I was, I ended up lying to my mom, explaining that we needed to sketch money for art class and I "borrowed" some from my mom's purse, fully intending to return it later but just forgot where I left it. My mom wasn't too mad, for I had a reputation of being a scatter-brained kid and forgetting where I left some cash was totally something I would do. I saved my little sister from a beating, she has thought of me as a hero and worshipped me from then on, and always lets me have the biggest slice when we get pizza. That's quite a nice thing to gain from a harmless lie, isn't it?

Whenever I think of this event, it will vividly come to my mind as if it had happened yesterday. To conclude, I support lying—if you can be sure that it's not going to really hurt anyone's feelings. In fact, a lot of games people play, such as most card games, are based on lying and more lying. It's true that we won't ever know what others really think if everyone lies in some way or another. But just imagine a world in which no one lies, where you have to watch brutally honest salespeople call your sweet grandma old and wrinkly and fat! You'd prefer the alternative too, wouldn't you?

我這人很好說話，所以最後我騙了我媽，跟她說我們美勞課要畫錢的素描，所以我從媽媽的錢包「借」了一些，打算晚點要還，但忘記放到哪去了。我媽並不太生氣，因為我本來就是出了名的健忘，忘記自己把錢放在哪裡確實是我會做的事。我幫我妹妹躲過一劫沒被揍，她從此都把我當英雄來供奉，每次我們吃披薩她都會讓我吃最大塊的。一個無傷大雅的謊言，能得到這樣的好處也不錯吧？

每當我想到這件事，它就會生動地出現在我心裡，好像昨天才發生的一樣。結論是，我是支持說謊的，如果你可以確定不會傷害到別人的話。其實我們玩的很多遊戲（像是大部分的紙牌遊戲），不都是建立在數不清的謊言上嗎？如果大家都多少會說謊，我們確實不會完全明白其他人真實的想法，但想像一下，如果這世界上沒人說謊，你會看到超誠實的店員說你可愛的奶奶又老又皺又胖耶！你也寧可大家說點謊吧，對不對？

\ 老師告訴你 /

套上顏色的文字都是你在前面就學過的句型喔！在SAT的考題中，主要還是要論述自己的論點為主，描述經驗的篇幅就只有中間的幾段而已。SAT的考題多半非常正經、考的是思辨能力，但不代表你就一定要用非常死板的方式回答，引用自己的經驗反而是加分的好方法喔！

你還可以這樣應用：
SAT全真模擬試題02

SAT全真模擬試題02

Is solitude—spending time alone—necessary for people to achieve their most important goals?

（中譯：擁有一個人獨處的時間，對於達成最重要的目標是必要的嗎？）

Does one need to be alone once in a while in order to achieve something? I would say yes, a hundred times yes. Don't get me wrong, I'm not advocating that working together with others actually hinders work progress (it doesn't), I just mean that everyone needs some time alone. Let's say, for example, that you're doing a job that requires a lot of your attention. But you aren't alone—around you are your friend Joey who believes blasting loud music helps him work faster, your classmate Linda who leaves her cat on your desk and assures you that he's very quiet and won't bother you (he is chewing on your hair at the moment) and your elderly teacher who wants to discuss profound principles of the universe with you. Can you work like that? Absolutely not!

And that's just a general example. Let's say you're trying to brainstorm, to think. All those little cells and neurons in your head are trying to form a connection with each other, to create new ideas. But you keep getting interrupted because your

一個人是否需要偶爾獨處以達成目標呢？我覺得需要，真的超級需要。別誤會，我不是説和其他人一起工作會讓效率變差（並不會），我只是説任何人都會需要一點獨處的時間。舉例來説，如果你正在做一個需要高度專注的工作，但你並不是一個人，你四周有你那自認放很吵的音樂能提高工作效率的朋友喬伊、把自家的貓放在你桌上還跟你説牠很安靜不會吵你（同時牠正在嚙你頭髮）的同學琳達、以及很想跟你討論宇宙奧祕的年長老師。這樣你能工作嗎？怎麼可能啊！

這也只是個比較概括的例子。假設你想要腦力激盪、想點事情好了。你腦中的所有細胞和神經元都在努力形成連結，以創造新的點子。但你一直

friends keep messaging you every 0.2 seconds. You would be working for two hours and ending up with zero ideas. Or, let's say your idea of an "important goal" is to write an epic novel. But you don't want others to see it before it's finished because you're shy. How do you expect to work on your masterpiece if you never get any solitude?

That's, in fact, what happened to me once. Whenever I recalled this event, I always felt **really mortified**. I can still remember that it happened when I was **a junior high school student**. I never had any time for myself at home, so I tried to write my novel at school during breaks. But my classmates soon saw what I was doing, and they snatched the notebook out of my hands and read my work out loud! It was terrifying. From this **embarrassing** experience, I learned how to **be more careful**, and now I know that if I want to achieve anything worthwhile I have to be left alone!

被打斷,因為你朋友每隔 0.2秒就會傳訊息給你。 結果你工作了兩個小時, 還是想不出任何點子。或 者,假設你的「重要目 標」指的是寫一本超偉大 的小說,可是你不想要在 完成前給其他人看到,因 為你很害羞。如果你都沒 機會獨處,你要怎麼完成 你的傑作?

這正是一件曾發生在 我身上的事。每當我回想 起這件事,我總會覺得超 級丟臉。我還記得事情發 生時,我是個國中生。我 在家從來沒有時間獨處, 所以我便在學校下課的時 候寫作。但我的同學們 很快地發現我在做的事, 於是他們把筆記本從我手 中奪走,還把我的作品大 聲唸出來。那真是太可怕 了。從這次難堪的經驗, 我瞭解到我必須更小心, 而且我也瞭解到,如果我 想要達成任何有意義的事 情,就一定得獨處才行!

\ 老師告訴你 /

套上顏色的文字都是前面就學過的句型喔! 這篇作文一直到最後一段才引用自己的經 驗,不過你也可以考慮試試看作文一開始就 開門見山地舉出自己的例子,以印證自己的 看法,也有讓人更印象深刻的效果喔!

讀完了這麼多的範例作文，現在你一定已經躍躍欲試，想套用模板句型自己寫寫看了吧！請你以「**一次難忘的生日**」（**An Unforgettable Birthday**）為題，套用模板句型寫一篇作文。所有的句型都在框框中為你列出來囉！

文章開頭參考句型

(1) I will never forget the [1]（形容詞）experience that happened to me when I was a [2]（名詞）.

(2) I am fond of recalling my past experiences, despite the fact that some of them are delightful or sorrowful. It is an undeniable fact that in the journey of life, we may come across many events, which may be hard to figure out. One of my unforgettable experiences happened in my [1]（名詞）.

(3) No matter when I think of this [1]（形容詞）experience, I still feel [2]（形容詞）and cannot help [3]（動詞+ing）.

(4) Whenever I recalled this event, I always felt [1]（形容詞）.

文章開展參考句型

(1) I can still remember that it happened when [1]（句子，說明時間點）.

(2) The [1]（名詞或名詞片語）has always remained crystal clear in my mind.

(3) Whenever I think of this event, it will vividly come to my mind as if it just happened yesterday.

Part
2

抄這本就對了！
寫出有趣的

「人物與物品
描述類」作文

抄這本就對了！寫出有趣的「人物與物品描述類」作文

　　作文的主題總和人脫不了關係。我的父母、我的朋友、我最崇拜的人、最喜歡的卡通人物⋯⋯這些都是可以好好發揮的題材。而就算題目中沒有提到人物，講述經驗、描述事件，一樣也會遇到要形容人物的時候。這個時候只要知道如何生動靈活地形容一個人，就能讓作文活起來，對讀了無數篇作文、卻發現裡面的每個角色怎麼都長一樣的閱卷老師來說，也是大加分！

　　同樣地，寫作文時也會碰到描述對自己重要的物品。重要的物品常和重要的回憶有關連，因此別忘了我們在Part 1經驗敘述篇中學到的句子也可以應用在這類作文中喔！快翻回去複習看看！

一定要知道「人物與物品描述類」作文的寫作重點

描述人物與物品 Step 1.
想好需描述的人物、物品有哪些特點？

　　每個人都是獨一無二的，所以無論想要形容的人是誰，一定能想出一些讓他和其他人不一樣的特點。就靠這些特點讓你形容的人栩栩如生地出現在大家面前吧！

　　假設題目偏向正面，就想一些好的特點。若是不見得一定正面、中庸性質的題目，則朝正面或負面發展都可以，看你覺得哪一個角度方便下手。若能想出三個特點，在結構上來說是很理想的數量。

例 **My Idol**（我的偶像）
My Favorite Teacher（最喜歡的老師）
My Best Friend（最好的朋友）

　　這些明顯地就是要你寫出這些人令你喜歡的地方，所以可以舉出優點。

例 **My Neighbor**（我的鄰居）
My Teacher（我的老師）
An Unforgettable Person（一個難忘的人）

　　這樣的題目就不一定要寫優點，因為鄰居和老師不見得都是你喜歡的人，而難忘的人也可能是討厭得令你難忘。這時就看你覺得從哪個角度來寫比較容易發揮了。

　　同樣地，描述物品時，也可以從它的特點下手。這個物品長什麼樣子呢？摸起來是軟的（soft）、硬的（hard）？有多大呢？方便攜帶嗎？盡量把它的特點描述清楚，讓閱讀的人光看你的文字，就能想像出這個物品的長相。

描述人物與物品 Step 2.

光是舉出特點還不夠，再以它們造成的影響或實例加以證明

例 **My friend is a very strong and brave person.**「我朋友是個很強壯、很勇敢的人。」這樣還不夠，光是看這句讀者無法知道他到底有多強壯、多勇敢。

　　你可以說：**Because my friend is a very strong person, people always ask him to carry heavy things for them.**「因為我朋友是個很強壯的人，人們總是請他幫忙搬重物。」

　　或是：**My friend is very brave. All my classmates scream and hide when they see a cockroach in the classroom, but my friend just calmly picks it up and throws it out of the window.**「我朋友很勇敢。我同學在教室裡看到蟑螂的時候都慘叫、到處躲，但我朋友都會很平靜地把蟑螂撿起來丟出窗外。」

　　這樣一來，你所形容的人就變得立體了一點，文章內容也會因此豐富一些。把每個特點和這些特點造成的影響或實際例子按照順序對應排好，文章就可以變得有條理、循序漸進。同樣地，在描述物品的時候，也不能只將它的特點呆板地列出，這樣讀者可不知道你描述這項物品要做什麼喔！除了特點之外，也將這件物品對你而言代表的意義、用途、讓你能夠產生的聯想等等，和讀者說得更清楚吧！

描述人物與物品 Step3. 光是說完特點就結束也不行，再加上結論，文章看起來更完整

　　以上所敘述的這個人的特點，讓你有什麼想法？你也想要擁有這些特點嗎？還是完全不想要呢？你會希望身邊有更多人有這些特點嗎？你會希望這個人繼續保持這些特點，還是最好不要呢？這個人的特點改變了你的人生嗎？將自己的感想寫出來，為文章做個收尾吧！同樣地，在描述物品後，也可以說明這個物品對你的重要性、對你的生活產生什麼影響……等等。像是如果最後來一句**「Without this object, my life would be so much more boring!」**（要是沒有這個東西，我的生活一定超無聊的！），就是個清楚表達這項物品重要性的結論。

「人物與物品描述類」作文必備單字片語

　　要讓你所敘述的人物、物品「活過來」，你就一定需要形容詞，而且是大量的形容詞！這裡為大家整理出描述人的外表、個性、儀態等等的形容詞或片語，並加上一些生動的動詞，在文章中使用，絕對能讓整篇內容畫龍點睛。此外，也提供一些描述物品外型的簡單形容詞，請把它大膽地活用在文章中吧！

描述「人的外表」，可以用這些字詞

❶	近視眼的	**near-sighted**
❷	戴眼鏡的	**wearing glasses**
❸	身材很高的	**tall in stature**
❹	身材很矮的	**short in stature**
❺	六呎高	**six feet tall**
❻	胖的	**heavy / fat**

⑦	圓胖的	chubby
⑧	矮矮壯壯的	chunky
⑨	粗壯的	stout
⑩	結實的	stocky
⑪	健壯的	robust
⑫	留短髮的	wearing short hair
⑬	留長髮的	long-haired
⑭	留平頭的	wearing a crew cut
⑮	留辮子的	wearing braids
⑯	擁有運動員的體格	have an athletic build
⑰	憔悴的	wan and sallow
⑱	骨瘦如柴的	all skins and bones
⑲	苗條的	slender
⑳	硬朗的	virile
㉑	結實的	solid
㉒	面黃肌瘦的	sallow
㉓	弱不禁風的	too frail to stand a gust of wind
㉔	體格	constitution
㉕	強健的	with a strong constitution
㉖	彪形大漢	burly chap
㉗	老當益壯的	old but vigorous
㉘	身高	height
㉙	體重	weight
㉚	優雅的	graceful
㉛	矮小的	diminutive
㉜	瘦小的	slight of figure
㉝	豐滿的	round out / plump
㉞	鬢髮	hair on the temples
㉟	柳腰	small waist
㊱	過胖的	obese

㊲	有肚子的	big-bellied
㊳	臃腫的	encumbered
㊴	枯瘦的	gaunt
㊵	衰弱的	emaciated
㊶	柔弱的	delicate
㊷	虛弱的	debilitated
㊸	有氣無力的	feeble
㊹	有活力的	vigorous

 描述「人的個性」，可以用這些字詞

❶	性急的	hot-tempered
❷	樂觀的	optimistic
❸	悲觀的	pessimistic
❹	體貼的	considerate
❺	小心眼的	narrow-minded
❻	思想開放的	open-minded
❼	外向的	extroverted
❽	內向的	introverted
❾	好問的	inquisitive
❿	好辯的	argumentative
⓫	頑固的	stubborn
⓬	無私心的	fair-minded

 描述「人的儀態與給人的感受」，可以用這些字詞

❶	存在感	presence
❷	儀表	appearance
❸	容貌	looks

④	舉止	bearing
⑤	賞心悅目的	pleasing to the eye
⑥	婀娜的	supple and graceful
⑦	高雅的	graceful
⑧	膚色	complexion
⑨	國色天香的	surpassing beauty
⑩	小巧玲瓏的	small and exquisite
⑪	其貌不揚的	undistinguished appearance
⑫	面目可憎的	repulsive in appearance
⑬	化妝化太濃的	heavily made-up
⑭	齜牙咧嘴	fierce-looking
⑮	鬼鬼祟祟的	thievish-looking
⑯	蓬頭垢面的	unkempt and untidy
⑰	尖嘴猴腮的	have a wretched appearance
⑱	眼睛發亮的	bright-eyed

 描述「家庭」，可以用這些字詞（因描述人物的作文常會提到家人）

❶	小家庭	a small family
❷	大家庭	a big family
❸	核心家庭	a nuclear family
❹	小康家庭	a middle-class family

 描述「身體狀態」，可以用這些字詞

❶	生病	be ill
❷	痼疾	obstinate illness
❸	染病	be infected with
❹	奄奄一息	at one's last gasp

❺	發病	come down with illness
❻	危在旦夕	on the verge of death
❼	臥病在床	bedridden
❽	九死一生	a narrow escape from death
❾	垂危	in dire danger
❿	絕症	incurable disease
⓫	病癒	recover from an illness
⓬	復原	rally from (an illness)
⓭	保養	take good care of oneself
⓮	療養	recuperate
⓯	積勞成疾	fall ill from constant overwork

 想要生動描述「眼睛與臉部動作」，可以用這些字詞

❶	垂頭	hang one's head
❷	抬頭	raise one's head
❸	拋媚眼	make eyes at
❹	仰望	look up at
❺	瞥視	glance at
❻	睜眼	open one's eyes
❼	瞪眼	glower at
❽	闔眼	shut eye
❾	遠眺	overlook
❿	凝視	fix one's eyes on / gaze at
⓫	掃視	glance around
⓬	在眾目睽睽之下	under the watchful eyes of the people
⓭	刮目相看	look at sb. with new eyes
⓮	偷看	peek
⓯	瞇著眼睛	narrow one's eyes

⑯ 眨眼	blink one's eyes
⑰ 目擊	witness
⑱ 注視	look at
⑲ 怒視	glare at
⑳ 回眸	glance back
㉑ 眨眼示意	wink at

 描述「物品的形貌」，可以用這些字詞

❶ 大的	big / large / huge / enormous
❷ 小的	small / tiny / little
❸ 重的	heavy
❹ 輕的	light
❺ 厚的	thick
❻ 薄的	thin
❼ 方形的	square-shaped
❽ 三角形的	triangle-shaped
❾ 長方形的	rectangle-shaped
❿ 圓形的	round
⓫ 軟的	soft
⓬ 硬的	hard
⓭ 溫暖的	warm
⓮ 冰涼的	cold / icy

「人物與物品描述類」作文 必備實用句型

　　踏進英文作文考場之前，總得知道寫一篇作文要如何開頭、承接與結尾。以下提供一些「人物與物品描述類」作文中超好用的句型，依照自己的狀況在劃底線的空格處放入適合的單字（想不出填什麼的話，也可以參考前面「實用單字」的部分找尋靈感），就能輕鬆寫出考場必備的超實用金句，一口氣加好幾分！

這樣抄就對了 Step1. 文章開頭抄這些句型就對了！

❶ **Because of** [1] （名詞或名詞片語）**, and because of** [2] （名詞或名詞片語）**,** （某人） **is the person I** [3] （動詞） **the most.**

因為_____和_____，_____是我最_____的人。

> **1 處可填入：**her good looks 她的美貌／her lovely voice 她悅耳的聲音／
> his amazing personality 他極好的個性
> **2 處可填入：**her passion for art 她對藝術的愛好／
> his athletic build 他運動員的體格／his cute smile 他可愛的笑容
> **3 處可填入：**admire 欣賞／love 愛／hate 討厭

👆 **整句可以這樣寫：**

Because of his guitar skills**, and because of** his great singing**,** this singer **is the person I** admire **the most.**

因為他的吉他技巧和厲害的歌喉，這位歌手是我最欣賞的人。

❷ As everyone knows, （某人） is famous as [1] （名詞，身分）. However, as （某人）'s [2] （名詞，身分）, I like him/her more because of [3] （名詞或名詞片語）.

如大家所知，＿＿＿以身為＿＿＿聞名。但是，身為＿＿＿的＿＿＿，＿＿＿才是我仰慕他的真正原因。

> **1 處可填入：** a great football star 厲害的足球明星／a talented singer 天才歌手／the proud winner of two Oscars 兩次奧斯卡獎獲獎人
>
> **2 處可填入：** close friend 好朋友／diehard fan 超級粉絲
>
> **3 處可填入：** the story behind her success 她的成功背後的故事／her sincerity 她的真誠

整句可以這樣寫：

As everyone knows, Leo is famous as a very talented actor. However, as Leo's number one fan, I like him more because of his friendly personality.

如大家所知，李奧以身為極有天賦的演員聞名。但是，身為他的頭號粉絲，他友善的個性才是我仰慕他的真正原因。

❸ Well goes an old saying, "[1] （名言）". We can tell how true this is from [2] （名詞或名詞片語）.

俗話說得好：＿＿＿＿。這句話的真實性可以從＿＿＿＿得證。

> **1 處可填入：** When there's a will, there's a way 有志者事竟成／Haste makes waste 欲速則不達
>
> **2 處可填入：** our interactions with people 我們與他人的互動／our experiences with our teachers 我們與老師相處的經驗

Well goes an old saying, "birds of a feather flock together". We can tell how true this is from our friendships.

俗話說得好：物以類聚。這句話的真實性可以從我們的交情中得證。

• •

❹ **When it comes to** [1] （複數名詞，身分）**,**（某人）**is definitely the first one that comes to my mind.**

說到_____，_____一定是我第一個想到的。

> **1 處可填入**：artists 藝術家／basketball players 籃球員／dancers 舞蹈家

When it comes to actors, Jet Li is definitely the first one that comes to my mind.

說到演員，李連杰一定是我第一個想到的。

• •

❺ **It is no secret that I consider** （某人）[1]（名詞）**.**

我把_____當作_____，這已經不是秘密了。

> **1 處可填入**：my favorite person 我最喜歡的人／
> the best singer 最強的歌手／my idol我的偶像

It is no secret that I consider John my best friend.

我把約翰當作我最好的朋友，這已經不是秘密了。

• •

⑥ My favorite [1]（名詞）**is my** [2]（名詞）**, which is** [3]（顏色）, [4]（形容詞）**and** [5]（形容詞）**.**

我最喜歡的_____是我的_____，它是_____的、_____的、_____的。

> **1 處可填入**：gift 禮物／furniture 家具／room 房間
> **2 處可填入**：bed 床／photo album 相簿／teddy bear 泰迪熊
> **3 處可填入**：red 紅色的／brown 棕色的／green 綠色的
> **4~5 處可填入**：furry 毛毛的／heavy 重的／large 很大的

🖐 **整句可以這樣寫：**

My favorite toy is my stuffed rabbit, which is pink, small and soft.
我最喜歡的玩具是我的絨毛兔子娃娃，它是粉紅色的、小小的、軟軟的。

· ·

❼ I received my [1]（名詞）**when I was** [2]（年紀）**.**

我是在我_____的時候得到我的_____。

> **1 處可填入**：book 書／radio 收音機／piano 鋼琴
> **2 處可填入**：four 四歲／a kid 孩子／in kindergarten 幼稚園時

🖐 **整句可以這樣寫：**

I received my toy car when I was three.
我是在我三歲的時候得到我的玩具車。

❶ I [1]（動詞）（某人）**for many reasons. First of all,** [2]（句子）**.**
Secondly, [3]（句子）**. Last but not least,** [4]（句子）**.**

我_____ _____有很多原因。首先，_____。然後，
_____。最後（但同樣重要的是），_____。

> **1 處可填入**：love 愛／admire 欣賞／don't like 不喜歡
> **2~4 處可填入**：she's very nice 她人很好／he's never around 他總是不在／
> she's quite strong 她很強壯

✋ **整句可以這樣寫：**

I don't like her **for many reasons. First of all,** she's very vain. **Secondly,**
she's always bullying people. **Last but not least,** she kicks puppies.

我不喜歡 她有很多原因。首先，她很虛榮。然後，她每次都在霸凌別人。最後
（但同樣重要的是），她會踢小狗。

··

❷ **After experiencing** [1]（名詞或名詞片語，不好的事），（某人）
didn't give way to the cruel destiny; instead,（某人）**still**
held a [2]（形容詞，正面的）**attitude towards** [3]（名詞或名詞片
語）**.**

在經歷了_____之後，_____不但沒有一蹶不振，反而依舊對_____抱持著
_____的態度。

> **1 處可填入**：such a failure 如此的失敗／painful surgeries 痛苦的手術／
> multiple setbacks 許多的阻礙
> **2 處可填入**：positive 正面的／determined 有決心的
> **3 處可填入**：life 生命的／her games 她的比賽／her work 她的工作

👆 **整句可以這樣寫：**

After experiencing <u>the loss of his mentor,</u> <u>Rob</u> didn't give way to the cruel destiny; instead, <u>he</u> still held a <u>bright</u> attitude towards <u>the future</u>.

在經歷了**失去良師的痛苦**後，**羅伯**不但沒有一蹶不振，反而依舊對<u>未來</u>抱持著<u>光明</u>的態度。

---

❸ **Although** （某人） **is** [1] （形容詞）, **he/she still holds a** [2] （形容詞） **attitude in dealing with people and his/her work.**

雖然_____ _____，他還是帶著_____的態度來面對其他人，以及他的工作。

> **1 處可填入：** successful 成功的／talented 天賦異稟的／beautiful 美麗的
> **2 處可填入：** modest and polite 謙虛有禮的／responsible 負責任的

👆 **整句可以這樣寫：**

Although <u>Scarlet</u> is <u>young and famous</u>, she still holds a <u>professional</u> attitude in dealing with people and her work.

雖然**史嘉蕾** **年輕又有名**，她還是帶著**專業的**態度來面對其他人，以及她的工作。

---

❹ （某人） **may look** [1] （形容詞）, **but he/she is actually a very** [2] （形容詞） **person.**

也許看起來_____，但他其實是個很_____的人。

> **1 處可填入：** weak 虛弱的／stupid 愚笨的／mean 兇惡的
> **2 處可填入：** strong 強壯的／clever 聰明的／nice 友善的

👆 **整句可以這樣寫：**

<u>Alice</u> may look <u>friendly</u>, but she is actually a very <u>spiteful</u> person.

愛麗絲雖然看起來**友善**，但她其實是個**個性惡劣**的人。

❺ ＿＿＿＿（某人）**is the prime example of a** [1]（名詞）**.**

＿＿＿是＿＿＿最好的例子。

> **1 處可填入**：saint 聖人／crybaby 愛哭鬼／snitch 愛打小報告的人

✋ **整句可以這樣寫：**

Benny is the prime example of a coward.

班尼是膽小鬼最好的例子。

---

❻ **When I look at my** [1]（名詞）**, I always feel** [2]（形容詞）**and** [3]（形容詞）**.**

每當我看到我的＿＿＿，我總會覺得＿＿＿又＿＿＿。

> **1 處可填入**：sketchbook 素描本／painting 畫／toy dog 玩具狗
> **2~3 處可填入**：happy 快樂的／excited 興奮的／nostalgic 懷舊的

✋ **整句可以這樣寫：**

When I look at my toy soldiers, I always feel content and safe.

每當我看到我的玩具士兵，我總會覺得安心又安全。

---

❼ **My** [1]（名詞）**bring(s) me back to my** [2]（時間）**days.**

我的＿＿＿總能把我帶回那段＿＿＿時光。

> **1 處可填入**：photos 照片／posters 海報／dress 洋裝
> **2 處可填入**：childhood 兒童／elementary school 國小

✋ **整句可以這樣寫：**

My doll brings me back to my childhood days.

我的娃娃總能把我帶回那段孩童時光。

這樣抄就對了 Step3.　結論收尾抄這些句型就對了！

❶ It is because of his/her [1] **（名詞） that （某人） is depicted as** [2] **（名詞）. Indeed, （某人） is an excellent example for** [3] **（名詞，某類人） to follow.**

正因＿＿＿，＿＿＿被描述為＿＿＿。的確，＿＿＿是＿＿＿的絕佳典範。

> **1 處可填入**：amazing performance 驚人的表現／great personality 極好的個性／remarkable achievements 極佳的成就
> **2 處可填入**：a modern hero 現代的英雄／the Glory of the country 國家之光
> **3 處可填入**：us 我們／teenagers 十幾歲的年輕人／students 學生

整句可以這樣寫：

It is because of his brave deeds that the man is depicted as a hero of the nation. Indeed, he is an excellent example for everyone to follow.

正因為他勇敢的表現，這個男人被描述為本國的英雄。的確，他是所有人的絕佳典範。

- -

❷ Some people may think that （某人） is [1] **（形容詞）, but I don't think so at all.**

有些人認為＿＿＿很＿＿＿，但我一點都不這麼覺得。。

> **1 處可填入**：lazy 懶惰的／indifferent 冷漠的

整句可以這樣寫：

Some people may think that Joe is dull, but I don't think so at all.

有些人認為喬很遲鈍，但我一點都不這麼覺得。

- -

❸ From （某人） I learned to [1] **（動詞或動詞片語）.**

我從＿＿＿身上學到如何＿＿＿＿＿。

1 處可填入：work hard towards my goals 朝著我的目標努力／
be a considerate person 成為一個體貼的人

✋ **整句可以這樣寫：**

From my mom **I learned to** be strong and independent.

我從**媽媽**身上學到如何**成為一個堅強而獨立的人**。

❹ **This is why I find** （某人） **my** [1] （名詞或名詞片語，身分）**.**

這就是為什麼我覺得_____是我的_____。

1 處可填入：favorite actor 最喜歡的演員／idol 偶像

✋ **整句可以這樣寫：**

This is why I find Chris **my** favorite person in the world.

這就是為什麼我覺得**克里斯**是**我全世界最喜歡的人**。

❺ **It is undeniable that** （某人） **has a huge influence on the way I** [1] （動詞）**. I'm very glad that I have the chance to get to know such a(n)** [2] （形容詞） **person.**

毋庸置疑地，_____對我_____的方式有很大的影響。我很高興我有機會認識這麼_____的人。

1 處可填入：treat others 對待他人／view life 看待人生
2 處可填入：wonderful 很棒的／inspiring 啟發性的

✋ **整句可以這樣寫：**

It is undeniable that my teacher **has a huge influence on the way I** strive towards my goals. **I'm very glad that I have the chance to get to know such an** amazing **person.**

毋庸置疑地，**我的老師**對我**朝著目標努力**的方式有很大的影響。我很高興我有機會認識這麼**棒**的人。

❻ Personally, I think ＿＿＿（某人）**is a modern day** [1]（已過世的名人名字）**!** 我個人認為，＿＿＿是現代的＿＿＿。

> **1 處可填入：** Mother Teresa 泰瑞莎修女／Beethoven 貝多芬

✋ **整句可以這樣寫：**

Personally, I think <u>my brother</u> **is a modern day** <u>Albert Einstein</u>**!**

我個人認為，**我弟弟**是現代的**愛因斯坦**。

- -

❼ While most people focus their attention on [1]（名詞或名詞片語，複數）**, they often forget that they should cherish small things like** [2]（名詞或名詞片語，複數）**.**

許多人都專注於＿＿＿，但他們卻常忘了要珍惜像是＿＿＿這樣的小東西。

> **1 處可填入：** expensive things 昂貴的物品／brandname products 名牌產品
> **2 處可填入：** gifts 禮物／handmade items 手工藝品

✋ **整句可以這樣寫：**

While most people focus their attention on <u>famous brands</u>**, they often forget that they should cherish small things like** <u>presents from their family</u>**.**

許多人都專注於**名牌**，但他們卻常忘了要珍惜像是**家人給的禮物**這樣的小東西。

- -

❽ Nothing can replace the good memories my [1]（名詞）**bring(s) me .** 沒有什麼能取代我的＿＿＿帶給我的美好回憶。

> **1 處可填入：** diary 日記／DVDs 光碟

✋ **整句可以這樣寫：**

Nothing can replace the good memories my <u>books</u> **bring me.**

沒有什麼能取代我的**書**帶給我的美好回憶。

這樣抄就對了！
示範一：親愛的人物

前面我們已經看過了「人物與物品描述」題型中超實用的單字片語和句型了！現在就把這些單字與句型組合起來，一篇完整的文章就完成囉！一起來看看幾個例子，都是老師精心為你寫成的高分參考作文喔！注意，裡面套色的地方都是你在前面已經學過的句型。你看，會了這些句型是不是整篇文章就可以完成八成了呢？真的夠實用吧！

My Idol

Because of her **gentle yet strong personality**, and because of **her kindness to everyone**, **my mother** is the person I **admire** the most. It is no secret that I consider **her my idol**.

I **love my mother** for many reasons. First of all, **she is always patient with me and is a good listener**. Secondly, **she is happy to help strangers she meets**. Last but not least, **she is willing to deal with difficult people, such as my grandma**.

After experiencing **a lot of problems with grandma**, **my mom** didn't give way to the cruel destiny; instead, she still held a **positive** attitude towards **life**. She is still nice to grandma so as to ensure peace in the family, but she doesn't let her walk all over her. Some people may think that **my mom** is **weak**, but I don't think so at all. To me she is the strongest woman in the world.

我的偶像

因為她溫柔而堅強的個性、和她對所有人都很親切，我的媽媽是我最欣賞的一個人。我把她當作我的偶像，這已經不是秘密了。

我愛我媽媽有很多原因。首先，她總是對我很有耐心，也是個很好的聆聽者。第二，她很樂意幫助她遇到的陌生人。最後（但同樣重要的是），她願意對付麻煩人物，例如我奶奶。

在經歷了與我奶奶的很多問題之後，我媽媽不但沒有一蹶不振，反而還是對人生抱持著樂觀的態度。她還是對奶奶很好，以維持家裡的和平，但她也不會完全順著奶奶。有些人認為我媽媽很柔弱，但我一點都不覺得。對我來說，她是全世界最堅強的女人。

★別忘了劃底線處可以依自己的
狀況套入別的單字或片語喔！

這樣抄就對了！

示範二：討厭的人物

接下來嘗試寫寫看「討厭的人物」吧！注意，裡面套色的地方都是你在前面已經學過的句型。你看，會了這些句型是不是整篇文章就可以完成八成了呢？真的夠實用吧！

My Neighbor

Well goes an old saying, "**A hedge between makes friendship green**." We can tell how true this is from **our experiences of interacting with our next door neighbors**. When it comes to **memorable next door neighbors**, **Mrs. Lee** is definitely the first one that comes to my mind.

Mrs. Lee may look **kind**, but she is actually a very **violent** person. She beats up all the stray dogs she sees with a broom. When she sees a spider in her garden, she lights it on fire! However, when she talks to others, she pretends to be a nice old lady who can't stand seeing animals get hurt. Therefore, some people may think that **Mrs. Lee** is **very sweet**, but I don't think so at all. From **Mrs. Lee** I learned to **not trust people so easily**, because they might not always be what they pretend to be!

我的鄰居

俗話說得好：「籬笆築得牢，人就處得好」。這句話的真實性可以從我們和隔壁鄰居相處的經驗得證。說到令人印象深刻的隔壁鄰居，李太太一定是我第一個想到的。

李太太看起來似乎很親切，但她其實是個暴力的人。她看到流浪狗就拿掃把打；如果在院子裡看到蜘蛛，她會點火燒牠！然而，當她和別人交談時，她都假裝自己是個和藹的老太太，不忍看到動物受傷。所以，有些人認為李太太是個善良的人，但我一點都不這麼覺得。從李太太身上，我學到不要隨便信任人，因為他們不見得是外表看起來的那個樣子！

★別忘了劃底線處可以依自己的狀況套入別的單字或片語喔！

這樣抄就對了！

示範三：珍貴的物品

接下來嘗試寫寫看「珍貴的物品」吧！注意，裡面套色的地方都是你在前面已經學過的句型。你看，會了這些句型是不是整篇文章就可以完成一大部分了呢？真的夠實用吧！

A Toy that is Important to Me

My favorite **toy** is my **stuffed bunny**, which is **yellow**, **small** and **soft**. It is very old and the color is faded now, but I still cherish it because it is a gift from my grandmother.

I received my **bunny** when I was **three**. My grandmother gave it to me for my birthday. I considered it my best friend and brought it with me everywhere. We even slept together and ate together! I would have brought it to school too, but my mom wouldn't hear of it of course!

When I look at my **bunny**, I always feel **peaceful** and **happy**. I suppose I can say that my **bunny** brings me back to my **carefree childhood days**. I think I will keep it with me even when I become an adult and leave home.

一個對我來說很重要的玩具

我最喜歡的一個玩具是我的絨毛兔子，它是黃色的、小小軟軟的。它現在已經很舊了，顏色也褪色了，但我還是很珍惜它，因為它是我奶奶給的禮物。

我是在我三歲的時候得到這隻兔子。我奶奶把它送給我當生日禮物。我把它當作我最好的朋友，去哪裡都帶著。我們甚至都一起睡覺、一起吃飯呢！我本來也想帶它去學校，但我媽當然不同意。

每當我看到這隻兔子，我就覺得平靜又開心。我想，我可以說我的兔子能夠把我帶回到我無憂無慮的孩提時期。我想就算我長大離家了，還是會帶著它。

★別忘了劃底線處可以依自己的
狀況套入別的單字或片語喔！

這樣抄就對了！

示範四：想要的物品

接下來嘗試寫寫看「想要的物品」吧！注意，裡面套色的地方都是你在前面已經學過的句型。你看，會了這些句型是不是整篇文章就可以完成一大部分了呢？真的夠實用吧！

What I Want for my Birthday

While many people focus their attention on **popular songs by famous singers**, they often forget that they should cherish small things like **the voices of people they love**. For example, their brother's off-key singing, their dad's whistling, or the content purrs of their fat kitten.

These may all be considered "annoying noise" by some, but for me they are important and memorable sounds that I want to keep with me for my whole life. That is why, on my birthday, I would like a recording of the daily sounds my family members make. It doesn't even have to be a beautiful song, and no one has to say any words. It might not sound as pleasing as some famous tunes, but I'm sure that when I'm sad in the future, my **recording** will bring me back to my **happiest** days.

我想要的生日禮物

許多人會把注意力放在知名歌手唱的名曲上，而他們經常會忘記要珍惜一些小事，例如他們所愛的人的聲音。舉例來說，弟弟走音的歌聲、爸爸吹口哨的聲音、胖貓咪滿足的呼嚕聲都是。

某些人可能會認為這些是「煩人的噪音」，但對我來說這些都是重要而難忘的聲音，我希望它們能伴我度過一生。因此，我生日的時候，我想要的禮物是一段錄音，錄進我的家人每天發出的聲音。不需要是什麼好聽的歌曲，他們也不用講什麼內容。和許多名曲比起來，聽起來可能不是很好聽，但我相信當我以後心情不好時，這段錄音能夠帶我回到我最快樂的時光。

自我挑戰試試看：
2017年指考作文題目

有了完整的句型模板，現在的你寫起作文絕對無往不利，大考的題目也難不倒你了！現在我們就來使用模板當武器，挑戰歷屆指考與學測中出現過的「人物與物品描述」類題型。

2017年指定科目考試英文作文試題
提示：每個人從小到大都有覺得寂寞的時刻，也都各自有排遣寂寞的經驗和方法。當你感到寂寞時，有什麼人、事或物可以陪伴你，為你排遣寂寞呢？請以此為主題，寫一篇英文作文，文長至少120個單詞。文分兩段，第一段說明你會因為什麼原因或在何種情境下感到寂寞，第二段描述某個人、事或物如何伴你度過寂寞時光。

Being the only child in the nuclear family of mine, I coexisted with solitude for a long time before I had the concept of it. Even though I am quite an expert in getting along with myself, there are still times when I feel lonely. It is when the obsessiveness took over, would I realize how enclosed my mind was. I believed that loneliness isn't something fully blank or a brick wall. To me, it is one's self-identity being in a state of lack. It might present as endless self-doubt, unable to accept any advice, or easily affected by comments from the others. In my opinion, the strongest effect lonesome could cause is, one feeling isolated from the outside and being unable to evaluate themselves fairly. Such status can cause serious damage to self-esteem and the confidence in others, which leads to a vicious cycle.

身為核心家庭中唯一的小孩，在理解什麼是寂寞前，我就已經與它共存了許久。但是即便是獨處專家如我，也會有感到孤單的時刻。那就是當執念盤踞心頭時，我才意識到自己的內心有多麼封閉。我認為孤寂並不是一片空白或是像面磚牆。對我來說，那是個缺乏自我認同的狀態。它可能讓人產生自我懷疑、無法接受任何建議，或是輕易被他人意見影響。在我看來，寂寞所能造成最嚴重的影響，是讓人感到與世隔絕導致無法公允地評價自我。這樣的狀態對自尊和對他人的信任都可能造成嚴重損害，進而導致惡性循環。

The most efficient cure for me is to cook. I was close with my grandma since I lived with her for three years in my childhood, and we talked about all kinds of thoughts in life. On sleepless nights feeling isolated, I would read the recipes my grandma wrote to me, and go grocery shopping the next day. It is no secret that I consider **my grandma the best chef**. Mapo tofu is her signature dish, which I've been trying hard to reproduce since she passed away. The scenes she magically blended all the sauce still came to me vividly. Cooking the dishes brings me back to my **childhood** days, which helps me reorganize all the growth experience once again, and define who I really am. While most people focus their attention on **fine dining**, they often forget that they should cherish small things like **dishes made by their family**. Cuisines can not only fill the stomach, but bear a great amount of feelings and memories which can comfort the souls.

對我來說最有效的解方就是下廚。兒時我和奶奶同住了三年,分享彼此生活中的種種想法讓我們變得很親近。在寂寞來襲的失眠夜晚,我會拿出祖母寫給我的食譜來讀,隔天出門採購食材。我認為我奶奶是最棒的廚師早已不是秘密。其中麻婆豆腐是她的招牌菜,也是在她過世後我一直努力試圖重現的一道。做這些料理總能帶我回到童年時光,她像施法般調製醬料的畫面在腦中仍舊鮮明,這讓我再一次重新組織自己的成長經驗,並定義自己究竟是誰。當人們在乎著高級料理,卻常常忘記應該要珍惜像是家人做的料理這種小事。佳餚不僅能填飽肚子,也乘載著能撫慰靈魂的大量情感與記憶。

\ 老師告訴你 /

套上顏色的文字都是你在前面就學過的句型喔!寫這種題目時,可別光是描述這個人、事物的模樣,更要提到它背後的意義,否則如果顧著描述外觀卻沒有提到他如何陪伴你,會被認為是偏離題目而扣分的。

你還可以這樣應用：
SAT全真模擬試題03

　　以下的題目都是專家綜觀先前的SAT試題所整理出的全真模擬試題，題目內容大多以論說為主，別忘了，在論說的同時也會需要描述人或物作為舉例啊！這裡就帶著大家試試看如何利用模板句型寫出自然又流暢的SAT作文。SAT作文一般建議長度要寫到300～400字左右，趕快來參考一下老師的寫法吧！

SAT全真模擬試題03

If people worked less, would they be more creative and active during their free time?

（中譯：如果人們不要工作那麼久，他們在閒暇時間就會變得比較有創意、比較有活力。你同意這個說法嗎？）

I'm a huge advocator of the mantra "all work and no play makes Jack a dull boy". My own cousin, Daniel, is the perfect example. I remember how he used to be my role idol. I **admired him** for many reasons. First of all, **he was always brimming over with excitement and adventurousness**. Secondly, **he was always coming up with new ways to entertain us younger relatives**. Last but not least, **he was an amazing musician**; his guitar skills were to die for. It was no secret that I considered **him my hero**.

　　我深信一句名言：「只工作不玩耍，聰明人也變傻」。我的表哥丹尼爾就是最好的例證。我記得他以前曾是我的偶像。我欣賞他的理由有很多，首先，他總是充滿精力與冒險精神。然後，他總是能想出各種新方法逗我們這些年紀小一點的親戚開心。最後（但同樣重要的是），他是個超厲害的音樂家，他彈吉他的技巧無人能及。我把他當作我的英雄，這已經不是秘密了。

All of these ended after Daniel began to work in a prestigious company. He no longer had time to hang out with us or to think up new ways to have fun, and his guitar skills became rusty. He is often sick, and his cheerful grin is usually hidden behind a mask because he doesn't want to give his cough to everyone else. He used to sing with such an amazing voice as he played his guitar, but his voice has now become cracked and emotionless. My parents loved him; it is because of his **dedication to his job and the mad bucks he made** that he is depicted as a **worthy role model**. But to me, I find the old Daniel much more preferable.

I asked Daniel once why he never had fun anymore, and the answer he gave me was depressing. "You'll understand when you start working, kiddo. You use your brain so much at work, you simply don't have any mental strength to do anything else after work except maybe play boring cell phone games. You know that your life is getting boring, but you simply can't muster up the will power to do anything less boring. You need the will power, you see, to get up for work the next day!"

I also asked Daniel why he would no longer write songs on his guitar. He told me: "It doesn't work that way. You need time to get into creative mode, to let the inspiration flow. If you have less than one hour of free time because you have so much work, there's no way you can write anything. The inspiration gets cut off before it can really grow into something worthwhile. Just when you finally feel like you've gotten into the right mode and your brain and body is all warmed up and ready to create some good stuff, you have to put your

但這一切在丹尼爾開始在一家知名公司工作後都結束了。他再也沒有時間陪我們玩或想出各種新玩法，而他的吉他技巧也變得生疏。他常常生病，而且他開朗的笑容都被口罩遮住了，因為他不想把長期的咳嗽傳播給別人。他以前總是一邊彈吉他一邊用好聽的聲音唱歌，但他的聲音現在已經啞了，而且毫無感情。我的父母都超愛他的，因為他對工作全心投入，而且又賺很多錢，所以被當作是個值得效法的模範。但對我來說，還是以前的丹尼爾好。

我曾問過丹尼爾他為什麼都不再玩樂了，他給我的答案非常令人難過。「等你開始工作你就懂了，小朋友。你在工作的時候用腦用得太多，下班後除了可能玩點無聊的手機遊戲以外，根本就沒有力氣做任何事情。你自己也知道你的人生越來越無趣，但你根本就沒有精神做一些比較不無聊的事，因為要留點精神，明天早上才有辦法起床工作啊！」

我也問了丹尼爾他為什麼不再彈著吉他寫歌。他告訴我：「事情不是這樣的，要進入創作的狀態需要時間，才能讓你的靈感好好發揮。如果你因為工作太多，連一個小時的空閒時間都沒有，你絕對什麼歌都寫不出來的。你的靈感還沒成長成什麼值得一聽的樂曲，就已經被硬生生切斷了。正當你終於覺得你已經進入狀況、

instrument away and go to bed because work is in six hours, and if you spend all night writing a song you'd probably be fired from your job!"

And that, ladies and gentlemen, is why I believe that long work hours do curb creativity and activity. From **Daniel** I learned to **prioritize my life over my job**. I will let nothing, I repeat, nothing, kill the creativity I have inside, and I certainly will not become another Daniel.

身體和大腦都暖身完畢，準備好可以創作一點好東西了，你就必須把樂器收起來去睡覺，因為再過六個小時就要上班了。如果你整夜不睡寫歌，大概會被開除吧！」

各位懂了吧，這就是為什麼我相信工作太久會傷害到創意和活力。從丹尼爾身上，我學會了要把自己的生活放在工作之前。我絕不會讓任何事情抹煞我的創意，而我也絕不會成為下一個丹尼爾。

\ 老師告訴你 /

套上顏色的文字都是你在前面就學過的句型喔！在SAT的考題中，經常會出現和「人」有關的考題，而這時以描述身邊的人當作例證就是個讓文章十分生色的好方法。這篇作文花了大篇幅介紹寫作者的表哥，讓讀者藉由表哥的例子感受到作者的強烈觀點，就是個在考SAT時很適用的方法。

美國高中升大學的SAT也無往不利！

你還可以這樣應用：
SAT全真模擬試題04

SAT全真模擬試題04

Do we benefit from learning about the flaws of people we admire and respect?

（中譯：我們能從我們欣賞與敬重的人的缺點中學習，因而讓自己變得更好嗎？）

Everyone has flaws, even the person you adore and respect the most. Thus, blindly believing someone you like to be perfect is no different from lying to yourself, and definitely not healthy—once you are able to accept that your idol has imperfections just like everyone else, you'll find that you can learn even more from your idol, and not like them any less in the process. In fact, learning about someone's flaws may very well help you like them even more!

Take my idol, a Japanese singer named Yamamoto, for example. Because of **her strong personality** and because of **her lovely voice**, **she** is the person I **admire** the most. I have lots of her posters on my bedroom wall, and I used to react angrily when anyone dared to insult her. In my heart, **Yamamoto** was the prime example of a **perfect angel**.

However, I gradually came to realize that Yamamoto may look **strong**, but she is actually a very **shy** person. Even though she seems cool when she sings, she doesn't know how to handle

每個人都有缺點，就連你最喜愛與尊敬的人也一樣。因此，盲目相信你喜歡的人一切完美，就和對自己說謊沒什麼兩樣，而且這樣的心態也不太健康。一旦你能夠接受你的偶像和其他人一樣都有缺點，你就會發現你可以從你的偶像身上學到更多，而且過程中對他們的喜愛不會減少。其實，瞭解某人的缺點，很可能會讓你變得更喜歡他們呢！

讓我來舉個例子。我的偶像是一名叫做山本的日本歌手。因為她堅強的個性和她甜美的聲音，她是我最欣賞的人。我的臥室牆上有很多她的海報，而如果有誰敢說她不好，以前我都會很生氣。在我心中，山本是個完美的天使。

然而，我漸漸發現山本雖然看起來很堅強，但她其實很害羞。雖然她唱

paparazzi and is always spotted running away from the cameras. Some call her unprofessional because of that, but to me it is very relatable, since I get all tongue-tied when put into the spotlight too! I began to learn more about Yamamoto's background story, in which she used to be overweight and very self-conscious about it, and she took a long time to find the courage to perform onstage.

The more I learn about Yamamoto's flaw of being painfully shy and unconfident, the more I can identify with her, and I ended up being an even more devoted fan. From **Yamamoto** I learned to **try to become more confident**, or at least not let my lack of confidence hinder me in doing the things I enjoy. This is why I find **Yamamoto** my **role model**, not in spite of her flaws but precisely because of them.

歌時看起來很酷，但她卻不知道如何對付狗仔隊，每次她都會害羞得從鏡頭前逃走。有人因此說她不夠專業，但對我來說這卻很能理解，因為我每次成為注目焦點時，也會害羞得什麼也說不出來。我開始更瞭解山本的背景，才知道她以前體重過重，而且非常在意這件事，她花了很長的一段時間才找到上台表演的勇氣。

我越瞭解山本害羞而沒自信的缺點，我就越能認同她的感受。我也成為更加死忠的粉絲了。從山本的身上，我學到要盡量讓自己更有自信，或至少不讓缺乏自信這點影響到我做一些喜歡的事情。因此，我才覺得山本是我的模範，並不是因為她毫無瑕疵，而正是因為她有瑕疵。

\ 老師告訴你 /

套上顏色的文字都是你在前面就學過的句型喔！這篇文章中從頭到尾沒有明確點出「人們能從我們欣賞與敬重的人的缺點中學習，因而讓自己變得更好」這一句話，但從作者舉的例子與內容，就可以看出作者對於此一議題的觀點。

　　讀完了這麼多的範例作文，現在你一定已經躍躍欲試，想套用模板句型自己寫寫看了吧！請你以**「我在我包包裡最喜歡的一個東西」（My Favorite Item in My Bag）**為題，套用模板句型寫一篇作文。所有的句型都在框框中為你列出來囉！

文章開頭參考句型

(1) Because of [1]（名詞或名詞片語）, and because of [2]（名詞或名詞片語），（某人）is the person I [3]（動詞）the most.

(2) As everyone knows,（某人）is famous as [1]（名詞，身分）. However, as（某人）'s [2]（名詞，身分），I like him/her more because of [3]（名詞或名詞片語）.

(3) Well goes an old saying, "[1]（名言）". We can tell how true this is from [2]（名詞或名詞片語）.

(4) When it comes to [1]（複數名詞，身分），某人 is definitely the first one that comes to my mind.

(5) It is no secret that I consider（某人）[1]（名詞）.

(6) My favorite [1]（名詞）is my [2]（名詞）, which is [3]（顏色），[4]（形容詞）and [5]（形容詞）.

(7) I received my [1]（名詞）when I was [2]（年紀）.

文章開展參考句型

(1) I [1]（動詞）（某人）for many reasons. First of all, [2]（句子）. Secondly, [3]（句子）. Last but not least, [4]（句子）.

(2) After experiencing [1]（名詞或名詞片語，不好的事），（某人）didn't give way to the cruel destiny; instead,（某人）still held a [2]（形容詞，正面的）attitude towards [3]（名詞或名詞片語）.

(3) Although （某人） is [1]（形容詞）, he/she still holds a [2]（形容詞） attitude in dealing with people and his / her work.

(4) （某人） may look [1]（形容詞）, but he / she is actually a very [2]（形容詞） person.

(5) （某人） is the prime example of a [1]（名詞）.

(6) When I look at my [1]（名詞）, I always feel [2]（形容詞） and [3]（形容詞）.

(7) My [1]（名詞） bring(s) me back to my [2]（時間） days.

結論收尾參考句型

(1) It is because of his/her [1]（名詞） that （某人） is depicted as [2]（名詞）. Indeed, （某人） is an excellent example for [3]（名詞，某類人） to follow.

(2) From （某人） I learned to [1]（動詞或動詞片語）.

(3) This is why I find （某人） my [1]（名詞或名詞片語，身分）.

(4) It is undeniable that （某人） has a huge influence on the way I [1]（動詞）. I'm very glad that I have the chance to get to know such a(n) [2]（形容詞） person.

(5) Personally, I think （某人） is a modern day [1]（已過世的名人名字）!

(6) While most people focus their attention on [1]（名詞或名詞片語，複數）, they often forget that they should cherish small things like [2]（名詞或名詞片語，複數）.

(7) Nothing can replace the good memories my [1]（名詞） bring(s) me .

抄這本就對了！
寫出清楚的
「圖表分析類」
作文

抄這本就對了！寫出清楚的「圖表分析類」作文

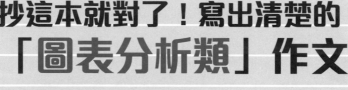

Part 3

　　無論在課本上或是報章雜誌上，一定都會看到各式各樣的圖表。圖表只有單字和數字，那麼要如何用完整的一段話來描述所看到的圖表呢？學會這一點可是很重要的，畢竟在職場上或是校園裡，都必須要知道如何分析圖表、再加上自己的意見。這一篇就教你如何寫出不能不會的圖表分析作文！

一定要知道

「圖表分析類」作文的寫作重點

圖表分析 Step 1. 先說明是哪一種圖表

　　常見的圖表包括柱狀圖（bar graph）、線型圖（line graph）、圓餅圖（pie chart）或表格（table）等。除了點明是哪一種圖表以外，更重要的是要說明這個圖表的主題是什麼？用來傳達怎樣的訊息？例如：如果這張圖表中訪問了一百名高中生最想要的寵物種類，就可以這麼說：**A hundred high school students were interviewed on what kind of pet they want the most. The results are shown in this bar graph.**「一百名高中生被訪問他們最想要哪種寵物。結果如這張柱狀圖所示。」

圖表分析 Step 2. 再描述整體趨勢、特別的現象

　　圖表中總會有幾項特別突出，如在圓餅圖中比例特別大一塊、或是在柱狀圖中只有某一根特別短之類的。這種時候，一定要把這些特別的狀況提出來描述。例如你發

現在一百名高中生中，高達七十名想要養狗，遠遠勝過其他種類的動物，就非得提一下這個狀況不可：**Seventy out of one hundred students said they wanted dogs as a pet.**「一百名中有七十個學生説他們想要養狗當寵物。」

　　若是線型圖，多半是用來表達「演變」的狀況。像是如果要表示從2016年到2024年中，班上有手機的學生數量，就不會用圓餅圖。如果從線型圖中發現有手機的人數一直在增加，就可以把這個趨勢點出來，甚至預測未來可能的狀況：**It's obvious in this line graph that more and more students have cell phones over the past years. In 2030, perhaps, it will be mandatory for all students to have cell phones!**「從這線型圖可以明顯看出每年都有越來越多學生有手機。也許到了2030年，學生們都會被規定一定要有手機才行！」

圖表分析 Step**3.** 也可以討論自己的狀況

　　要是每個人都只分析圖表中的數字而已，文章會千篇一律，閱卷老師也會看到睡著。要讓自己的文章與眾不同、吸引注意，就可以加入自己的親身體驗。例如當你發現一百名學生中有七十名都想養狗，而覺得很驚訝：難道他們不會想養其他的動物嗎？這種時候就可以寫：**I'm surprised that so many students want dogs. What about birds and cats? Aren't fish good pets too?**「我很驚訝這麼多學生想要養狗。鳥和貓呢？魚難道不是好的寵物嗎？」

　　不過，要注意的是撰寫圖表首重分析，分析要盡量客觀，且應該避免口語跟情緒化字眼。所以就算你很討厭狗，也不要説出「這些受訪的學生真沒品味」之類的話。而若題目中只要你描述圖表的狀況，沒有提到任何分析方面的事情，那就最好不要加入自己的感想，且盡量使用精簡的文字，以免被視為離題。

實戰必備

「圖表分析類」作文必備單字片語

　　圖表分析其實和「數學」非常有關係！因此，在寫圖表分析類作文時，我們必須知道如何描寫數據的變化（如增加、減少……等等），而如果遇到的是圓餅圖，就更要知道如何用英文說「幾分之幾」等等的「比例」。這可是很重要的，就算是英文很好的人，如果沒有學過「用英文算數學」，還不見得會說呢！快來一起看看這些實用的單字吧！

 ### 表示「增加」的動詞

❶	增加	increase	❺	湧升	surge
❷	上升	go up / rise	❻	飆升	shoot up
❸	成長	grow	❼	爬升	climb
❹	竄升	jump			

 ### 表示「減少」的動詞

❶	減少	decrease	❺	被減少	is reduced
❷	下降	go down	❻	下沉	sink
❸	衰退	decline	❼	墜落	dip / plunge
❹	掉落	fall / drop			

表示「增加」的名詞

❶	增加	increase	❹	竄升	jump
❷	上升	rise	❺	湧升	surge
❸	成長	growth			

表示「減少」的名詞

❶	減少	decrease	❸	掉落	fall / drop
❷	衰退	decline	❹	縮減	reduction

 表示「增加與減少幅度」的副詞

❶	輕微地	slightly	❼	急遽地	sharply
❷	緩慢地	slowly	❽	戲劇性地	dramatically
❸	漸漸地	gradually	❾	大幅地	drastically
❹	穩定地	steadily	❿	相對地	relatively
❺	快速地	rapidly	⓫	明顯地	noticeably
❻	適度地	moderately			

 表示「維持不變」的單字片語

❶	維持不變	remain the same
❷	達到穩定	reach a plateau
❸	穩定	stabilize
❹	維持平穩	remain stable
❺	維持穩定	remain constant

 描述「比例」的單字

❶	百分之七十五（四分之三）	75 percent = three quarters
❷	百分之六十六（三分之二）	66 percent = two-thirds
❸	百分之五十（一半）	50 percent = half
❹	百分之三十三（三分之一）	33 percent = a third
❺	百分之二十五（四分之一）	25 percent = a quarter
❻	百分之二十（五分之一）	20 percent = one-fifth

實戰必備
「圖表分析類」作文 必備實用句型

　　踏進英文作文考場之前，總得知道寫一篇作文要如何開頭、承接與結尾。以下提供一些「圖表分析類」作文中超好用的句型，依照自己的狀況在劃底線的空格處放入適合的單字（想不出填什麼的話，也可以參考前面「實用單字」的部分找尋靈感），就能輕鬆寫出考場必備的超實用金句，一口氣加好幾分！

這樣抄就對了 Step 1. 文章開頭抄這些句型就對了！

❶ The ¹（名詞，圖表種類名稱） shows the general picture of ²（名詞子句）.

這張＿＿＿＿顯示＿＿＿＿的概況。

> 1 處可填入：pie chart 圓餅圖／line graph 線圖／table 表格
> 2 處可填入：the ways students use computers 學生使用電腦的方式／
> 　　　　　　people's preferences in movies 人們對於電影的喜好

✋ **整句可以這樣寫：**

The **bar graph** shows the general picture of <u>the ways of music listening people prefered</u>.

這張**長條圖**顯示了<u>人們偏好的聽音樂方式</u>的概況。

❷ This ¹ （名詞，圖表種類名稱） **shows the change of** ² （名詞子句） **over a** ³ （數字）**-year period.**

這張＿＿＿＿顯示在＿＿＿＿年間，＿＿＿＿有哪些改變。

> **1 處可填入**：table 表格／line graph 線圖／bar graph 長條圖
> **2 處可填入**：people's preferences in books 人們偏好的書種類／
> opinions on new technology 對於最新科技的想法
> **3 處可填入**：ten 十／five 五／three 三

✋ **整句可以這樣寫：**

The bar graph shows the change of people's feelings about idols over a fifteen-year period.

這張長條圖顯示在十五年間，人們對偶像的看法有哪些改變。

❸ The ¹ （名詞，圖表種類名稱） **shows the number of** ² （名詞子句） **between** ³ （時間and時間）**.**

這張＿＿＿＿顯示在＿＿＿＿＿＿＿＿之間，＿＿＿＿的數量。

> **1 處可填入**：chart 圖表／table 表格／graph 圖表
> **2 處可填入**：students with smartphones 有智慧型手機的學生／
> people who have pets 有寵物的人
> **3 處可填入**：2014 and 2015 2014年到2015年／
> October and December 十月到十二月

✋ **整句可以這樣寫：**

The graph shows the number of students who have a tablet between 2011 and 2012.

這張圖表顯示在2011到2012年之間，擁有平板電腦的學生數量。

❹ **The** [1] （名詞，表格名稱） **illustrates the difference between** [2] （名詞and名詞） **in choices of** [3] （名詞）**.**

這張_____顯示_____ _____對_____的選擇有什麼差別。

> **1 處可填入：** chart 圖表／table 表格／bar graph 圖表
> **2 處可填入：** male students and female students 男學生與女學生／
> girls and boys 女生與男生
> **3 處可填入：** snacks 點心／fruit 水果

✋ **整句可以這樣寫：**

The graph illustrates the difference between teenagers and adults in choices of transportation.

這張圖表顯示青少年與成人對交通方式的選擇有什麼差別。

· ·

❺ **It is** [1] （被動態動詞，表現） **in this** [2] （名詞，表格名稱） **how people** [3] （動詞或動詞片語）**.**

在這張_____裡，_____了人們如何_____。

> **1 處可填入：** shown 被表現／exhibited 被展現／demonstrated 被展現
> **2 處可填入：** graph 圖表／chart 表格／table 表格
> **3 處可填入：** spend their vacations 度假／sleep 睡覺

✋ **整句可以這樣寫：**

It is shown in this graph how people go to work.

在這張圖表裡，展現了人們如何去上班。

這樣抄就對了 Step2. 文章開展抄這些句型就對了！

❶ **Overall, they spend** [1] ＿＿＿（比例） **of their** [2] ＿＿＿（名詞） [3] ＿＿＿（動詞+ing子句）.

整體來說，他們花＿＿＿＿的＿＿＿＿來做＿＿＿＿。

> **1** 處可填入：two-thirds 三分之二／twenty percent 百分之二十
> **2** 處可填入：weekends 週末／time 時間／money 錢
> **3** 處可填入：surfing the Internet 上網／buying clothes 買衣服

✋ 整句可以這樣寫：

Overall, they spend two-thirds of their money paying mortgage.
整體來說，他們花三分之二的錢來繳房貸。

❷ **Overall, the number of** [1] ＿＿＿（複數名詞） **shows a(n)** [2] ＿＿＿（名詞，增加或減少） **from** [3] ＿＿＿（時間 to 時間）.

整體來說，＿＿＿＿的數量從＿＿＿＿＿＿＿＿呈現＿＿＿＿的狀態。

> **1** 處可填入：students 學生／cars 汽車
> **2** 處可填入：increase 增加／decrease 減少／rise 上升
> **3** 處可填入：2012 to 2013 2012年到2013年／
> January to February 一月到二月

✋ 整句可以這樣寫：

Overall, the number of residents shows an increase from last year to this year.
整體來說，居民的數量從去年到今年呈現上升的狀態。

❸ ¹ _____（名詞） take(s) a ² _____（形容詞） lead of _____（數字）percent over
³ _____（名詞）.

_____ _____領先_____百分之_____。

> **1 處可填入：** Motorcycles 機車／Cats 貓
> **2 處可填入：** huge 很大的／little 小的／surprising 驚人的
> **3 處可填入：** bicycles 腳踏車／mice 老鼠

✋ **整句可以這樣寫：**

<u>Motorcycles</u> take a <u>surprising</u> lead of <u>20</u> percent over <u>bicycles</u>.
<u>機車</u> <u>驚人地</u>領先了<u>腳踏車</u>百分之二十。

- -

❹ ¹ _____（名詞）, which has a meager proportion of _____（數字）
percent, apparently is under disfavor.

_____只有_____％，明顯地不受歡迎。

> **1 處可填入：** Swimming 游泳／Snakes 蛇

✋ **整句可以這樣寫：**

The <u>pineapple</u>, which has a meager proportion of <u>10</u> percent, apparently is
under disfavor.

<u>鳳梨</u>只有**10**％，明顯地不受歡迎。

- -

❺ In contrast, ¹ （名詞） takes up ² （比例） of ³ （名詞或名詞片語）.

相對地，＿＿＿＿佔了＿＿＿＿的＿＿＿＿。

> **1 處可填入**：dancing 跳舞／Mexican food 墨西哥菜
> **2 處可填入**：one-third 三分之一／30 percent 百分之三十／
> two-thirds 三分之二
> **3 處可填入**：people's weekends 人們的週末／my time 我的時間

✍ **整句可以這樣寫：**

In contrast, rice **takes up** 50 percent **of** people's daily diet.

相對地，米佔了人們每日飲食的百分之五十。

這樣抄就對了 Step3. **結論收尾抄這些句型就對了！**

❶ Overall, from ¹ （時間） to （時間）, there was ² （形容詞，描述大小） change in ³ （名詞片語）.

整體來說，從＿＿＿＿＿＿＿，在＿＿＿＿方面有＿＿＿＿改變。

> **1 處可填入**：autumn to winter 秋天到冬天／
> Monday to Friday 禮拜一到禮拜五
> **2 處可填入**：no 沒有／little 非常少／a huge 非常大
> **3 處可填入**：the average income 平均收入／
> people's preferences in clothing 人們對服飾的選擇

✍ **整句可以這樣寫：**

Overall, from 2014 to 2015, **there was** very little **change in** people's interests in movie genres.

整體來說，從2014到2015年間，在人們感興趣的電影種類方面，改變非常地小。

❷ In conclusion, mostly, ¹ （名詞） **for** ² （複數名詞，族群） **are to** ³ （動詞） **with, whereas** ⁴ （複數名詞，另一族群） **opt for** ⁵ （名詞） **to** ⁶ （動詞） **.**

結論是，大抵而言，_____對_____來說是用來_____，而_____選擇___則是為了_____。

> **1 處可填入：** food 食物／books 書
> **2 處可填入：** men 男人／students 學生
> **3 處可填入：** entertain 娛樂／stay slim 維持身材
> **4 處可填入：** women 女人／adults 成人
> **5 處可填入：** drinks 飲料／television 電視
> **6 處可填入：** enjoy themselves 享樂／have fun 享樂

✍ **整句可以這樣寫：**

In conclusion, mostly, smartphones for retired people are to play games with, whereas students opt for smartphones to stay in touch with their friends.

結論是，大抵而言，智慧型手機對退休人士來說是用來玩遊戲，而學生選擇智慧型手機則是為了和朋友保持聯絡。

❸ This ¹ （名詞，圖表名稱） **clearly illustrates that** ² （複數名詞，族群） **view** ³ （名詞） **as an indispensable part of their lives.**

這張_____明確地顯示，_____把_____看作是生活中不可或缺的一部分。

> **1 處可填入：** chart 圖表／table 表格
> **2 處可填入：** children 兒童／men 男人
> **3 處可填入：** cell phones 手機／cosmetics 化妝品

✍ **整句可以這樣寫：**

This chart clearly illustrates that women view music as an indispensable

part of their lives.

這張**表格**明確地顯示，**女人**把**音樂**看作是生活中不可或缺的一部分。

---

❹ **According to this** [1] （名詞，圖表名稱）**, we can expect that, in the future, more and more** [2] （複數名詞，族群） **will** [3] （動詞）**.**

根據這張_____，我們可以預期在未來會有更多_____能夠_____。

> **1 處可填入**：bar graph 長條圖／pie chart 圓餅圖
> **2 處可填入**：families 家庭／girls 女生
> **3 處可填入**：enjoy books 喜歡看書／like rock music 喜歡搖滾樂

✋ **整句可以這樣寫：**

According to this diagram, we can expect that, in the future, more and more students will have access to online libraries.

根據這張**圖表**，我們可以預期在未來會有更多的**學生**能夠**有權使用線上圖書館**。

---

❺ **To conclude,** [1] （名詞所有格） **preferences for** [2] （複數名詞，種類名稱） [3] （動詞，表示改變、不變） **with time.**

結論是，_____對_____的喜好隨著時間_____。

> **1 處可填入**：people's 人們的／students' 學生們的
> **2 處可填入**：book genres 書籍種類／ice cream flavors 冰淇淋口味
> **3 處可填入**：fluctuate 波動／remain stable 持續穩定

✋ **整句可以這樣寫：**

To conclude, boys' preferences for video game genres remain the same with time.

結論是，**男孩們**對於**電動種類**的喜好隨著時間**維持不變**。

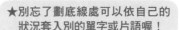
★別忘了劃底線處可以依自己的
狀況套入別的單字或片語喔！

這樣抄就對了！

示範一：圖表〈一〉

　　前面我們已經看過了「圖表分析」題型中超實用的單字片語和句型了！現在就把這些單字與句型組合起來，一篇完整的文章就完成囉！一起來看看幾個例子，都是老師精心為你寫成的高分參考作文喔！注意，裡面套色的地方都是你在前面已經學過的句型。你看，會了這些句型是不是整篇文章就可以完成八成了呢？真的夠實用吧！

　　範文題目：以下的圓餅圖是關於NBA高中的學生在週末時對各項活動時間分配的調查。寫一篇短文分析說明此數據，並與自己的時間表做比較。

 # Time Arrangement on Weekends

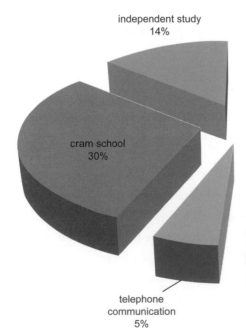
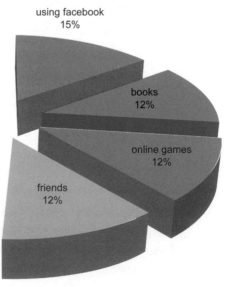

independent study
14%

using facebook
15%

books
12%

online games
12%

cram school
30%

friends
12%

online games
12%

telephone
communication
5%

The **pie chart** shows the general picture of **the way students in NBA high school allocate their time on weekends**. Overall, they spend **two-thirds** of their **schedule dealing with personal business, using facebook, reading books, playing online games, hanging out with friends and talking on the phone**. Among them, **using Facebook** takes a **little** lead of **15** percent over **books, games and friends**, all of which have equal shares of 12 percent. **Telephone communication**, which has a meager proportion of **5 percent**, apparently is under disfavor now that contacting friends has been a lot easier, more convenient, and cheaper via the internet. In contrast, **after-school learning** takes up **one-third** of **the timetable**, with an amazing division of 30 percent on the cram school, twice more than that on independent study.

Compared with the above schedule, my weekends are outlined likewise as study for 60 percent and leisure, 40 percent. Yet the arrangement differs. Mostly, I study and discuss schoolwork with classmates in school. In addition, there are a number of differences in leisure activities. Firstly, while using Facebook and online games account for half of the leisure time in NBA school, the two of them take the least proportion in my schedule. What parallels with the pie chart is the telephone hours, which I don't take much interest in either, since my friends and I stick together for most of the daytime.

In conclusion, while there are diverse choices how NBA students and I arrange the weekends, as high school students, the contour of the timetable is similar.

週末的時間安排

這張圓餅圖顯示NBA高中的學生在週末運用時間方式的概況。整體來說,他們花三分之二的時間來處理個人的事務,包含使用臉書、看書、玩網路遊戲、和朋友一起玩、講電話。在這之中,使用臉書有15%,稍稍領先看書、玩遊戲和朋友聚會,這三項都同樣有12%。而電話聯絡只有小小的5%,明顯地不受歡迎,因為現在使用網路聯絡朋友更簡單、更方便、更便宜。相對的,課後學習佔了時間表的三分之一,而且驚人地有30%的部份都在補習班,比獨立學習多了兩倍。

與以上的時間表相比,我的週末大致也一樣,讀書佔60%,休閒佔40%,但分配稍有不同。大部分的時候我都在學校讀書並和同學討論課業。另外,在休閒活動方面也有一些不同。首先,使用臉書和網路遊戲佔了NBA高中的學生一半的休閒時間,但它們兩個在我的時間表佔了最少的部分。和圓餅圖狀況相同的是通話時間,我也對那個沒什麼興趣,因為我和我的朋友白天大部分的時間都在一起。

結論是,雖然NBA的學生跟我分配週末時間的選擇有些不同,身為高中生,時間表大致上還是相似的。

這樣抄就對了！

示範二：圖表〈二〉

接下來看看以下的圖表吧！注意，裡面套色的地方都是你在前面已經學過的句型。你看，會了這些句型是不是整篇文章就可以完成一大部分了呢？真的夠實用吧！

範文題目：以下是2009到2012年間台灣某城市的平均家庭年收入圖，請寫兩到三段敘述來說明四年間平均家庭收入的變化。

Average Household Income

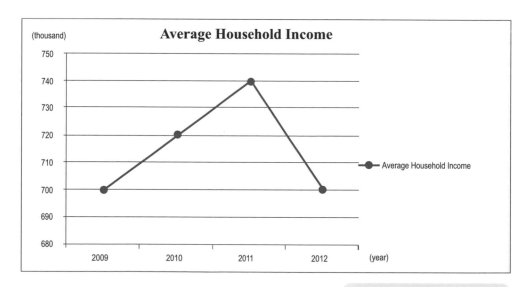

The above **chart** shows the change in **average yearly income** over a **four**-year period. From 2009 through 2011, average income rose steadily at a rate of $20,000 per year. However, from 2011 to 2012, incomes dropped $40,000 and returned to the average yearly income of 2009.

平均家庭收入

以上的表格顯示四年內平均年收入的改變。從2009到2011，平均收入穩定地以一年20000元的速率上升。但是從2011到2012，收入跌落了40000元，回到2009年的平均年收入。

Overall, from **2009 to 2012**, there was **no** change in **average household income**. However, this doesn't mean that no changes occurred between 2009 and 2012—the average household income did rise, it's just that it dropped again in 2012. We will need to see the data for the next few years to figure out whether the drop will continue, or the number will go up again.

We might be able to deduce a few things from the chart, such as the state of our economy. The general economy appears to be steadily getting better during the 2009 to 2011 period, as can be seen from the rising average household income. However, perhaps something happened to the global market from 2011 to 2012, causing the numbers to go down. We can only hope that they don't go down any further!

整體來説，從2009到2012年，平均家庭收入沒有改變。但是，這並不表示從2009到2012沒有發生任何改變：平均的家庭收入是有上升，只是在2012又下降罷了。我們必須看到接下來幾年的數據，才能知道究竟這個下降的趨勢會持續，還是數字會再度上升。

我們可以從這張圖表推斷出一些事情，例如社會上的經濟狀態。從2009到2011這段時間，經濟似乎穩定成長，從平均家庭收入就能看出來。然而，在2011到2012年間全球市場或許發生了什麼變化，造成數字下滑。我們只能希望不要再繼續下滑了！

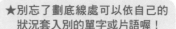

這樣抄就對了！

示範三：圖表〈三〉

接下來看看以下的圖表吧！注意，裡面套色的地方都是你在前面已經學過的句型。你看，會了這些句型是不是整篇文章就可以完成一大部分了呢？真的夠實用吧！

範文題目：以下這張圖表示訪問了20名男學生與20名女學生喜歡的冰淇淋口味的結果，每個人都可以選一種以上。請寫一篇文章來表述這張圖表，並加入自己的感想。

 # Favorite Ice Cream Flavors

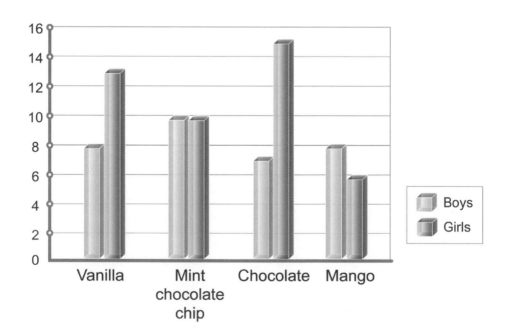

This **bar graph** illustrates the difference between **male students** and **female students** in choices of **ice cream flavors**. Twenty male students and twenty female students were interviewed, and they can choose more than one flavor if they want to. We can see from this chart that an overwhelming number of 15 out of 20 girls chose chocolate flavored ice cream, while only seven boys picked chocolate. We can also see that more boys seem to prefer mango flavored ice cream than girls, and the numbers of boys and girls enjoy mint chocolate chip ice cream are the same.

We can see from this **bar graph** that **girls** prefer **chocolate** over **other flavors**, which surprised me somewhat. In my opinion, chocolate ice cream tastes terrible! I love chocolate, but I still can't stand chocolate ice cream. I've heard that some brands of chocolate ice cream taste great, but those must be very rare because all the ones I tried seemed to taste positively terrible. On the other hand, I'm glad that many share my love for vanilla ice cream. Overall, this chart shows that my preference is a bit different, but not too different from other girls'.

.

「圖表分析類」作文

最喜歡的冰淇淋口味

這張長條圖顯示了男學生與女學生在挑選冰淇淋口味時的差異。共有20名男學生和20名女學生受訪，他們可以選擇超過一種口味。我們可以從這張表格看出20名女學生中就有壓倒性的15名選了巧克力口味，而只有7個男生選了巧克力口味，我們也可以發現，比起女生，更多男生喜歡芒果口味的冰淇淋，而男生和女生喜歡薄荷巧克力口味冰淇淋的人數是一樣的。

我們可以從這張長條圖看出，比起其他口味，女生還是最喜歡巧克力。這讓我有點驚訝。在我看來，巧克力冰淇淋超難吃的！我喜歡巧克力，但我可受不了巧克力冰淇淋。我聽說有些品牌的巧克力冰淇淋很好吃，但那應該是很罕見，因為我吃過的那些都超級難吃。另一方面，我很高興大家都喜歡我也喜歡的香草口味。整體來說，從這張表格看來，我的喜好和其他女生的喜好有一點點不同，但相去不遠。

這樣抄就對了！

示範四：圖表〈四〉

接下來看看以下的圖表吧！注意，裡面套色的地方都是你在前面已經學過的句型。你看，會了這些句型是不是整篇文章就可以完成一大部分了呢？真的夠實用吧！

範文題目：下方的圖表列出男、女學生喜歡的點心選項。寫一篇至少兩段的文章，分析解說圖表，並與你個人喜歡的喜好做比較。

 Students' Preferences in Snacks

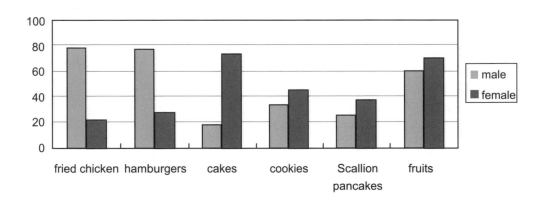

The **bar graph** illustrates the difference between **male** and **female students** in choices of **snacks**. Apparently, boys prefer fried and salty food whereas girls favor sweets. For boys, fried chicken and hamburgers win the most votes, both accounting for over 75 percent. **Cakes**, which have a meager proportion of less than **20 percent**, apparently are under disfavor. **On the other hand, girls' likes and**

學生對點心的喜好

這張柱狀圖描述男女學生對點心選擇的差別。明顯地，男生喜歡油炸和鹹的食物，而女生喜歡吃甜的。對男生來説，炸雞和漢堡得到最多票，都超過75%。蛋糕只有不到20%，明顯地不受歡迎。另一

dislikes go drastically opposite to those of boys. Well-loved refreshments for boys are least popular with girls, while cakes, which barely attract boys, hit girls' top choice.

Interestingly, among the diversities, boy and girl students do share one thing in common—their love for fruits. 60 percent of boys and 70 percent of girls have fruits for snacks according to the figure. As a girl, my choices are similar with most female students, only that fruits come first and cakes and cookies follow after.

In conclusion, mostly, **snacks** for **boys** are to **satiate hunger** with, whereas **girls** opt for **sweets** to **acquire a sense of comfort**. Yet without doubt, boys and girls at this stage are health-conscious to a certain degree, for over half of them would take fruits between meals.

方面，女生喜歡和討厭的東西和男生的喜好完全相反。受到男生喜愛的點心最不受女生歡迎，幾乎不吸引男生的蛋糕，卻是女生的最佳選擇。

有趣的是，在眾多不同之中，男女學生有一件事相同：他們對水果的喜好。根據數據，60%的男生和70%的女生都吃水果當點心。身為女生，我的選擇和大部分的女學生類似，只是水果是第一名，再來才是蛋糕和餅乾。

結論是，大致上點心對男生來說是為了滿足食慾，而女生選擇甜點來得到慰藉。但毋庸置疑，這個階段的男女生某種程度上都滿注重健康，因為他們超過一半的人都會在正餐之間吃水果。

自我挑戰試試看：
2014年指考作文題目

有了完整的句型模板，現在的你寫起作文絕對無往不利，大考的題目也難不倒你了！現在我們就來使用模板當武器，挑戰歷屆指考與學測中出現過的「圖表分析」類題型。

> 2014年指定科目考試英文作文試題
> 下圖呈現的是美國某高中的全體學生每天進行各種活動的時間分配，請寫一篇120個單詞的英文作文。文分兩段，第一段描述該圖所呈現之特別現象；第二段請說明整體而言，你一天的時間分配與該高中全體學生的異同，並說明理由。

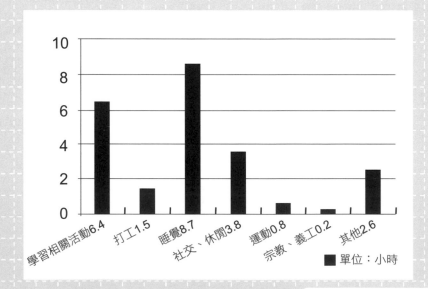

學習相關活動6.4　打工1.5　睡覺8.7　社交、休閒3.8　運動0.8　宗教、義工0.2　其他2.6　■單位：小時

The **bar graph** shows the general picture of the way **high school students in a certain American high school spend their time in one day.** It is quite easy to see that their time allocation is drastically different from that of us Taiwanese

這張長條圖展現的是某一美國高中的學生一天的時間分配概況。很容易就能看出，他們的時間分配和我們台灣學生差得很多。例如，整體來說，他

students. For one, overall, they spend about **six hours** of their **day doing study-related activities**. Which aren't very much compared to us! In contrast, **sleeping** takes up **eight hours** of their **days**. This is, of course, something that we Taiwanese students can only envy.

It's obvious that my daily timetable would be very different from the one above, for school hours plus cram school and commuting to and from both places already take up more than fourteen precious hours, and of the remaining ten, one would go to eating meals, taking showers, and other routine household chores. Around seven would be slept away. That leaves less than two hours free time— which are spent doing, guess what, homework and reports! It's quite a terrible life we students lead here.

們會一天花六個小時在學習相關的活動上。這跟我們比算什麼啊！相反地，他們一天要睡八個小時。當然，這點我們台灣學生也只能羨慕了。

很明顯，我每天的行程表和以上這張會差很多，因為我們上學的時間，加上補習班時間和其間的通勤時間，就已經花上超過14個小時了，而剩下的十個小時裡有一個小時用來吃飯、洗澡、做其他的例行家事；七個小時用來睡覺；只剩下不到兩個小時的時間要做什麼呢？猜對了，拿來做功課、寫報告。我們學生的生活實在很慘啊。

\ 老師告訴你 /

套上顏色的文字都是你在前面就學過的句型喔！千萬注意在題目中提到的兩段內容架構：第一段描述特點，第二段描述你個人的經歷，一定要照著它寫，不然馬上就會被扣分囉。

讀完了這麼多的範例作文，現在你一定已經躍躍欲試，想套用模板句型自己寫寫看了吧！請你以前面之「2014年指考作文題目」為題，套用模板句型寫一篇作文。所有的句型都在框框中為你列出來囉！

文章開頭參考句型

(1) The [1] （名詞，圖表種類名稱） shows the general picture of [2] （名詞子句）.

(2) This [1] （名詞，圖表種類名稱） shows the change of [2] （名詞子句） over a [3] （數字）-year period.

(3) The [1] （名詞，圖表種類名稱） shows the number of [2] （名詞子句） between [3] （時間and時間）.

(4) The [1] （名詞，表格名稱） illustrates the difference between [2] （名詞and名詞） in choices of [3] （名詞）.

(5) It is [1] （動詞，表現） in this [2] （名詞，表格名稱） how people [3] （動詞或動詞片語）.

文章開展參考句型

(1) Overall, they spend [1] （比例） of their [2] （名詞） [3] （動詞+ing子句）.

(2) Overall, the number of [1] （複數名詞） shows a(n) [2] （名詞，增加或減少） from [3] （時間 to 時間）.

(3) [1] （名詞） take(s) a [2] （形容詞） lead of （數字）percent over [3] （名詞）.

(4) [1] （名詞）, which has a meager proportion of （數字）percent, apparently is under disfavor.

(5) In contrast, [1] （名詞） takes up [2] （比例） of [3] （名詞或名詞片語）.

結論收尾參考句型

(1) Overall, from [1] （時間） to （時間）, there was [2] （形容詞，描述大小） change in [3] （名詞片語）.

(2) In conclusion, mostly, [1] （名詞） for [2] （複數名詞，族群） are to [3] （動詞） with, whereas [4] （複數名詞，另一族群） opt for [5] （名詞） to [6] （動詞）.

(3) This [1] （名詞，圖表名稱） clearly illustrates that [2] （複數名詞，族群） view [3] （名詞） as an indispensable part of their lives.

(4) According to this [1] （名詞，圖表名稱）, we can expect that, in the future, more and more [2] （複數名詞，族群） will [3] （動詞）.

(5) To conclude, [1] （名詞所有格） preferences for [2] （複數名詞，種類名稱） [3]（動詞，表示改變、不變） with time.

Part **4**

抄這本就對了！
寫出連貫的

「連環圖片類」
作文

抄這本就對了！寫出連貫的「連環圖片類」作文

　　所謂看圖作文，就是根據圖畫的內容和命題的要求寫成一篇作文（大多以寫人、記事、寫景物為主）。目前考試中常出現的連環圖片類作文，通常都有一個簡單的劇情貫串，只需要將整體的劇情敘述完即可，不需要太多的想像力。但適時的加油添醋，總會有錦上添花的效果。連環圖片類作文的寫法，簡單地說來要把握以下三點，我們一起來看看吧！

一定要知道

「連環圖片類」作文的寫作重點

寫連環圖片題 Step 1. 抓住圖片重點

　　進行連環圖片的寫作時，使用「定體→審圖→立意→聯想」的四步驟，能幫助你全盤掌握圖片重點。首先讓我們找出圖片中的主角是誰吧：

 定體：主體是誰？

　　看圖作文中，畫面的主體往往是人物。要從畫面中人物的形體、相貌、服飾等，弄清人物的性別、年齡、身分；從人物的表情、動作，推測人物在想什麼。確認主角的個人檔案（定體）之後，接下來便是要觀察跟主角互動的事件、地點和時間。

 審圖：觀察圖片中的周圍環境

　　一張只有主角的圖片，是無法開展成一篇故事的。因此需要觀察圖片中的周圍環境，弄清事件發生的時間、地點以及和事件有關的物品，這個步驟就是「審圖」。

寫連環圖片題 Step2. 安排故事架構並完成作文

 立意：訂出寫作題旨

根據圖片的事件、時間與地點，你可以從中發展出不同的寫作路線；集合上述所有的條件，把事情的來龍去脈交代清楚，建構出一篇完整的作文。這個步驟的寫作，也就是「立意」。

 聯想：佈局作文內容，加上聯想畫龍點睛

雖然有人物、有景物，但沒有聲音也不會動。而看圖作文，則要藉助圖片提供的形象進行合理想像，把圖上的人物寫活。經過前面的「定體→審圖→立意」三步驟，這時要注意，按照從整體到部分，由遠到近等順序寫作；要抓住重點，突出中心。利用已掌握的事件、地點和時間等寫作素材，將作文寫得「有色有聲」，既有事物的靜態，還有事物的動態；將靜止的畫面「動起來」，平面的事物「立體化」，就是一篇生動又充滿感情的連環作文了。

寫連環圖片題 Step3. 創意思考，將文章引導至自己有利之處

改作文的老師一天要看千百篇作文，如果這些作文總是長得千篇一律，也就只能拿到不怎麼突出的分數。想要拿高分，就一定要發揮創意，寫出讓閱卷老師印象深刻的作文才行！而這種時候，創意思考就是你最需要的武器。不過，也別覺得慌張：「我就是沒有創意，那怎麼辦？」事實上，正是因為連環圖片作文可以切入的角度如此多，各種千奇百怪的角度都可以當作出發點，所以你才更能將它轉為對自己有利的角度啊！

舉例來說，相信你的生活中一定多多少少都會有一些興趣吧！如果你喜歡看像是《哈利波特》系列的書或電影，那你對於「魔法」、「巫師」這方面所知道的英文單字就可能比別人多。那何不把你作文中的角色寫成一個巫師呢？連環圖片中什麼也沒規定，當然也沒規定你的角色不能是巫師。從巫師的角度來展開文章，絕對夠有創意，也能讓閱卷老師眼睛為之一亮。

或者，如果你對唱歌有興趣呢？或許你是學校管樂隊的成員？那你一定知道一些別人不知道的音樂術語。如果你喜歡看籃球，常會看外國的籃球比賽，那你也一定知道一些別人不知道的籃球術語。怎麼把你所知道的東西融入文章中呢？這就考驗你的

創意了。幸好連環圖片題目中的角色都不會有太過強烈的特色，你想讓他們變成籃球員、音樂家⋯⋯都沒人限制你，可以盡量使用自己擅長的角度和領域來發揮，這樣不但能讓使用的單字變得更有深度，也可以自然而然地表現出和別人不同的創意囉！

寫連環圖片題 Step 4. 看圖作文還需要注意什麼？

 選擇陳述觀點

撰寫故事時，可以從很多種觀點切入：你可以是故事中的某個角色（會用I/We第一人稱），或是講故事的旁觀者（會用He/She/They第三人稱）。在寫作時，你可以幫主角取好名字，避免一直出現our English teacher或是the classmate sitting next to me這樣重複的單字。要注意的是，全文只能選定一個觀點，且主詞、時態及相關描述都必須符合這個觀點。

 使用正確時態

注意「時態」的掌握：一般看圖寫作都是描述文或記敘文，寫的都是過去已發生的事，主要都用「過去式」。若中間有一些說明「習慣」或是「不變的真理」的句子，則可用現在式。

 聯想相關詞彙

為了避免內文多次重複出現相同的字，有時候要尋找相關的替代詞彙。例如：

中文說法	英文寫法	其他替換寫法
「寫」東西	to write	to scribble、to jot down
「信件」	note	letter、message
「生氣」	angry	furious、irritated

實戰必備

「連環圖片類」作文必備單字片語

連環圖片雖然每張圖表達的故事不盡相同（甚至可以說天差地遠），但多少還是會有一些共通點，例如裡面一般會有「主角」（有角色才能開展故事嘛），而要發展故事，也就需要提到各種時間點。因此，在這裡便為大家整理了一些修飾主角的形容詞，以及表達時間用的單字與片語。

描述「人的外表」，可以用這些字詞

❶	好看的	**good-looking / beautiful / pretty**
❷	可愛的	**cute / lovely**
❸	英俊的	**handsome**
❹	善良的	**kind / good-hearted / kind-hearted**
❺	壞心的	**evil / bad-hearted**
❻	溫柔的	**tender / gentle**
❼	正直的	**decent**
❽	細心的	**careful**
❾	粗心的	**careless**
❿	誠實的	**honest**
⓫	驕傲的	**proud**
⓬	自大的	**(self-)conceited**
⓭	自私的	**selfish**
⓮	幼稚的	**childlike / immature**
⓯	成熟的	**mature**
⓰	勇敢的	**brave / courageous**
⓱	膽小的	**timid / cowardly / shy**

⑱	好脾氣的	good-tempered
⑲	壞脾氣的	bad-tempered / ill-tempered
⑳	受歡迎的	popular
㉑	好相處的	easy-going
㉒	愛吹牛的	boastful
㉓	心胸寬大的	open-minded
㉔	有自信的	(self-)confident
㉕	自我中心的	self-centered
㉖	有禮貌的	polite / well-mannered / courteous
㉗	沒禮貌的	impolite / ill-mannered / rude

 表達「時間」的單字片語

❶	有一天	one day
❷	有一天早上	one morning
❸	那一天	that day
❹	那一天早上	that morning
❺	明天早上	tomorrow morning
❻	上週	last week
❼	上課中	in class
❽	放學後	after school / after class
❾	在一個晴朗的早上	on a sunny morning
❿	在一個星期天早上	on a Sunday morning
⓫	前一晚	the night before
⓬	隔一天	the next day
⓭	隔天早上	the next morning

實戰必備

「連環圖片類」作文
必備實用句型

　　連環圖片類作文題目有千百種，當然不太可能有同樣一個句型能夠涵蓋全部的連環圖片題目。況且，連環圖片類作文題目考的是你的創意，想展現創意，似乎也很難只侷限在幾個句型中。然而，如果你是那種看到考卷就腦筋一片空白的人，一定很希望有幾個可以參考的句子當作「出發點」，才能夠藉由這個「基石」盡情揮灑創意吧！所以在這裡為大家列出一些連環圖片類作文中，「說故事」時可以使用的萬用句型做個參考，讓大家寫作時有個方向喔！

這樣抄就對了 Step **1.** 故事的開頭抄這些句型就對了！

❶ <u>　¹（時間）　</u>, a(n) <u>²（形容詞）</u> **thing happened to** <u>（人）</u>.

　　<u>　　　</u>，一件<u>　　　　</u>事發生在<u>　　　　</u>身上。

> **1 處可填入：**Last week 上禮拜／Yesterday 昨天／This Monday 這禮拜一
> **2 處可填入：**embarrassing 丟臉的／funny 好笑的／crazy 瘋狂的

🖐 整句可以這樣寫：

This morning, an exciting thing happened to me.
今天早上，一件刺激的事發生在我身上。

· ·

❷ <u>　¹（時間）　</u>, **something really** <u>²（形容詞）</u> **happened to** <u>（人）</u>, **who would never forget it for the rest of** <u>³（所有格）</u> **life.**

　　<u>　　　</u>，一件很<u>　　　</u>事發生在<u>　　　</u>身上，<u>　　　</u>一輩子也不會忘記的。

> **1 處可填入：** This morning 今天早上／Two days ago 兩天前／
> Yesterday 昨天
> **2 處可填入：** stupid 愚蠢的／hilarious 好笑的／unbelievable 難以置信的
> **3 處可填入：** his 他的／our 我們的／her 她的

✋ **整句可以這樣寫：**

Last week, something really surprising happened to John, who would never forget it for the rest of his life.

上禮拜，一件很驚人的事發生在約翰身上，他一輩子都不會忘記的。

- -

❸ **Everyone has his or her own story to tell. Here is [1] （所有格）.**

每個人都有自己的故事。以下就是_____故事。

> **1 處可填入：** mine 我的／my dad's 我爸的／Susan's 蘇珊的

✋ **整句可以這樣寫：**

Everyone has his or her own story to tell. Here is Jenny's.

每個人都有自己的故事。以下就是珍妮的故事。

- -

❹ **Now, allow me to share this [1] （形容詞） story with you.**

現在就讓我和你分享這個_____故事。

> **1 處可填入：** happy 快樂的／sad 傷心的／strange 奇怪的

✋ **整句可以這樣寫：**

Now, allow me to share this funny story with you.

現在就讓我和你分享這個好笑的故事。

- -

❺ Although ＿＿＿（某人）would rather keep this story a secret, it's so
¹＿（形容詞）that I can't help but share it with you.

雖然＿＿＿＿希望把這故事保密，但這故事太＿＿＿＿了，我忍不住想跟你們分享。

> **1 處可填入**：interesting 有趣的／funny 好笑的／crazy 瘋狂的

✋ **整句可以這樣寫：**

Although <u>my friend</u> would rather keep this story a secret, it's so
<u>fascinating</u> that I can't help but share it with you.

雖然**我朋友**希望把這故事保密，但它太**有意思**了，我忍不住想和你們分享。

- -

❻ It was ¹＿＿＿（時間點）, and ＿＿＿＿（人物）was ²＿＿（動詞+ing）. That was
how our story began.

當時是個＿＿＿＿，＿＿＿＿在＿＿＿＿。我們的故事就是這樣開始的。

> **1 處可填入**：morning 早上／June 六月／a hot summer day 一個炎熱的夏日
> **2 處可填入**：sleeping 睡覺／doing homework 做功課／
> eating breakfast 吃早餐

✋ **整句可以這樣寫：**

It was <u>a cool evening</u>, and <u>Jason</u> was <u>jogging</u>. That was how our story began.

當時是個**涼爽的傍晚**，**傑森**在**慢跑**。我們的故事就是這樣開始的。

- -

❼ ＿＿＿＿（某人）thought it was going to be an ordinary day. But it
ended up being anything but that.

＿＿＿＿＿以為這會是很普通的一天，結果這天卻非常不一般。

✋ **整句可以這樣寫：**

<u>I</u> thought it was going to be an ordinary day. But it ended up being
anything but that.

我以為這會是很普通的一天，結果這天卻非常不一般。

這樣抄就對了 Step2. 故事的收尾抄這些句型就對了！

❶ It was the [1] （形容詞最高級） experience that （某人） has (have) ever had.

這是_____經歷過_____經驗。

> **1 處可填入：** most unforgettable 最難忘／sweetest 最甜美的／
> most confusing 最令人困惑的

🖐 **整句可以這樣寫：**

It was the strangest experience that Jodie has ever had.

這是**裘蒂**經歷過**最奇怪**的經驗。

⋯⋯⋯⋯⋯⋯⋯⋯⋯⋯⋯⋯⋯⋯⋯⋯⋯⋯⋯⋯

❷ （某人） felt very [1] （形容詞） after what happened.

在事情發生後，_____覺得很_____。

> **1 處可填入：** regretful 懊悔的／worried 焦慮的／exhausted 疲累的

🖐 **整句可以這樣寫：**

I felt very grateful after what happened.

在事情發生後，**我**覺得很**感激**。

⋯⋯⋯⋯⋯⋯⋯⋯⋯⋯⋯⋯⋯⋯⋯⋯⋯⋯⋯⋯

❸ （某人） really learned a lesson and swore never will （某人） make the same mistake again.

_____真的學到了一課，並發誓再也不會犯一樣的錯誤。

🖐 **整句可以這樣寫：**

Bob really learned a lesson and swore never will he make the same mistake again.

鮑勃真的學到了一課，並發誓再也不會犯一樣的錯誤。

⋯⋯⋯⋯⋯⋯⋯⋯⋯⋯⋯⋯⋯⋯⋯⋯⋯⋯⋯⋯

❹ **The moral of the story is that we should never** [1]（動詞或動詞片語）.

這個故事帶來的啟示就是我們絕不能＿＿＿＿。

> **1 處可填入：**waste food 浪費食物／take things for granted 把事情視為理所當然

✋ **整句可以這樣寫：**

The moral of the story is that we should never trust strangers.

這個故事帶來的啟示就是我們絕對不能信任陌生人。

❺ （某人）**decided never to** [1]（動詞或動詞片語） **again.**

＿＿＿＿決定再也不＿＿＿＿＿了。

> **1 處可填入：**be careless 不小心／drive while drunk 酒後駕車

✋ **整句可以這樣寫：**

Benny decided never to procrastinate again. 班尼決定再也不拖延了。

❻ **To** （某人）**, the story would be forever memorable because it taught** （某人）**to be a(n)** [1]（形容詞比較級）**person from then on.**

對＿＿＿來說，這個故事很令人印象深刻，因為它教會了＿＿＿從此成為一個＿＿＿人。

> **1 處可填入：**better 更好的／more careful 更小心的

✋ **整句可以這樣寫：**

To David, the story would be forever memorable because it taught him to be a nicer person from then on.

對大衛而言，這個故事很令人印象深刻，因為它教會了他從此成為一個更好的人。

❼ **Real life is indeed sometimes stranger than stories, isn't it?**

現實生活有時候就是比故事更奇怪，不是嗎？

這樣抄就對了！

★別忘了劃底線處可以依自己的狀況套入別的單字或片語喔！

示範一：連環圖片〈一〉

前面我們已經看過了「連環圖片」題型中超實用的單字片語和句型了！現在就把這些單字與句型組合起來，一篇完整的文章就完成囉！一起來看看幾個例子，都是老師精心為你寫成的高分參考作文喔！注意，裡面套色的地方都是你在前面已經學過的句型。你看，會了這些句型是不是整篇文章就可以完成八成了呢？真的夠實用吧！不過別忘了，連環圖片題型是很考驗創意的，所以使用以上句型之外，還要加入一些自己的個人特色，否則分數高不了的。

 The Bloody Tie

Strange things happen, even to the most innocent people. That is why everyone has his or her own story to tell. Here is **my friend, Terry's**.

It was **Terry's first wedding anniversary**, and he was **looking for an anniversary gift for his wife**. That was how our story began. Being a rather careless person, Terry spent too much time picking out a suitable gift for his sweetheart, and thus had to run all the way to the park where he and his wife were

濺血領帶

　　就算是最無辜的人，也可能會發生奇怪的事。所以每個人都有自己的故事。以下是我朋友泰瑞的故事。

　　當時是泰瑞結婚週年紀念日，他在找送給太太的紀念禮物。我們的故事就是這樣開始的。泰瑞這個人有點粗心，所以花了

scheduled to meet so as to not be late. When turning a corner, he bumped into a man in a sleek suit, his gift as well as the man's package went tumbling to the ground.

Terry would have apologized and helped the man up, he really would, but there was no time! He snatched up his things and took off towards his destination without looking back once. When he arrived, he was out of breath, but at least his wife was happy and excitedly ripped open the present. And in the box, she found a tie with fresh blood on it!

Both Terry and his wife were horrified. It was the **strangest** experience that they have ever had. Terry swore that the gift he chose was a silver necklace, and luckily his wife believed him. They decided to take the tie to the police, and since they both felt very **woozy** after what happened, they went to get expensive steak to help calm themselves down.

They never found out why the man in the suit was carrying a bloody tie. Real life is indeed sometimes stranger than stories, isn't it?

太多時間在為他的愛人挑選適合的禮物，因此為了不要遲到，他必須一路跑到他跟太太相約的公園去。在跑過轉角時，他撞到了一個穿著俐落西裝的男子，而他的禮物與男子的包裹都滾落到地上了。

泰瑞本來想道歉、拉那個男子起來的，但就真的沒時間了啊！他把東西隨手一抓，然後頭也不回地朝著目的地狂奔。他抵達時都快喘不過氣來，但至少他太太很開心，並很興奮地把禮物拆開。在盒子裡，她發現一條上面沾著鮮血的領帶！

泰瑞跟他太太都嚇傻了。這是他們經歷過最奇怪的事。泰瑞發誓他挑的禮物明明是條銀項鍊，幸好他太太也相信他。他們決定把領帶拿去警察局，然後因為事情發生過後兩人都有點暈頭轉向，他們就決定去吃很貴的牛排來壓壓驚。

他們永遠也不知道那個穿西裝的男子為什麼會帶著一條染血的領帶。真實生活有時真的比故事還要奇怪，對吧？

這樣抄就對了！

★別忘了劃底線處可以依自己的狀況套入別的單字或片語喔！

示範二：連環圖片〈二〉

接下來嘗試寫寫看下面的這四張連環圖片，試著描述裡面的故事吧！注意，裡面套色的地方都是你在前面已經學過的句型。你看，會了這些句型是不是整篇文章就可以完成一大部分了呢？真的夠實用吧！

 Superhero in Disguise

 ① ②

③ ④

Ella thought it was going to be an ordinary day. But it ended up being anything but that. It was **one Sunday afternoon**, and **Ella** was **heading towards the park**. That was how our story began.

隱藏的超級英雄

艾拉以為這天會是個很一般的日子，結果這天卻非常不一般！那是個星期天下午，艾拉正在走向公園。我們的故事就是在這裡開始的。

As Ella walked, she felt a tug at her handbag. Instinctively looking down, she witnessed a boy stick his hand in her bag and snatch away her purse! Ella was naturally quite pissed off. She was not going to let the boy get away with her precious purse—there wasn't much money in it, but she happened to keep all her favorite family photos in the purse and there was no way she would hand them over to some ugly boy.

Ella shouted loudly for help and began to chase after the boy. Since she was wearing heels, which were very hard to run in, she even took off her shoes so as to run faster. However, the boy was too nimble for her. He soon disappeared into the park, much to Ella's dismay. She watched unhappily, ready to give up, as the boy ran past the resident blind old man who always sits idly on a park bench.

Suddenly, the boy fell forward onto the ground, and began to groan and cry. The purse fell out of his clutch, and Ella walked over to pick it up. But it was all very strange; the boy was agile, and there was nothing for him to trip over. How did he fall?

Ella glanced at the blind old man, who was still sitting there calmly like nothing was out of the ordinary. She was about to say something when the corner of his mouth twitched, like he was suppressing a smile.

Perhaps the old man knew telekinesis? Ella wondered, but she didn't dare ask. It was the **most curious** experience that **she** has ever had. Real life is indeed sometimes stranger than stories, isn't it?

艾拉正走著，忽然感覺到有人在拉她的手提包。她直覺地往下看，看到一個男孩把手放進她的包包裡，搶走了她的錢包！艾拉當然很生氣。她才不會讓那男孩拿走她珍貴的錢包。裡面的錢是不多，但她最喜歡的家人相片都在裡面，她才不會讓這醜醜的男孩拿走呢。

艾拉大聲地求救，並開始追那個男孩。因為她穿高跟鞋很難跑，還為了跑快一點乾脆把鞋脫了。然而男孩太敏捷了，很快就消失在公園中，讓艾拉很不高興。她難過地看著男孩跑過那個總是閒閒沒事坐在公園長凳上的失明老人前面，準備要放棄追他了。

突然，男孩往前摔到地上，開始又哭又呻吟。錢包從他手中掉了出來，艾拉便走過去把它撿了起來。但這實在滿奇怪的，這男孩這麼敏捷，地上又沒有東西會絆倒他，他到底怎麼跌倒的？

艾拉看了一眼失明的老人，他還是很平靜地坐在那裡，好像什麼也沒發生一樣。她正想說什麼，卻注意到老男人的嘴角微微揚起，好像在忍笑一樣。

也許他有心靈遙控的超能力吧？艾拉這樣想，但她不敢問。這是她遇過最奇怪的一個經驗。真實生活有時候真的比故事還奇怪，不是嗎？

這樣抄就對了！

★別忘了劃底線處可以依自己的狀況套入別的單字或片語喔！

示範三：連環圖片〈三〉

接下來嘗試寫寫看下面的這四張連環圖片，試著描述裡面的故事吧！注意，裡面套色的地方都是你在前面已經學過的句型。你看，會了這些句型是不是整篇文章就可以完成一大部分了呢？真的夠實用吧！

 # It Didn't Go as Planned

Last summer, something really **embarrassing** happened to **my best friend Josh**, who would never forget it for the rest of **his** life, because we laugh at him about it whenever we get the chance. Although **poor Josh** would rather keep this story a secret, it's so **stupid** that I can't help but share it with you.

It was **a lovely day**, and **Josh** was **surfing at the beach**. That was how our story began. He noticed a pretty lifeguard with amazing assets and curves in all the right places, and decided that he wanted her attention. To catch the eye of a lifeguard, the best way, of course, would be to drown. Therefore Josh stepped into the water, and pretended to be flailing and screaming for help. Soon, with glee, he saw the pretty lifeguard swim towards him in all her glory, and began to excitedly imagine the girl kissing his lips in order to perform CPR.

However, the girl did not kiss him, and instead slapped him across the face. "Are you insane?" she yelled. "We can tell at a glance that you're acting. Pretending to drown is an honestly terrible thing. What if someone really needs help, yet we lifeguards are rescuing idiots like you and don't have time to save the ones in need?"

Josh was speechless. He had never thought of it that way before. He felt very **regretful** after what happened. Yes, he still occasionally jokes about being slapped by a pretty girl, but he told me that **he** really learned a lesson and swore never will he make the same mistake again. A human life is much more important than kissing pretty girls.

計畫失敗

去年夏天,我最好的朋友喬許發生了一件很丟臉的事,他一輩子都不會忘記,因為我們隨時會拿出來嘲笑他。雖然可憐的喬許希望保密,但這件事實在太蠢,我忍不住想拿出來和你們分享。

這天天氣很好,喬許在海邊衝浪。我們的故事就是這麼開始的。他注意到有個漂亮的救生員,身材相當均稱,所以他想要得到她的注意。要讓救生員注意你,最有效的方法當然就是溺水了,所以喬許便踏入水中,假裝在掙扎、喊救命。很快地,他很開心地看到那名正妹救生員朝他游來,他興奮地想像著這個女孩將如何為他做人工呼吸、親吻他的嘴唇。

然而,這個女孩不但沒親他,還甩了他一巴掌。「你瘋了喔?」她大吼。「我們一看就知道你是演的。假裝溺水真的是一件很糟糕的事情。如果有人真的需要救援,我們救生員卻在救像你這種白目,沒空去救真正有需要的人怎麼辦?」

喬許說不出話來。他不曾想過這樣的事,也覺得發生的事讓他很懊悔。沒錯,他現在還是偶爾會自嘲自己被正妹甩巴掌的事,但他告訴我,他真的學了一課,並發誓再也不犯同樣的錯誤。人命比和正妹接吻重要太多了。

★別忘了劃底線處可以依自己的
狀況套入別的單字或片語喔！

示範四：連環圖片〈四〉

接下來嘗試寫寫看下面的這四張連環圖片，試著描述裡面的故事吧！注意，裡面套色的地方都是你在前面已經學過的句型。你看，會了這些句型是不是整篇文章就可以完成一大部分了呢？真的夠實用吧！

這題連環圖片特別的地方在於，許多的連環圖片題都是「最後一張」空白，要你以自己的想像力補滿。然而這題卻是「第三張」空白，也就是說你需要自己想像的不是「結局」而是「過程」。一起來試試看吧！

 An Unlikely Hero

(1)

(2)

(3)

(4)

Anyone can be a hero, even you and me. Huh? You don't think you could be a hero? Lisa didn't either. She was just Lisa, boring and average. Her one passion was baseball, but could one be a hero by playing baseball? She didn't think so.

That is, she didn't think so until one day. It was **a Saturday**, and <u>Lisa</u> was <u>**heading home after baseball practice**</u>. That was how our story began. Now, allow me to share this <u>**incredibly touching**</u> story with you.

Lisa had a crush on the guy who worked in the convenience store on her way home. She always tried to act all girly and flirty to get his attention, but it never worked. Still, she persevered, because Lisa wasn't one to give up. That day, she went into the convenience store to get some water, but also to sneakily peek at her crush. However, she realized that the atmosphere in the store was different as soon as she walked in. Turning towards the counter, she saw a masked robber pointing a gun at her crush, demanding money. Her crush was trembling, nearly in tears. It broke her heart to see him like that.

Lisa acted fast. Using her trusty baseball bat, she whacked the robber on the back of the head and watched as the man crumpled to the ground. It felt better than hitting a homerun!

意想不到的英雄

誰都有可能成為英雄，你我都有可能。啊？你覺得自己不可能成為英雄嗎？麗莎以前也不覺得。她就只是麗莎，無聊又一般般的麗莎。她唯一一個興趣是棒球，但打棒球能讓人變成英雄嗎？她可不這麼認為。

應該說，她一直到某天之前，都不這麼認為。當時是個星期六，麗莎正在練完棒球回家的路上。我們的故事就是從這裡開始的。現在，讓我來跟你們分享這個非常感人的故事。

麗莎一直暗戀著在她回家路上便利商店裡打工的一個男生。她每次都想要表現得很淑女、很曖昧，讓那個男生注意她，然而總是沒有成功。她依舊繼續努力，因為她不是會輕言放棄的那種人。那天，她到便利商店買水，順便偷看她的暗戀對象。然而她一走進店裡，就發現氣氛非常不同。她一轉頭看櫃台，就看到一個戴著面罩的搶匪，拿著槍指著她暗戀的對象，和他要錢。他一直在發抖，都快哭了，讓麗莎簡直要心碎。

麗莎很快便行動了。她拿起她可靠的球棒，用力地打了搶匪的頭，看著那男人倒地不起。感覺比打全壘打還要爽！

Lisa's crush was very grateful. Since they had to go to police interviews and whatnot together, they soon became friends with each other, and he asked her out one day. **Lisa** felt very **happy** after what happened. **She** decided never to **pretend to be girly** again. After all, it was not her girliness that made her crush notice her! Instead, it was her kickass baseball skills, which she used to think weren't anything worth bragging about. Now, whenever friends ask Lisa for love advice, she tells them "just be yourself", because being herself and doing what she does best were what made her a hero and landed her a boyfriend!

麗莎的暗戀對象非常感激她。因為他們必須一起去警局面談做筆錄什麼的,他們後來就變成好朋友了,而他後來也有天約她出去。發生了這些事,麗莎很開心。她決定再也不要假裝自己很淑女了。畢竟她暗戀的人注意到她,可不是因為她的淑女表現啊!反而是因為她本來以為不值一提的超強棒球球技。現在,每當有朋友請麗莎給一點戀愛相關的意見,她都會告訴他們「做自己就好了」,因為做自己、做自己最擅長的事,正是讓麗莎成為英雄、並交到男朋友的原因。

學測指考歷屆試題實戰驗證！

自我挑戰試試看：
2011年學測作文題目

有了完整的句型模板，現在的你寫起作文絕對無往不利，大考的題目也難不倒你了！現在我們就來使用模板當武器，挑戰歷屆指考與學測中出現過的「連環圖片」類題型。

2011年學科能力測驗英文作文試題
提示：請仔細觀察以下三幅連環圖片的內容，並想像第四幅圖片可能的發展，
　　　寫出一個涵蓋連環圖片內容並有完整結局的故事。

Last month, a **hilarious** thing happened to **my brother Charlie**. Although **Charlie** would rather keep this story a secret, it's so **funny** that I can't help but share it with you, so that we can all laugh at him together.

It was Halloween, and Charlie went to a masquerade ball with his college friends. At the ball, he saw a lovely girl dressed as a princess, and he

上個月，一件爆笑的事發生在我哥哥查理的身上。雖然查理希望保密，但這件事太好笑，我忍不住要和你們分享，這樣我們就可以一起笑他了。

當時是萬聖節，查理和他的大學朋友們一起去了化裝舞會。在舞會他看

immediately went over to talk to her. The girl was gentle and sweet, and when he asked her for her address she wrote it down for him shyly, eyes downcast.

Charlie was more than excited; he thought he would finally land his first girlfriend. The very next night, he rode his motorbike to the girl's apartment, guitar in hand, ready to serenade his girl with a love song he composed himself overnight. However, what you need to know about Charlie is that he's tone-deaf, completely tone-deaf. As he sang, more and more windows opened in the neighborhood, and angry residents began to yell at him to shut up. An elderly lady even threw eggs at him. Charlie was devastated to find that even though all these people heard him, his girl did not show up at all. He finally realized that she had given him a fake address.

Charlie felt very **disappointed** after what happened. He realized that asking a girl her address the first time they met wasn't a good idea and **he** decided never to **be that foolish** again. To his shock and horror, his singing that night was recorded by a resident in the neighborhood and uploaded to YouTube. It was so terrible that it went viral in one day. It was the most **embarrassing** experience that **Charlie** has ever had, though the rest of us find great joy in recounting this story to others like you!

＼老師告訴你／

套上顏色的文字都是你在前面就學過的句型喔！這篇作文中的主角是唱歌的男生，但也可以嘗試從女孩、鄰居、男主角的朋友的角度為出發點描寫，我甚至還讀過從「吉他」的角度寫的作文……。

到了一個漂亮的女孩，打扮成公主的樣子，他馬上就過去和她說話。這個女孩溫柔甜美，他和她要地址時，她害羞地垂眼寫給他。

查理非常興奮，他覺得他終於要交第一個女朋友了。第二天晚上，他騎著機車到女孩的套房那裡，手上拿著吉他，準備要唱一首他熬夜寫的情歌給那女孩聽。然而，你要知道查理是個音痴，徹徹底底的音痴。他唱著歌的同時，整個社區中越來越多窗戶打了開來，憤怒的居民嚷著要他閉嘴。有個年邁的太太還拿雞蛋丟他。查理很絕望地發現，雖然這麼多人聽到他唱歌，他喜歡的女孩卻根本沒出現。他終於瞭解到，她給他的是假地址。

事情發生後，查理很失望。他發覺，第一次見面就跟女生要地址實在不是個好主意，他決定不要再這麼蠢了。讓他驚慌的是，他當晚的歌聲被社區中的一個居民錄下來上傳到了YouTube。因為他唱得太難聽，影片一天內就爆紅。這是查理有過最丟臉的經驗，不過我們大家倒是很喜歡把這個故事告訴其他人，就像你們！

學測指考歷屆試題實戰驗證！

自我挑戰試試看：
2013年學測作文題目

2013年學科能力測驗英文作文試題
提示：請仔細觀察以下三幅連環圖片的內容，並想像第四幅圖片可能的發展，
寫出一個涵蓋連環圖片內容並有完整結局的故事。

Everyone has his or her own story to tell. Here is **mine**. But first, let me introduce myself. My name is Grace, and I used to be the laughingstock of my school. Please note the past tense. I'm not longer that now, for I am dead.

每個人都有自己的故事，而這就是我的故事。但先讓我自我介紹一下。我叫葛蕾斯，我以前是我們學校裡的笑柄。請注意我用了過去式。我現在已經不再是笑柄，因為我已經死了。

Anyway, like I was saying, I used to be the laughingstock of my school. I was ugly, I had too much acne, my hair was untamable. Among my bullies was a guy called Derek. He not only made fun of me but was also impolite in general—I'd seen him refuse to yield priority seats to the elderly countless times.

It was **one of those normal school days**, and **we were playing basketball in PE**. That was how our story began. Except it ended right away too. Derek was laughing at my clumsy dribbling skills and shoved me. I fell backwards, hitting my head on a statue. I was in a coma for two days before passing away.

Derek did not get punished, claiming it to be an accident, but he had been plagued with bad luck ever since. He injured himself on the basketball courts. When he was taking the MRT, no one would ever let him have their seat, even though he had a broken leg. His love life was nonexistent. And guess who caused it. I did, of course. I cursed him with every fiber of my soul.

The moral of the story is that we should never **be intentionally mean to people**. If only **Derek** had really learned a lesson and sworn never to make the same mistake again. Maybe that would have saved him from his fate. Maybe, or maybe not, I think, as I float towards his home, ready to burn it down.

總之，我以前是我們學校裡大家嘲笑的對象。我很醜，我的青春痘太多，我的頭髮完全不聽話。霸凌我的人之中，有一位叫德瑞克的。他不但拿我開玩笑，平常也很沒禮貌，我看過他佔用博愛座不讓給老人不知道幾次了。

當時是個普通的上學日，我們在體育課打籃球。我們的故事就是從這裡開始，不過這個故事馬上就結束了。德瑞克在嘲笑我差勁的運球技術時推了我一把。我往後倒，頭撞上一座雕像。我昏迷了兩天後過世了。

德瑞克沒有受到處罰，因為他說那是意外，但他從此一直受到噩運纏身。他打籃球時受傷，就算他斷了一條腿，搭捷運時從沒人讓座給他。他的感情生活一片空白。是誰害他這麼慘呢？當然是我啦。我用我全部的靈魂狠狠地詛咒他。

這個故事的啟示就是我們不該惡意欺負人。要是德瑞克有學到教訓、發誓不再犯同樣的錯就好了，或許他就不會遭受這樣的命運了。或許吧，我這麼想著，飄向他的家，準備放火燒掉它。

\ 老師告訴你 /

套上顏色的文字都是你在前面就學過的句型喔！這個題目很貼心，把博愛座的英文說法寫出來了，無論如何可千萬不要連這個都拼錯！

2014年學科能力測驗英文作文試題
提示：請仔細觀察以下三幅連環圖片的內容，並想像第四幅圖片可能的發展，
　　　寫出一個涵蓋連環圖片內容並有完整結局的故事。

When I was **in my first year of high school**, an **unforgettable** thing happened to me. Now, allow me to share this **memorable** story with you.

It was **a normal school day**, and I was **walking to school**. That was how our story began. As usual, I was texting my friends on my phone as I walked. Some of my friends are in different

我在高一時，發生了一件難忘的事。現在，就讓我和你們分享這個難忘的故事。

當時是個普通的上課日，我正在走路去學校。我們的故事就是這樣開始的。我一如往常地在用

127

schools, you see, so we don't get to talk face to face much. Walking beside me was my childhood friend and classmate Peter. Peter was an aspiring musician and was immersed in his own little world, wearing his amazing hi-fidelity new headphone set.

I was so busy texting that I didn't watch where I was going, and walked straight into a tree. I felt very **embarrassed** after what happened, and I was surprised that Peter didn't stop to help me, but then I guess he was just too busy listening to music. In fact, he was too busy listening to music to even notice a car honking at him in warning. A car came swerving around by the corner, and ran straight into Peter.

It was the **scariest** experience that I have ever had. Peter lived, but he was paralyzed from the waist down. To **me**, the story would be forever memorable because it taught **me** to **be a** more careful **person from then on**. I decided never to **fiddle with gadgets when walking** again. Instead, when walking, I would be, well, just walking. That might not necessarily guarantee me a safer life, but I hope to at least not end up like Peter.

手機傳訊息給我朋友。因為我有些朋友在不同的學校,所以我們很少可以當面聊天。走在我旁邊的是我的青梅竹馬兼同學彼得。彼得想成為音樂人,正沉浸在他自己的小小世界裡,戴著他新買的高傳真耳機。

我忙著傳訊息,沒注意自己在往哪裡走,結果直直撞到樹。事情發生後,我覺得很丟臉,也有點驚訝,彼得居然沒停下來幫我一把。但我想他應該是聽音樂聽得太認真了。事實上,他聽得之認真,甚至沒注意到有車子在按喇叭警告他。一輛車從轉角快速開來,直接撞上了彼得。

這是我遇過最可怕的經驗。彼得活下來了,但他從腰以下都癱瘓了。對我來說,這個故事永遠難忘,因為它教會我從此成為一個更小心的人。我決定再也不要邊走邊玩小東西了。反之,在走路時,我就專心走路。也許這不保證我的生活會更加安全,但我希望自己至少不要變成另一個彼得。

\老師告訴你/

套上顏色的文字都是你在前面就學過的句型喔!你可以發現這些連環圖片中有很多的角色,包含男女主角、開車的人、後面的媽媽和小孩。可以試試用不同角色的角度來寫,不過如果從小小朋友的角度就勢必要用非常簡單的單字和句型,在正式考試時可能沒有加分的效果,所以要注意。

學測指考歷屆試題實戰驗證！

自我挑戰試試看：
2017年學測作文題目

2017年大學學科能力測驗英文作文試題
提示：請仔細觀察以下三幅連環圖片的內容，並想像第四幅圖片可能的發展，
　　　然後寫出一篇涵蓋每張圖片內容且結局完整的故事。

Last weekend, something really **thrilling** happened to **me**, who would never forget it for the rest of **my** life. It was **a sunny morning**, and **my whole family** was **loading the luggage with humming excitedly.** Yet the highway traffic to Hualien was totally stuck! Fortunately, we had lots of interesting things to share with each other since my

　　上個週末發生了一件很驚險的事，讓我永生難忘。那是個晴朗的上午，我們全家人正邊哼著歌邊裝行李。然而通往花蓮的高速公路完全塞住了！幸好我們有一堆趣事可以跟彼此分享，因為我爸才

father had just got back from a long business trip in Shanghai. He talked about how marvelous the buildings and cuisine there were, and said he's gonna take me with him next time. When we finally made it to Hualien, it was overcrowded everywhere. Therefore, we made a decision: let's discover unknown places, create a journey of our own!

So the adventure embarked, we headed towards a natural cave recommended by the locals. The scenery was spectacular, it had been preserved well because there's not many tourists there. Just when I thought the trip was getting better, things went wrong. As I finally found the perfect angle to take a panoramic photo of the cave, I wasn't aware that I was also in something's crosshair. The moment I pressed the shutter, my camera was lifted by a tremendous eagle. I saw them off in stunned speechlessness, pitched my thighs to verify if I was dreaming or not. To **me**, the experience would be forever memorable because it taught **me** to be a **more careful** person from then on. Because you'll never know what kind of magical things could happen to you. Real life is indeed sometimes stranger than stories, isn't it?

剛結束長期出差從上海回來。他聊了許多讓人驚豔的當地建築和料理，而且說有機會一定要帶我一起去。當我們終於抵達花蓮，發現到處都人滿為患。我們因此決定去探索未知的地方，創造屬於自己的旅程！

於是旅程開始了，我們前往當地人推薦的一處天然洞穴。景色相當壯觀，而且因為遊客不多環境維護得非常好。正當我以為這趟旅程要變得順利時，事情直轉急下。當我終於找到了一個可以拍攝洞穴全貌的好角度時，渾然不覺自己也成了別人準星中的獵物。我按下快門的那個瞬間，一隻碩大的老鷹抓走了我的相機。在無言的震驚中我目送他們離開，一邊掐著大腿確認自己是不是在作夢。我將永遠記得這個經驗，因為它讓我從此變成一個更加小心的人。你永遠不會知道有什麼樣神奇的事會發生。真實世界有時真的比故事還離奇，對吧？

美國高中升大學的SAT也無往不利！

你還可以這樣應用：
SAT全真模擬試題05

以下的題目都是專家綜觀先前的SAT試題所整理出的全真模擬試題，題目內容大多以論說為主，別忘了，在論說的同時也會需要輔以故事進行說明啊！這裡就帶著大家試試看如何利用模板句型寫出自然又流暢的SAT作文。SAT作文一般建議長度要寫到300～400字左右，趕快來參考一下老師的寫法吧！

SAT全真模擬試題05

Are people better off if they do not listen to criticism?

（中譯：人們如果不聽人家的批評指教，會過得比較好。你同意嗎？）

It appears that not listening to criticism is the new trend. Criticism, people explain, takes away what little self-confidence most people have left, and leaves them unable to create new innovations simply because they're too unsure of themselves to do so. Besides, people may argue, most people who give criticism to others aren't exactly qualified to do so, and in fact the less knowledgeable people are about a subject the more likely they are to force their own ignorant opinions on others.

This is all true, and personally I absolutely hate it when people criticize me. But are we really better off if we do not listen to criticism? I don't think so. Let's take my friend George for an example. Although **George** would rather keep this story a secret, it's so **relevant to the subject** that I can't help but share it with you.

不聽別人的批評指教看來已經成為近期趨勢了。有些人說，批評會讓本來已經很沒自信的人更沒自信，而變得無法發揮創意，因為他們對自己太沒有信心了。還有人可能會說，許多批評別人的人其實沒有資格這麼做，而且通常對某個主題越不瞭解的人，越喜歡強迫別人接受自己愚蠢的意見。

這都沒錯，我自己也很討厭別人批評我。但不聽別人批評，真的就會比較好嗎？我覺得不會。拿我朋友喬治來舉例好了。雖然喬治希望把這個故事保密，但它和這個主題非常有關，我忍不住想要與你們分享。

George had always wanted to become a professional writer; whenever I saw him, he was writing. It was **last year**, and **George** was **bragging about a novel he wrote that he considered a masterpiece**. That was how our story began. George decided to post his work online before searching for an editor to help him get published. However, the feedback George received was less than encouraging. He had too many spelling errors, one said. The plot was cliché, said another.

George immediately lashed out angrily, calling the readers a bunch of haters and some other words unfit for virgin ears. But when I read the comments, I noted that they weren't really that bad—most were kind and helpful, and some even provided links and articles that could help George in improving his writing skills. George would have none of it. He went straight to a professional editor, believing that amateurs were not good enough to criticize his work. Yet the editor merely read through the first paragraph of his 500-paged book before declaring the very same thing the readers told him: he had too many spelling errors, and the plot was cliché.

It was the most **humbling** experience that **George** has ever had. He felt very **regretful** after what happened, and decided never to be **stubborn and not listen to criticism** again.

To **George**, the story would be forever memorable because it taught **him** to be a **less obstinate** person from then on. And to me, it was definitely a lesson that you can't disregard criticism

喬治一直都想成為一名職業作家。每當我看到他,他都在寫東寫西。當時是去年,喬治一直在吹噓自己寫了一部傑出的小說。我們的故事就是這麼開始的。在找一個編輯幫他出版這本書前,他決定先把作品貼在網路上。然而,他得到的回應並不是很正面。有人說他拼錯太多單字了,另一個人則說他的故事情節很老套。

喬治馬上生氣地反擊了,他罵讀者們都是一群「酸民」,並用一些不堪入耳的字罵他們。但我讀了那些評論,發現其實也沒那麼糟,大部分都很親切、很有幫助,也有人提供了連結與一些文章,以幫助喬治增進文筆。但喬治才不管那麼多,他直接去找一名專業編輯,因為他覺得業餘的人沒資格批評他的作品。然而,那個編輯只看了這本500頁的書的第一段,就說了和那些讀者一樣的話:喬治的錯字太多了,而且故事情節很老套。

這是喬治經歷過最羞愧的經驗。事情發生後,他覺得很懊悔,決定不要再堅持己見、不聽別人的批評。

對喬治來說,這個故事永遠都會令他難忘,因為它教會了他成為一個從此不那麼倔強的人。而對我來說,這絕對像是上

completely—not all criticism is ill-intentioned, and a lot of it can in fact make you become a much better person.

了一課,我學到人真的不能完全不理會批評指教。並不是所有批評指教都是惡意的,很多的批評反而能夠讓你成為一個更好的人。

\ 老師告訴你 /

套上顏色的文字都是你在前面就學過的句型喔!參考看看這篇範文如何利用模板句型的引導,把「故事」不著痕跡地融入論點中作為例證。模板句型同時也可以幫助為整篇文章作一個漂亮的收尾。

你還可以這樣應用：
SAT全真模擬試題06

SAT全真模擬試題06

Does tradition prevent people from doing things in new or more sensible ways?

（中譯：傳統會害人們無法用一些較新或較合理的方式做事嗎？）

As someone who grew up in a very traditionally Chinese society, I can easily tell you that tradition does prevent people from doing things in ways that make better sense (sorry, grandma). You can see evidence of it every day, in people's thoughts, in people's actions. Married women have to live with their in-laws despite it being a huge hassle for both sides, because tradition deems it appropriate. Old people should not wear colorful clothes even if they'd really like to, because tradition says so. Giving birth to a son makes you automatically more favorable than if you had had a daughter, because tradition is like that. None of this makes any sense, but there you have it—our tradition.

My sister Abby, who recently gave birth (luckily, to a son) could tell you all about the troubles tradition caused her. Now, allow me to share **her crazy** story with you. It was **last month**, and **Abby** was **resting at home after she gave birth**. That was how our story began.

身為一個在傳統華人社會中成長的人，我可以肯定地告訴你傳統絕對會害人們無法用比較合理的方式做事（抱歉啦奶奶）。你天天都可以看到相關證據，從人們的想法中、舉動中。已婚的女性必須和公婆住，雖然兩邊都覺得很麻煩，但是傳統認為這樣是洽當的。老人不應該穿太花俏的衣服，就算他們很想穿也一樣，因為傳統說了算。生男孩比生女孩更好，因為傳統就是這樣。這根本就沒有意義，但我們的傳統正是如此。

我姊姊艾比最近剛生孩子（是個男孩，幸好），她可以告訴你傳統造成了她哪些麻煩。現在就讓我來和你們分享她瘋狂的故事。事情發生在上個月，艾比生完孩子後在家裡休息。我們的故事就是這麼開始的。

Feeling tired and greasy, Abby wanted to take a shower and wash her hair. Her in-laws would not hear of it, because women who gave birth weren't traditionally supposed to wash their hair. Abby complied. The next day, she got bored and texted her friends on the phone. Her in-laws came in and snatched her phone away, because women who gave birth weren't traditionally allowed to use electronic products. So Abby decided that, if she couldn't use her phone, she should go out and take a walk. Her in-laws were horrified! Traditionally, women who gave birth must not do anything that could potentially give them a cold, and therefore all fans and air conditioners were switched off in the house, despite it being July.

They also prohibited my sister from eating fruits and salads, from drinking water, and from doing laundry (which was strange enough, but it wasn't like Abby was complaining). All these "do"s and "don't"s, all because of some silly tradition!

It was the most **stifling** experience **Abby** ever had. But here, heaps of women suffer from the same fate after they give birth. No kidding! Even though it's the 21st century! Real life is indeed sometime stranger than stories, isn't it?

艾比覺得身體又累又油，想要淋浴洗頭，但她的公婆不同意，因為生完孩子的女性傳統上不能洗頭。艾比便同意了。第二天，她很無聊，就用手機傳訊息給朋友。她的公婆跑進來把她的手機拿走，因為生完孩子的女性傳統上不能用電子產品。艾比想說既然不能用手機，那她就出去散個步好了。她的公婆嚇死了！傳統上，生完孩子的女性不能做任何可能會感冒的事情，所以家裡的電扇和冷氣都關掉了，即便當時正值七月。

他們也不准我姊吃水果或沙拉、不准喝水、不准洗衣服（這也滿奇怪的，不過艾比倒是樂在其中）。這麼多該做、不該做的事，都是因為莫名其妙的傳統而來的！

這是艾比經歷過最沉悶的事。但在我們這裡，許多生完孩子的女性都要經歷這樣的命運。沒騙你耶！現在明明是二十一世紀耶！現實生活有時真的比故事還奇怪，是不是？

＼老師告訴你／

套上顏色的文字都是你在前面就學過的句型喔！參考看看這篇範文如何利用模板句型的引導，把「故事」不著痕跡地融入論點中作為例證。模板句型同時也可以幫助為整篇文章作一個漂亮的收尾。

讀完了這麼多的範例作文，現在你一定已經躍躍欲試，想套用模板句型自己寫寫看了吧！請你以前面之「**2014年學測作文題目**」為題，套用模板句型寫一篇作文。所有的句型都在框框中為你列出來囉！

_____

_____

_____

_____

_____

_____

_____

_____

_____

_____

_____

_____

_____

_____

_____

_____

_____

_____

_____

_____

_____

_____

_____

_____

_____

_____

_____

_____

_____

_____

_____

故事開頭參考句型

(1) [1] （時間）, a(n) [2] （形容詞） thing happened to （人）.

(2) [1] （時間）, something really [2] （形容詞） happened to （人）, who would never forget it for the rest of [3] （所有格）life.

(3) Everyone has his or her own story to tell. Here is [1] （所有格）.

(4) Now, allow me to share this [1] （形容詞） story with you.

(5) Although （某人） would rather keep this story a secret, it's so [1] （形容詞）that I can't help but share it with you.

(6) It was [1] （時間點）, and （人物）was [2] （動詞+ing）. That was how our story began.

(7) （某人） thought it was going to be an ordinary day. But it ended up being anything but that.

故事收尾參考句型

(1) It was the [1] （形容詞比較級最高級） experience that （某人） has (have) ever had.

(2) （某人） felt very [1] （形容詞） after what happened.

(3) （某人） really learned a lesson and swore never will （某人） make the same mistake again.

(4) The moral of the story is that we should never [1]（動詞或動詞片語）.

(5)（某人）decided never to [1]（動詞或動詞片語） again.

(6) To（某人）, the story would be forever memorable because it taught（某人）to be a(n) [1]（形容詞比較級）person from then on.

(7) Real life is indeed sometimes stranger than stories, isn't it?

Part
5

抄這本就對了！
寫出有故事的

「單張照片類」

作文

抄這本就對了！寫出有故事的 「單張照片類」作文

照片題型也就是「看圖作文」，也就是看著照片，寫出一篇富有故事性的文章。比起「連環圖片題」，單張照片並不會有明確的「劇情走向」，所以就更要靠著你的想像力發揮啦！先看看以下的步驟，照片題型寫作就並非難事喔！

一定要知道

「單張照片類」作文的寫作重點

單張照片 Step 1. 文章開頭：利用「5W1H」設定照片主題

還記得前面「經驗敘述篇」中提過的「5W1H」嗎？照片題型寫作多以寫人、記事、寫景物為主，所以同樣可以運用5W1H的寫作技巧。舉例來說，看到照片時你可以這樣想：

What? 什麼事？

照片裡看起來發生了什麼事？是好事還是壞事？照片裡有哪些景物和物品？我可以如何描述這些景物和物品？

Who? 誰？

照片裡的主角是誰？是男生還是女生？年紀多大？是否可以從他的穿著打扮看出身分（如：學生、警察或是上班族等等）？

When? 什麼時候？

照片裡看得出來是冬天或夏天嗎？看得出來是早上、下午、傍晚還是晚上嗎？是否可以從時鐘之類背景道具看出確切的時間點？

Where? 在哪裡？

場景是都市或鄉村？室內或室外？是否在特定建築內（如：學校、醫院等等）？或是家裡的某個房間（如：臥室、廚房或客廳等等）？

Why? 為什麼？

照片裡的人物為什麼正在做照片中的動作呢？如果光用看的實在看不出理由那更好，就可以依自己的揣測替他編一個理由，沒有標準答案。

How? 如何？

整張照片給你的感覺如何？是開心的、溫馨的、灰暗的或絕望的？考試卷上印的照片很可能是黑白的，但如果讓你來想像，整個畫面該是溫暖的色調還是冷暗的色調呢？

單張照片 Step2. 文章開展：運用想像力

單張的照片題型因為只有一張圖，所以只能展示一件事的部分內容，不會有完整的「過程」、「結局」，更別提有什麼起承轉合。這種時候，只好靠著想像力，從一張照片呈現的畫面，想像出故事的過去以及未來，幫故事杜撰之前曾經發生的事情，並且賦予故事未來的變化與結果，以便能順利展開文章、加深照片本身的故事性，讓內容看起來更豐富，與其他只能呆板地描述照片中景物的文章做出區隔。

怎麼訓練這方面的想像力呢？相信身為考生的你，應該有看過MV（音樂影片）吧！試試看挑幾支自己從來沒看過的MV，在影片的途中任一秒將畫面停頓，看著靜止的畫面想像一下：接下來的劇情會怎麼演？這部影片究竟是要表達什麼？相信你一定能從畫面上的色彩、人物的表情與動作，猜出一個端倪。這是練習從靜止圖片想像整段劇情的一個方法。

單張照片 Step3. 文章結尾：完整的收尾

可別以為只把照片裡看到的情境寫完就沒了！文章若有個好的結尾，可以讓整篇作文變得生動有趣、引人入勝。常見的照片題型結尾，會根據文章開展時所鋪陳的劇情做延伸，或是提出寓意，讓人有所領悟。只要能確認結尾涵蓋到前面的開頭與開展，互相呼應，就是一個完整的收尾了。

「單張照片類」作文必備單字片語

　　單張照片類作文和連環圖片類似，都是要述說一個故事，只是需要更多的想像力。由於照片裡能夠提供的資訊比較少，所以更要把握其中的每一個細節與線索。想要細細地描寫照片中背景環境裡的所有蛛絲馬跡，你需要的就是描寫「環境」的大量單字！現在就來介紹一些形容天氣、氣候的單字，以及和距離、方向有關的片語，這樣要描寫照片中出現的地點時便萬無一失了。那如果你想描寫的不只照片裡的地點，還想多寫一點和人物有關的描述呢？可以翻到「人物與物品描述類」（p.046）看看。

描述「天氣、氣候」，可以用這些字詞

❶	暴雨	**downpour / deluge**
❷	豪雨	**torrential rain**
❸	暴風雪	**blizzards**
❹	隨風飄飛的雪	**snowdrifts**
❺	冰雹	**hailstones**
❻	冷得刺骨的	**bitingly cold**
❼	寒風刺骨的	**nippy**
❽	濕冷發黏的	**clammy**
❾	炎熱的	**boiling hot**
❿	令人窒息地熱的	**stifling hot**
⓫	悶熱	**sweltering heat / oppressive heat**
⓬	悶熱的天氣	**sultry weather**
⓭	灼熱的豔陽	**scorching sun**
⓮	潮濕的	**humid**
⓯	乾燥的；不毛的	**arid**
⓰	風大的	**windy / blustery**

⑰	微風輕拂的	**breezy**
⑱	無風的	**windless**
⑲	有薄霧的	**hazy**
⑳	多霧的	**misty / foggy**
㉑	煙霧彌漫的	**smoggy**
㉒	星星多的	**starry**

 描述「地點、位置」的單字與片語

❶	面向東方／西方／南方／北方	**facing east / west /south / north**
❷	位於……的東方／西方／南方／北方	**in the east / west /south / north of...**
❸	比……這更東／西／南／北一點	**to the east / west / south / north of...**
❹	在……的左／右邊	**on the left / right side of...**
❺	離……很近	**close to / near...**
❻	在附近	**in the neighborhood**
❼	在……的邊緣	**at the edge of...**
❽	在……的中心	**at the center of...**
❾	在……的對面	**be opposite (to)...**
❿	在……的隔壁	**next to...**
⓫	在遠處	**in the distance**
⓬	位於……	**be located / be situated**
⓭	某地的視野不錯	**commanding a fine view**
⓮	被……所環繞	**be surrounded by...**
⓯	環境很美	**in a beautiful / lovely setting**

實戰必備

「單張照片類」作文
必備實用句型

　　單張照片類的作文有很多發揮的角度，所以當然也不能完全侷限於一些固定的句型。可是一下沒有靈感，不知道從哪裡發揮創意怎麼辦呢？沒關係，這裡提供一些簡單的句子，可以幫你開展你要說的整個故事，並做個完整的收尾。別忘了，單張照片類的作文考驗的一樣是你的創意，這些句型只是做一個參考，幫助你作為開展文章的引導，千萬別一股腦地把它們通通都用上去了，作文會亂成一團的。

這樣抄就對了 Step 1. 文章開頭抄這些句型就對了！

❶ I am fond of looking at old photos, because they never fail to transport me back to the good old times when I was still ¹（名詞片語或形容詞）.

我喜歡看舊照片，因為它們總能帶著我回到過去的美好時光，那時我還是
＿＿＿＿＿。

> **1 處可填入：** happy 快樂的／pretty 漂亮的／a child 一個孩子

✋ **整句可以這樣寫：**

I am fond looking at old photos, because they never fail to transport me back to the good old times when I was still a little boy.

我喜歡看舊照片，因為它們總能帶著我回到過去的美好時光，那時我還是個小男孩。

❷ Do you know what it's like to see a(n) [1] （名詞或名詞片語） **right in front of you? I do. Here's my story.**

你知道看到你面前有個_____是什麼樣的感覺嗎？我知道。這就是我的故事。

> **1 處可填入**：giant 巨人／car crash 車禍／angel 天使

✋ **整句可以這樣寫：**

Do you know what it's like to see a robber right in from of you? I do. Here's my story.

你知道看到你面前有個**搶匪**是什麼樣的感覺嗎？我知道。這就是我的故事。

---

❸ Picture this. A(n) [1] （名詞） **is happening. What would you do?**

想像一下這個畫面。有個_____正在發生。你會怎麼做？

> **1 處可填入**：tornado 龍捲風／snowstorm 雪暴／flood 水災

✋ **整句可以這樣寫：**

Picture this. An earthquake is happening. What would you do?

想像一下這個畫面。有場**地震**正在發生。你會怎麼做？

---

❹ Does this [1] （名詞） **shock you? It happens every day in** [2] （地名）**, actually.**

這個_____讓你驚訝嗎？在_____，這種事天天在發生。

> **1 處可填入**：picture 圖片／photo 照片／painting 圖畫
> **2 處可填入**：my hometown 我家鄉／my country 我的國家／America 美國

✍ **整句可以這樣寫：**

Does this image shock you? It happens every day in Mumbai, actually.

這個**畫面**讓你驚訝嗎？在**孟買**，這種事天天在發生。

· ·

❺ （人物） **makes it a habit to** [1] （動詞或動詞片語） [2] （時間頻率）**.** （人物） **didn't expect today to be any different.**

_____習慣_____ _____。_____沒想到今天會和以往不同。

> **1 處可填入：** jog 慢跑／go to the library 去圖書館／
> water his plants 幫植物澆水
> **2 處可填入：** every day 每天／every morning 每天早上／
> every week 每個禮拜

✍ **整句可以這樣寫：**

Johnson makes it a habit to exercise every evening. He didn't expect today to be any different.

強森習慣**每天晚上** **運動**。他沒想到今天會和以往不同。

· ·

❻ **Just by looking at** [1] （人物或景物）**, you would not be able to tell that** [2] （人物或景物的代名詞） **is actually** [3] （名詞片語或形容詞）**.**

光是看_____的樣子，你很難想像_____其實是_____。

> **1 處可填入：** Marie 瑪麗／the building 這棟建築／the bear 這隻熊
> **2 處可填入：** he 他／they 他們／it 它
> **3 處可填入：** a grand justice 大法官／a florist 花藝師

👆 **整句可以這樣寫：**

Just by looking at Lucy, you would not be able to tell that she is actually a mother of three.

光是看露西的樣子，你很難想像她其實是三個孩子的媽。

❼ **The** ¹（形容詞）² （地點名稱）**is my favorite place to go to when I'm feeling** ³（形容詞）**.**

_____ _____是我感到_____時最喜歡去的地方。

> **1 處可填入：**beautiful 美麗的／dark 黑暗的／calming 令人心情平靜的
> **2 處可填入：**park 公園／alley 巷子／house 房子
> **3 處可填入：**down 心情不好的／bad 不好的／unhappy 不開心的

👆 **整句可以這樣寫：**

The quiet café is my favorite place to go to when I'm feeling bored.

那家安靜的 咖啡廳是我感到無聊時最喜歡去的地方。

❶ This is why I enjoy looking at [1] **（複數名詞或名詞片語） so much. They not only bring me memories but also a lot of things to ponder on.**

就是因為這樣，我才這麼喜歡看_____，它們不但能帶給我回憶，也給了我很多思考的題材。

> **1 處可填入**：photos 照片／people's works 人們的作品／sketches 素描

✋ **整句可以這樣寫：**

This is why I enjoy looking at <u>doodles</u> so much. They not only bring me memories but also a lot of things to ponder on.

就是因為這樣，我才這麼喜歡看<u>塗鴉作品</u>，它們不但能帶給我回憶，也給了我很多思考的題材。

❷ What this incident really taught <u>（人物）</u> was that it's quite [1] **（形容詞） to** [2] **（動詞或動詞片語）.**

這次事件告訴_____的是，_____是_____事。

> **1 處可填入**：silly 愚蠢的／pointless 無意義的／fun 有趣的
> **2 處可填入**：ignore people's advice 忽略別人的意見／make mistakes 犯錯

✋ **整句可以這樣寫：**

What this incident really taught <u>us</u> was that it's quite <u>stupid</u> to <u>text while driving</u>.

這次事件告訴**我們**的是，**邊開車邊傳訊息**是**很蠢**的事。

❸ **I stuff the photo back into the album with a smile. I am no longer the** [1]（名詞片語）**I once was, but at least I've become** [2]（形容詞比較級）**.**

我微笑著把照片塞回相簿中。我已經不再是當年那個_____了，但至少我已經變得_____。

> **1 處可填入**：cute little girl 可愛的小女孩／young kid 小孩子／
> elementary school student 國小學生
> **2 處可填入**：smarter 更聰明的／more mature 更成熟的／
> less naïve 更不天真的

整句可以這樣寫：

I stuff the photo back into the album with a smile. I am no longer the <u>obedient child</u> **I once was, but at least I've become** <u>more independent</u>**.**

我微笑著把照片塞回相簿中。我已經不再是當年那個**聽話的孩子**了，但至少我已經變得**更獨立**。

---

❹ **The** [1]（形容詞）**scene will forever be inscribed in** [2]（所有格）**mind.**

那_____畫面永遠都會烙印在_____的心中。

> **1 處可填入**：terrible 糟糕的／frightening 嚇人的／beautiful 美麗的
> **2 處可填入**：his 他的／John's 約翰的／my 我的

整句可以這樣寫：

The <u>sad</u> **scene will forever be inscribed in** <u>Allie's</u> **mind.**

那**悲傷的**畫面永遠都會烙印在**艾麗**的心中。

---

❺ What we can learn from this [1]（名詞） **is that people really do all kinds of** [2]（形容詞） **things.**

我們可以從這個＿＿＿＿學到，人們真的什麼＿＿＿＿事都做得出來。

> **1 處可填入：** true story 真實故事／phenomenon 現象／tale 故事
> **2 處可填入：** strange 奇怪的／stupid 愚蠢的／crazy 瘋狂的

✍ **整句可以這樣寫：**

What we can learn from this <u>happening</u> is that people really do all kinds of <u>terrible</u> things.

我們可以從這個**事件**學到，人們真的什麼**糟糕的**事都做得出來。

----

❻ This is the type of [1]（名詞） **that always makes me** [2]（動詞） **whenever I see it.**

這是那種讓我每次看到就忍不住＿＿＿＿的＿＿＿＿。

> **1 處可填入：** picture 圖片／film 電影／photograph 相片
> **2 處可填入：** smile 微笑／laugh 大笑／tear up 流淚

✍ **整句可以這樣寫：**

This is the type of <u>drawing</u> that always makes me <u>grin</u> whenever I see it.

這是那種讓我每次看到就忍不住<u>微笑</u>的<u>圖畫</u>。

❼ **And this is where our story ends, but I know that our** [1] **（名詞）will last long, long after.**

我們的故事就在這裡結束，但我知道我們的_____還會持續很久很久。

> **1 處可填入：** friendship 友誼／memories 回憶

🖐 **整句可以這樣寫：**

And this is where our story ends, but I know that our <u>legacy</u> will last long, long after.

我們的故事就在這裡結束，但我知道我們的**傳說**還會持續很久很久。

這樣抄就對了！

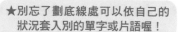

★別忘了劃底線處可以依自己的
狀況套入別的單字或片語喔！

示範一：照片〈一〉

　　前面我們已經看過了「單張照片」題型中超實用的單字片語和句型了！現在就把這些單字與句型組合起來，一篇完整的文章就完成囉！

　　一起來看看幾個例子，都是老師精心為你寫成的高分參考作文喔！注意，裡面套色的地方都是你在前面已經學過的句型。你看，會了這些句型是不是整篇文章就可以完成八成了呢？真的夠實用吧！不過，照片題型多的是你可以發揮創意的地方，這些句型當作你開頭與收尾的一個參考就好，中間的劇情發揮可要靠你自己囉！加油！

My Baby Brother

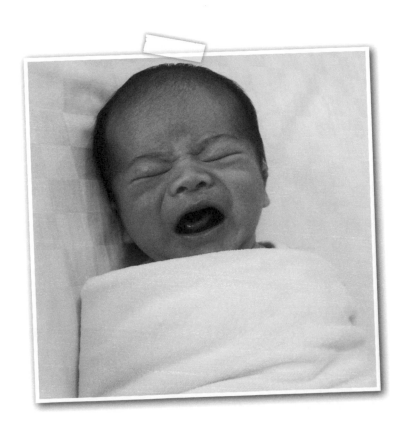

Picture this. A **thunderstorm** is happening. What would you do? Shut the windows and hide in the closet? I just did that, until I realized that it was not a thunderstorm but my little brother JJ crying. He was bawling so loudly that the room was literally shaking. Does this **volume** shock you? It happens every day in **my home**, actually.

I was naturally quite annoyed so I buried myself in my blankets. The **warm bed** is my favorite place when I'm feeling **irritated**. As soon as I made myself comfortable, however, I realized that JJ had stopped crying.

I peeked out under the sheets. JJ was so quiet, it couldn't be normal. I began to get worried, so I crawled out of bed towards JJ's crib. Was he breathing? I couldn't tell! I decided that this called for drastic measures, so I picked up the family cat and threw her into the crib.

JJ made a sound of pure delight and I was immediately relieved. He was alive! He smiled up at me, that is the type of **smile** that always makes me **feel all warm and fuzzy inside** whenever I see it. I tackled him in a hug.

Baby brothers can get so irritating sometimes, but mine will forever be my angel.

我的弟弟

想像一下，假如現在正在下大雷雨，你會怎麼做呢？把窗戶關上，躲在衣櫃裡嗎？我就這麼做了，然後我發現其實不是大雷雨，而是我弟JJ在哭。他哭得超大聲的，房間都開始震動了。這個音量有嚇到你嗎？其實在我家這是常態。

我當然覺得很煩，所以就躲在棉被裡。溫暖的床是我覺得心煩時最喜歡去的地方。我好不容易躺好了，卻發現JJ不哭了。

我從被單下面偷偷往外看。JJ太安靜了，這不正常。我開始擔心了，所以就從床上爬到JJ的嬰兒床旁邊。他到底有沒有在呼吸啊？我都看不出來啊！我決定該是時候使出非常手段了，所以我抓起家裡的貓扔進嬰兒床裡。

JJ 發出了十分開心的聲音，我馬上感到很放心，原來他還活著啊！他對著我笑，是那種讓我全身都覺得暖暖的笑容。我馬上狠狠擁抱他。

小弟弟有的時候真的很煩，但我弟弟永遠都會是我的天使。

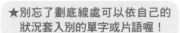
★別忘了劃底線處可以依自己的
　狀況套入別的單字或片語喔！

示範二：照片〈二〉

　　接下來嘗試寫寫看另一張照片吧！注意，裡面套色的地方都是你在前面已經學過的句型。你看，會了這些句型是不是整篇文章就可以完成一大部分了呢？真的夠實用吧！

A Place I Miss

I am fond of looking at old photos, because they never fail to transport me back to the good old times when I was still a **happy-go-lucky kid**. One of my favorite pictures is a photo of my favorite bench at my favorite park. Just by looking at the **photo**, you would not be able to tell that **the park** is actually quite **large**. It has not only a lake, but also dozens of little trails that meander through the trees.

The **quiet park** is my favorite place to go when I'm feeling **down**. The trees provide me shade from the cruel sun, and the birds hold multiple conversations in the trees, entertaining both themselves and me. It's a good place to actually be alone and clear my head.

I can no longer go to the park because I am too busy studying for exams, but the **tranquil** scene will forever be imprinted in my mind. When I close my eyes, I can see it: the lake, the trees, the bench, the lovely, lovely purple sky. They give me the strength to move forward.

我想念的一個地方

我喜歡看舊照片,因為它們總能帶我回到過去我還是個樂觀小孩的美好時光。我最喜歡的一張照片,就是我在我最愛的公園中最喜歡的一張長凳的照片。光是看照片,你應該看不出這公園其實滿大的。裡面不但有湖,還有很多小徑穿梭在樹林之間。

這座安靜的公園是我難過時最喜歡去的地方。這裡的樹讓我有蔭涼處可以躲太陽,小鳥們在樹上聊天,讓牠們和我都很開心。這個地方很適合獨處,能夠理清思緒。

我再也不能去公園了,因為我忙著準備考試,但這個平靜的畫面會永遠烙印在我心中。每當我閉上眼睛,我就會看到:湖、樹、長凳、美麗的紫色天空。它們給了我繼續前進的動力。

★別忘了劃底線處可以依自己的
狀況套入別的單字或片語喔！

這樣抄就對了！

示範三：照片〈三〉

　　接下來嘗試寫寫看另一張照片吧！注意，裡面套色的地方都是你在前面已經學過的句型。你看，會了這些句型是不是整篇文章就可以完成一大部分了呢？真的夠實用吧！

 # Love at First Sight

Do you know what it's like to see a **goddess** right in front of you? I do. This is my story.

一見鍾情

　　你知道看到你面前有個女神是什麼感覺嗎？我知道。這就是我的故事。

Just by looking at **me**, you would not be able to tell that **this simple young man** is actually **a billionaire**. I inherited a lot from my grandparents, you see, including one of the biggest companies in the city. Though I am successful at my job, I had never fallen in love, until my new secretary was introduced to me.

She had her silky brown hair in a bun, and was dressed in a graceful black suit. When she smiled, the heavens sang. We dated for two weeks, before I saw her kissing another man. It turned out that she was only using me for my money. I was devastated. My only consolation was a photo with her, shaking hands when we first met. I keep it in my wallet, and take it out to look at it from time to time to remind myself of how foolish I had been.

What this incident really taught me was that it's quite **impractical** to **fall in love at first sight**. I stuff the photo back into the wallet with a smile. I am no longer the **lovesick boy** I once was, but at least I've become **smarter**.

光是看我的外表，你應該看不出這個單純的年輕人其實是個億萬富翁。這是因為我從爺爺奶奶手上繼承了許多東西，包括全市最大的公司之一。雖然我事業有成，但我從來沒有談過戀愛，直到有人將我的新秘書介紹給我認識。

她絲滑的棕色頭髮綁成了包頭，穿著優雅的黑色套裝。她一笑，天使都要開始唱歌了。我們在一起兩週後，我看到她吻了另一個男人。原來她只是因為我有錢而利用我。我非常挫敗。我唯一的安慰就是一張與她的合照，是在我們初次見面握手時拍的。我把照片放在錢包裡，偶爾拿出來看看，提醒自己我當初有多愚蠢。

這件事告訴我，一見鍾情是不切實際的。我微笑著把照片塞回錢包中。我再也不是以前那個被愛沖昏頭的男生了，但至少我現在有變得比較聰明。

這樣抄就對了！

★別忘了劃底線處可以依自己的
狀況套入別的單字或片語喔！

示範四：照片〈四〉

接下來嘗試寫寫看另一張照片吧！注意，裡面套色的地方都是你在前面已經學過的句型。你看，會了這些句型是不是整篇文章就可以完成一大部分了呢？真的夠實用吧！

The Selfie Trend

Picture this. A **terrorist bombing** is happening. What would you do? Well, take selfies, of course— at least according to Sasha and Janie, two young ladies in their twenties. And many will agree with them, in fact. People take selfies everywhere now—

自拍風潮

想像一下，恐怖份子正在到處轟炸，你要怎麼辦？那當然是自拍了，至少薩莎和珍妮兩個二十幾歲的年輕女性是這樣想

on the toilet, while walking, during catastrophes even. Does this **phenomenon** shock you? It happens every day in **my hometown**, actually.

Just by looking at **a cell phone**, you would not be able to tell that **such a small thing** is actually **as good as any camera**. And now, since everyone has a phone, everyone also has means of picture-taking. Therefore, people take pictures anywhere and everywhere, and employ convenient photo-editing apps to beautify them or add layers to give the photos a sense of individuality.

Is this a good thing or not? I suppose it can be nice because we can now record all events in our lives easily. However, to be quite honest, taking selfies in front of disaster sites such as places where planes crashed isn't really in good taste in my opinion. But people really do things like that! What we can learn from this **example** is that people really do all kinds of **strange** things.

的。而且事實上還有很多人會同意她們的看法呢！現在的人到哪裡都可以自拍，在馬桶上拍、邊走邊拍、連災難發生的時候也拍。這個現象讓你驚訝嗎？其實這件事在我的家鄉天天都會發生。

光是看看一支手機，你應該很難想像這麼小的一個東西竟能和任何相機一樣厲害。而現在，既然每個人都有手機，每個人也就有拍照的工具。因此，人們到哪都要照相，並使用方便的修圖軟體讓照片變得更漂亮，或加上圖層讓照片顯得更獨特。

這是好事嗎？我想是不錯，我們現在可以輕鬆地記錄下生活中的所有事情。然而，老實說，我覺得在災難現場（例如墜機現場）自拍，實在不是件得體的事。但人們真的會做這樣的事耶！我們從這個例子可以學到，人們真的是怎樣奇怪的事都做得出來。

自我挑戰試試看：
2021年學測作文題目

　　有了完整的句型模板，現在的你寫起作文絕對無往不利，大考的題目也難不倒你了！現在我們就來使用模板當武器，挑戰歷屆指考與學測中出現過的「單張照片」類題型。

> 2021年大學學科能力測驗英文作文試題
> 下圖為遊客到訪某場所的新聞畫面。你認為圖中呈現的是什麼景象？你對這個景象有什麼感想？請根據此圖片，寫一篇英文作文。文分兩段，第一段描述圖片的內容，包括其中人、事、物以及發生的事情；第二段則以遊客或場所主人的立場，表達你對這件事情的看法。

歡迎賞花拍照，但請勿進入踐踏，謝謝合作！

Do you know what it's like to see a **hysterical girlfriend** right in front of you? I do. Here is my story. "Let's go to the garden! You gotta take some decent pictures for me, I was uglified in the previous ones." mumbled my girlfriend, Janice. Just by looking at **her**, you would not be able to tell that **Janice** is actually **an Instagramer with fifty-**

你知道面前有個歇斯底里的女友是什麼樣的嗎？我知道，這是我的故事。「我們去那個花園吧！你一定要幫我拍些好照片，前面我都被拍醜了。」珍妮絲，我的女友說道。光是看她的模樣，

thousand followers. She's really good at creating photos with chilling vibes and following the trends closely. As we reached the garden, I noticed that the owner had set up a billboard informing the tourists that trespassing is prohibited. Janice was so obsessed with taking nice photos that she shut her ears to any of my dissuasion and stepped into the garden like lots of people did. All of a sudden, she screamed and rushed out of the garden. Standing firmly on her knee was a gigantic, furry caterpillar. The **shocking** scene will forever be inscribed in **my** mind.

The disturbance subsided before long, yet no one dared to step into the garden again. What we can learn from this **happening** is that people really do all kinds of **selfish and blindful** things. I believe that a favorable environment requires lots to look after, and it is the duty of us tourists obeying the regulations while appreciating it. The way individualism prevails nowadays, people being so indifferent to others. They care about neither the troubles brought by violating the regulations, nor the real reasons behind. But the causes and effects in the world are intertwined, and a small leak will sink a great ship. Only if we learn to think for others could the world become a better place.

你不會知道珍妮絲其實是個擁有五萬追蹤者的IG網紅。她非常擅長拍出放鬆氛圍的照片並且跟緊流行。當我們走近時，我注意到花園主人立了一塊告示寫著請勿進入。但珍妮絲太執著於想要拍出好照片，根本聽不進任何勸言，就跟不少人一樣踏了進去。突然間，她尖叫著衝出花園。在她膝蓋上屹立不搖的是一隻毛茸茸的巨大毛毛蟲。這衝擊的畫面會永遠刻在我的腦中。

騷動不久後就平息了，但再也沒有人敢踏進花園。我們可以從這件事學到的是，人們真的會做各種自私又盲目的行為。我相信要照顧好環境需要費不少功夫，而身為遊客我們的責任就是在欣賞的同時遵守相應的規範。在個人主義興盛的現今，人們對他人漠不關心。無論是違反規則可能會對他人造成的困擾，或是背後真正的原因他們都不在乎。但世間的因果是糾纏不清的，可說是牽一髮而動全身。唯有學習為別人著想，我們才能讓這個世界變得更美好。

老師告訴你

套上顏色的文字都是你在前面就學過的句型喔！描寫圖片中發生的事時，可以觀察圖中人事物的特徵，賦予性格、身分或是情境，也可以發揮想像力，延伸至畫面外或是與照片拍攝有關的前後時間點，並使用模板句型位文章增色。雖然寫文章時要發揮創意，還是要基於圖中事實判斷，注意不要過分天馬行空了。

你還可以這樣應用：
SAT全真模擬試題07

　　以下的題目都是專家綜觀先前的SAT試題所整理出的全真模擬試題，題目內容大多以論說為主，別忘了，在論說的同時也會需要描述人事物和他們帶來的影響啊！這裡就帶著大家試試看如何利用模板句型寫出自然又流暢的SAT作文。SAT作文一般建議長度要寫到300～400字左右，趕快來參考一下老師的寫法吧！

SAT全真模擬試題07

Is it important to question the ideas and decisions of people in positions of authority?（中譯：質疑權威人士的決策是重要的事嗎？）

Most of the time, people in positions of authority are in said positions for a reason. They either have expertise on the subject, or years and years of experience in a particular field. Therefore, it's logical to believe that they can usually be trusted, and questioning their decisions may not only bring problems into whatever plans you're supposed to be carrying out, but also cause you to be kicked off your team or lose your job.

However, there are certain flaws in this reasoning. For one, people can also be in positions of authority because they simply ooze charisma or have influential relatives who put them there. These people may not necessarily be more knowledgeable in whatever subject you're dealing with than you are, and therefore if you have better ideas than theirs it's likely more profitable to bring them up instead of following their orders blindly. For another, people in high positions can also make mistakes, and not pointing them out

大部分的時候，權威人士之所以能夠擁有這樣的地位，都是有原因的。他們可能在在某個主題上有一定的專業，或在該領域有多年的經驗。因此，邏輯上可以推斷他們能夠信任，而且質疑他們的決策不但可能造成你們要執行的計畫出現問題，還可能會害你被踢出團隊或失去工作。

然而，這樣的想法還是有些瑕疵。首先，人們擁有權威地位，有可能是因為他們天生很有魅力、或是因為有影響力的親戚加持關說。這些人對你們將要處理的主題不見得比你瞭解，所以如果你的點子比他們的更好，最好還是提出來，而不是盲目跟從他們的指示。還有，

may lead to you being unfairly blamed for it with no way to prove your innocence. Either way, trusting people without knowing what they're actually about is quite a stupid thing in my opinion.

Let's look at my Aunt Joanie's story for an example. Just by looking at **her**, you would not be able to tell that **this fragile lady** is actually a **CEO of an important company**. Her employees are good people who follow her around like obedient dogs. But they really shouldn't have, because Aunt Joanie admitted openly over a family drinking session that she made most decisions based on what would benefit her the most. Note the "her"! She doesn't care about whether her employees benefit or not—in fact she takes away some of their profits so that she would have more.

What this incident really taught me was that it's quite **easy** to **trust the wrong people**. Aunt Joanie's employees probably still do not know about this and perhaps will never know. Do you still think we should trust authority blindly? I think not. What we can learn from this **confession** is that people really do a lot of **selfish** things. Therefore, when you have questions, ask them. When you have doubts, point them out. It may cause unpleasantness and maybe even cost you your job, but it's better than slaving away for someone who doesn't have your best interest in mind, right?

地位高的人一樣會犯錯，不指出這些錯誤的話，搞不好會被誣賴，你也無法證明自己的清白。無論如何，我覺得在不清楚某人到底是怎樣的人之前就全然信任他們是很蠢的。

就拿我瓊妮阿姨的故事當個例子好了。光看她的樣子，你很難想像這個虛弱的太太是個重要公司的總經理。她的員工都是好人，像很乖的狗一樣聽她的話。但他們真的不應該這樣，因為有一次在我們家庭聚餐喝酒的時候，瓊妮阿姨大方承認她做決策時主要都是考慮如何最大化她的利益。注意，是「她」的利益喔！她根本不管她的員工會不會有好處，事實上她還會拿走員工的一些收益，這樣她就可以得到更多錢。

這件事情教會我信任錯的人實在太容易了。瓊妮阿姨的員工大概還是不知道這件事，大概永遠也不會知道。你還覺得我們可以盲目信任權威嗎？我覺得不行。我們可以從阿姨這次坦白得知，人們真的會做很多自私的事情。所以，有問題的時候就要問，有疑慮的時候就提出來。這有可能造成不愉快，甚至害你丟工作，但總比為了一個不顧你的權益的人賣命來得好吧！

✑ 老師告訴你 ✑

套上顏色的文字都是你在前面就學過的句型喔！這篇範文中，論述的地方比較多，舉例的篇幅比較少。大家在寫SAT的作文時，也可以依自己的喜好選擇要寫比較多的論述，還是比較多的實際例證，甚至整篇論述都可以。可以翻到「假設與論述類」作文這一單元（p.206）看看論述類的英文作文該怎麼寫。

你還可以這樣應用：
SAT全真模擬試題08

SAT全真模擬試題08

Is persistence more important than ability in determining a person's success?
（中譯：比起「能力」，「堅持到底」更能夠決定一個人是否成功。你同意嗎？）

We've all been educated since we were kids on the importance of persistence. Everyone has heard of the story of the tortoise and the hare. The tortoise, despite being slow, was able to beat the lazy and arrogant hare in the race. However, real life is not a fairy tale, and most of the time, the people you're competing with aren't lazy and arrogant hares. In fact, most of the people you're going to meet are hardworking, diligent, humble, and to top it all, have better abilities than you do. Being a simple, persistent but slow tortoise doesn't cut it. You may succeed in reaching the finish line in the end, but others would have already been there and taken away all the prizes available.

Does this **bold statement** shock you? It happens every day in **a work environment**. Take my brother Harry's story for an example. Just by looking at **him**, you would not be able to tell that **this nondescript young guy** is actually a **manager**, despite having started work for only one year. And did he get the position because of persistence? No, one year is too short for one to

從我們還小時，就被教育要堅持到底。大家都聽過龜兔賽跑的故事吧。烏龜雖然動作慢，但賽跑時還是擊敗了懶惰又驕傲的兔子。然而，真實生活不是童話故事，你大部分的競爭對手都不會是懶惰又驕傲的兔子。事實上，你遇到的人大部分都會是努力、認真、謙虛的，而且更厲害的是能力還比你好。如果你只是一隻堅持到底但動作遲緩的烏龜，那是不夠的。你最後或許能夠成功到達終點線，但其他人都早就到那裡了，還把獎品都帶走了。

這個大膽的說法嚇到你了嗎？在職場上，這種事天天都在發生。舉我哥哥哈利的故事當例子好了。光是看他的樣子，你很難想像這個長相平平的年輕男人其實是個主管，雖然他才工作一年而已。他是因為堅持不懈而得到

show his persistence. Instead, he was appointed manager simply because he had amazing coordination skills and was able to lead his team with huge efficiency. On the other hand, my sister Kara is extremely persistent but slow. She's already been working for ten years, and hasn't gotten a salary raise even once!

What we can learn from this **contrast** is that there are all sorts of **unfair** things, and you're not guaranteed to excel just because you work hard. Face it: everyone works hard. You need skills to make you stand out from the crowd. It's a dog-eat-dog world, no one has the patience to wait for your perseverance to bloom into something profitable. But don't lose hope, you can use your persistence to learn skills! How about that? It's a win-win situation, isn't it?

這個職位的嗎？不是，才一年耶，根本看不出你的堅持不懈。反而是因為他極佳的協調能力、能夠有效率地帶領團隊，他才被任命為主管的。另一方面，我姊姊凱拉就是個堅持到底、但動作很慢的人。她已經工作十年了，一次都沒加薪耶！

從這個對比，我們可以瞭解到世界上真的有很多不公平的事，不會因為你工作努力，就能保證你會成功。面對現實吧！每個人都很努力啊！你需要有能力，才能讓自己與眾不同。這個世界很殘酷的，沒有人有耐心等著你的堅持開花結果。但別因此絕望，你可以用你堅持到底的性格學會一些能力與技術！你覺得如何？這樣不就雙贏了嗎？

＼ 老師告訴你 ／

套上顏色的文字都是你在前面就學過的句型喔！一般的文章會告訴你堅持努力的重要性，但這篇範文中，作者卻往相反的方向寫，以機車的語氣摧毀讀者的信心，這也是作文切入的一種角度，能夠讓閱卷老師留下印象。前提是要能寫出足夠的論證來支持自己的觀點。

讀完了這麼多的範例作文，現在你一定已經躍躍欲試，想套用模板句型自己寫寫看了吧！請你以前面之「**2021年學測作文題目**」為題，套用模板句型寫一篇作文。所有的句型都在框框中為你列出來囉！

_____

_____

_____

_____

_____

_____

_____

_____

_____

_____

_____

_____

_____

_____

_____

_____

_____

_____

_____

_____

_____

_____

_____

_____

_____

_____

文章開頭參考句型

(1) I am fond of looking at old photos, because they never fail to transport me back to the good old times when I was still [1]（名詞片語或形容詞）.

(2) Do you know what it's like to see a(n) [1]（名詞或名詞片語）right in front of you? I do. Here's my story.

(3) Picture this. A(n) [1]（名詞）is happening. What would you do?

(4) Does this [1]（名詞）shock you? It happens every day in [2]（地名）, actually.

(5) （人物）makes it a habit to [1]（動詞或動詞片語）[2]（時間頻率）.（人物）didn't expect today to be any different.

(6) Just by looking at [1]（人物或景物）, you would not be able to tell that [2]（人物或景物的代名詞）is actually [3]（名詞片語或形容詞）.

(7) The [1]（形容詞）[2]（地點名稱）is my favorite place to go to when I'm feeling [3]（形容詞）.

文章收尾參考句型

(1) This is why I enjoy looking at [1]（複數名詞或名詞片語）so much. They not only bring me memories but also a lot of things to ponder on.

(2) What this incident really taught （人物） was that it's quite [1] （形容詞） to [2] （動詞或動詞片語）.

(3) I stuff the photo back into the album with a smile. I am no longer the [1] （名詞片語） I once was, but at least I've become [2] （形容詞比較級）.

(4) The [1] （形容詞） scene will forever be inscribed in [2] （所有格） mind.

(5) What we can learn from this [1] （名詞） is that people really do all kinds of [2] （形容詞） things.

(6) This is the type of [1] （名詞） that always makes me [2] （動詞） whenever I see it.

(7) And this is where our story ends, but I know that our [1] （名詞） will last long, long after.

Part

6

抄這本就對了！
寫出動人的

「書信類」作文

抄這本就對了！寫出動人的 「書信類」作文

前面所學到的作文題型，以敘述文為主。無論是描述經驗、地方的寫作，或是題目提供了照片、連環圖片，讓同學進行一篇故事敘述。不過這一篇不同，是要讓大家寫書信！和以上所述題型不太相同的是，書信寫作除了需要具備基本的描述故事能力外，最重要的是注意「書信的寫作格式」。如何正確撰寫書信的開頭、信件內文、結尾、敬辭，並且將它們寫在信中的正確位置，這些都是在面對書信寫作時拿分的關鍵點。

以下將介紹「正式英文書信」與「電子郵件e-mail」的寫作形式與注意要點，跟著慢慢學習，英文書信其實一點都不困難喔！

一定要知道

「書信類」作文的寫作重點

書信類作文 Step **1.** 掌握正式英文書信的形式

要說書信類作文和其他作文最不一樣的地方，就是它必須照著一定的格式走，如果格式出了差錯，肯定會大扣分的！所以，一定要掌握最完整的書信類作文寫作格式，這樣就算寫的內容不精彩，至少格式上面的分數可以穩穩拿。下面提供正式英文書信的形式範例，其中❶至❼的標號，請看右頁的列點解釋說明。

---

❶寫信者的住址（Address）
寫信的日期（Date）

❷敬辭（Salutation）
❸寫信的內文（Body） ....
....
....
....
....

❹結尾語（Closing）

❺結尾敬辭
❻署名（Signature）

❼附筆（P.S.）

---

 ❶寫信者的住址（Address），寫信的日期（Date）：

所佔的空間一般為兩行（住址一行，日期一行）。若住址太長，則寫成兩行，然後第三行寫日期。

 ❷敬辭（Salutation）：

佔一行空間。注意：敬辭後要使用逗號「,」。敬辭就是英文書信本文開始上方要寫的「稱呼語」，如My dear sister、Dear John……等。寫法視寄信者和收信者雙方的熟識狀態而定，但最常見的還是以「Dear xxx」開頭，如「Dear friend」、「Dear Mr. Jones」、「Dear Madam」等等。

 ❸寫信的內文（Body）：

書信本文視需要可長可短。

 ❹結尾語（Closing）：

可寫也可不寫，視實際狀況來決定。結尾語就是簡短的問候語，如中文的「祝闔家安康」、「敬祈回音」等等。注意英文結尾語的書寫方式，後面不用句號「.」，而用逗號「,」。主要的寫法有三種：

1. 以With開始，如：
- **With my best wishes,**（祝福您）
- **With our kind regards,**（我們祝您安康）

2. 以命令句開始，如：

- **Please give my kindest regards to your family,** （請代我問候你的家人）
- **Take care,** （保重）

3. 以現在分詞-ing開始，如：

- **Expecting to hear from you soon,** （期待您早日回信）
- **Hoping that you'll get well soon,** （望您早日康復）

❺結尾敬辭：

佔一行空間。注意，後面要使用逗號「,」。中文信的結尾敬辭通常是寫「頓首」、「敬上」等等，而英文亦有類似的用語，如：Yours truly, / Sincerely yours, 等等。不過，和中文一樣，依照寄信者和收信者的關係不同，寫法也稍有相異之處，整理如下：

1. 家人或親戚

寫信給兄弟、姊妹、父母、叔嬸等，一般用Affectionately, 作為結尾敬辭即可，但是也可以在前面或後面加Yours等字，亦可把Affectionately的ly去掉，後面接關係的稱呼。例如：

- **Affectionately Yours, / Yours affectionately,**
- **Your affectionate son / daughter / nephew / niece,**
- **Yours very affectionately, / Yours ever most affectionately,**
- **Your loving son (or daughter), / Your affectionate brother (or sister)**

2. 朋友

寫信給比較親近的朋友，不管男生或女生，一般會使用：

- **Yours always, / Yours ever,**
- **Always yours, / Ever yours,**

如果寫信對象是比較不親近的友人，可以使用下列的用語：

- **Yours sincerely / Yours truly, / Your sincere friend,**
- **Sincerely yours, / Truly yours,**

3. 親友之外的其他人

寫信對象是親友之外的人，結尾敬辭使用：

- **Yours faithfully, / Faithfully yours,**
- **Yours very faithfully,**

如果對象是長輩或老師，則可用：

- **Yours respectfully, / Respectfully yours,**

❻署名（Signature）：

署名佔一行空間，且名字要寫在結尾敬辭的正下方。

 ❼附筆（P.S.）

可寫可不寫，視實際狀況而定。

書信類作文 Step2. 掌握電子郵件 e-mail 的形式！

因為網路時代的來臨，傳統耗時的書信方式（snail-mail）已經被便利的電子郵件（e-mail）取代了。電子郵件不但即時、私密，又低成本，更符合現代人「時間就是金錢」（Time is money）的觀念。下面提供電子郵件的形式範例，其中❶至❿的標號，請看下面的列點解釋説明。

▼❶From：	mia0101@kmail.com
▼❷Mail to：	james0202@umail.hinet.net
▼❸Cc：	
▼❹Bcc：	
❺Subject：	Congratulations!

Dear James,❻

❼

I've just heard the wonderful news about the birth of your daughter. Congratulations!

What's her name? She must be a beautiful baby. If I have time next month, I'll pay you a visit. Say hello to Joyce and the baby for me. I wish your family the happiest in the world. (^_^)❽

Sincerely, ❾

Mia ❿

P.S. Send me a photo of the baby, will you？

❶發信者姓名（From）：

這裡的「mia0101@kmail.com」，是發信人的e-mail信箱。從發信人的e-mail中也可以探出一些端倪：mia0101是使用者名稱（handle name），@在英文中念作「at」，kmail.com則是網域名稱（domain name）。

❷寄給（Mail to）：

也就是「收信人」。

❸副本收件人（Cc）：

指的就是「Carbon Copy」，也就是當我們發信給A時，若是也想將同一封信發給B、C、D，這時你只需在寄給A的e-mail中Cc的欄位輸入B、C、D的e-mail信箱發送出去，除了A之外，B、C、D三人也會同時收到這封信。

❹密件副本（Bcc）：

指的就是「Blind Carbon Copy」。在這一欄中輸入的電子郵件信箱，將不會被其他收件者看到。所以如果寄信時，不想讓A知道同封信還有寄給B，則可以選擇將B的信箱資訊打在這裡。

❺信件主旨（Subject）：

信件主旨要清楚，但也要掌握字數。不要把Subject的欄位當作本文使用，會讓收件者非常麻煩。主題盡量寫得簡短而明白即可。例如這篇e-mail要祝賀朋友生小寶寶，就可以使用「Congratulations!」來當信件主旨。

❻ 開頭敬辭：

在本文之前，對寄信者表示禮貌的「開頭敬辭」，通常都是用「Dear xxx,」開頭，像這封信的「Dear James,」一樣。注意在人名後要加上逗點「,」。

❼本文內容：

寫e-mail時必須注意「網路禮節」（netiquette），如「文章不全以大寫書寫」、「為文須精簡」、「不用攻擊或輕視字眼」等。

❽**表情符號（smiley / emoji）：**

E-mail中可以使用一些俏皮的圖形文字來表示情緒或表情。如：^_^（微笑）、:)（開心）、:(（不開心）等。

❾**結尾敬辭：**

信件完成後，在結尾的地方會加上「結尾敬辭」。通常結尾敬辭根據郵件性質會有不同的寫法。若是用於一般電子郵件，可以這樣寫：

- **Sincerely yours,**
- **Sincerely,**

若是私人性質的電子郵件，則可以這樣寫（均有「祝福你」、「敬上」的含意）：

- **With best regards,**
- **Best regards,**
- **Regards,**
- **With best wishes,**
- **Best wishes,**
- **Yours, / As ever, / Cheers,**

❿**署名**

在結尾敬辭之後，寫上自己的名字。若是第一次寫信，寫出全名比較禮貌，也可以在全名後面加上能表示性別的敬稱（Mr.、Mrs.、Miss、Ms.），方便收件者分辨寄件者是男生或女生。若是寫信給熟識的親朋好友，留名字即可，應該不至於會搞錯或有不禮貌之處。

實戰必備

「書信類」作文必備單字片語

　　書信類作文中，經常需要與對方述說寫信的來龍去脈，出現語氣轉折也是難免的事。以下就列出在寫書信時，可以用來開展、轉折語氣的單字片語。此外，我也替大家列出了常見的書信結尾敬辭供參考喔！

✏️ 表達書信中語氣轉折的單字或片語

①	譬如說	For instance,
②	除此之外	In addition,
③	此外；並且	Moreover,
④	同樣地	Also,
⑤	相同地	Similarly,
⑥	儘管	Although,
⑦	反而	Instead,
⑧	然而	Nevertheless,
⑨	但是	But,
⑩	由此；於是	Thus,
⑪	因而；所以	Therefore,
⑫	結果	Consequently,
⑬	結果；所以	As a result,
⑭	於是	Accordingly,
⑮	基於這個理由	For this reason,
⑯	同樣地	By the same token,
⑰	而且	And,
⑱	第一	First,

⑲	首先	In the first place,
⑳	第二	Secondly,
㉑	下一個；接下來	Next,
㉒	之後	After,
㉓	最後	Finally,
㉔	考慮到這一點	With this in mind,
㉕	依次	In turn,
㉖	總之	Anyway,

 書信結尾敬辭：正式電子郵件或信件

❶	感激地	With gratitude,
❷	溫暖的關懷	Warm regards,
❸	親切的關懷	Kind regards,
❹	誠摯地	Cordially,
❺	祝你好運	With all good wishes,
❻	（恭敬地）敬上	Respectfully (yours),
❼	（真誠地）敬上	Yours truly,
❽	（最由衷地）敬上	Most sincerely,
❾	（由衷地）敬上	Sincerely yours,
❿	謝謝	Thank you,
⓫	謝謝你的體貼	Thank you for your consideration,

 書信結尾敬辭：私人電子郵件或信件

❶	非常愛你的……	Lots of love,
❷	非常感謝	Many thanks,
❸	願愛與和平以及快樂	Peace, Love and Happiness,
❹	虔誠地	Prayerfully,

⑤	和平與祝福	Peace and Blessings,
⑥	保重	Take care,
⑦	好好保重	Take good care,
⑧	別太辛苦	Take it easy,
⑨	之後再聯絡	Talk to you later,
⑩	祝你一切順利	Thinking the best for you,
⑪	期待下次相會	Till we meet again,
⑫	下次再見	Until next time,
⑬	獻上我最溫暖的問候	Warmest greetings to all,
⑭	最溫暖的關懷	Warmest Regards,
⑮	願你一切順利	Wishing you all the best,
⑯	願你順利	Wishing you the best,
⑰	由衷地	With kind affection,
⑱	個人由衷地	With kindest personal regards,
⑲	熱烈地	With warmth,
⑳	祝你好運	With all good wishes,
㉑	敬愛地	With love,
㉒	你一直是我掛念的人	You're in my thoughts,
㉓	（真誠地）敬上	Yours truly,
㉔	（忠實地）敬上	Yours faithfully,
㉕	（最由衷地）敬上	Yours most sincerely,
㉖	（恭敬地）敬上	Yours respectfully,
㉗	敬上	Yours,

實戰必備
「書信類」作文
必備實用句型

　　踏進英文作文考場之前，總得知道寫一篇作文要如何開頭、承接與結尾。以下提供一些「書信類」作文中超好用的句型，依照自己的狀況在劃底線的空格處放入適合的單字（想不出填什麼的話，也可以可參考前面「實用單字」的部分找尋靈感），就能輕鬆寫出考場必備的超實用金句、一口氣加好幾分！

這樣抄就對了 Step 1. 書信開頭抄這些句型就對了！

❶ **I'm writing to tell you about** [1] （名詞片語）.

我寫信是要告訴你_____。

> **1 處可填入**：my new baby 我的新生寶寶／my engagement 我訂婚的事／
> some bad news 一些壞消息

✍ **整句可以這樣寫：**

I'm writing to tell you about a decision I made.

我寫信是要告訴你**我做的一個決定**。

・・

❷ **I hope this letter finds you well.**

我希望你收到信時一切安好。

・・

❸ I hope you're enjoying [1] （名詞片語）.

我希望你正在享受_____。

> **1 處可填入**：the lovely weather 美好的天氣／your vacation 假期

✋ **整句可以這樣寫：**

I hope you're enjoying your honeymoon.

我希望你正在享受你的蜜月。

---

❹ I was very happy to learn that you've [1] （過去分詞或過去分詞片語）.

我很高興聽說你_____。

> **1 處可填入**：gotten married 結婚了／recovered 恢復了／
> returned safely 安全地歸來了

✋ **整句可以這樣寫：**

I was very happy to learn that you've moved into the neighborhood.

我很高興聽說你搬到這附近。

---

❺ I was thrilled to find out about your [1] （名詞或名詞片語）.

我很高興聽說你_____的事。

> **1 處可填入**：graduation 畢業／big discovery 大發現／new job 新工作

整句可以這樣寫：

I was thrilled to find out about your <u>wedding</u>.

我很高興聽說你<u>婚禮</u>的事。

⋯⋯⋯⋯⋯⋯⋯⋯⋯⋯⋯⋯⋯⋯⋯⋯⋯⋯⋯⋯⋯⋯⋯⋯

❻ **I'd be grateful if you could ¹（動詞或動詞片語）.**

如果你能夠_____，我將感激不盡。

> **1 處可填入**：tell me about the proposal 告訴我提案的事／forward me the file 把那個檔案傳給我／give me some advice 給我一點建議

整句可以這樣寫：

I'd be grateful if you could <u>meet me this Thursday</u>.

如果你<u>這禮拜四可以跟我見面</u>，我將感激不盡。

⋯⋯⋯⋯⋯⋯⋯⋯⋯⋯⋯⋯⋯⋯⋯⋯⋯⋯⋯⋯⋯⋯⋯⋯

❼ **I hope you're doing well.**

希望你現在一切安好。

⋯⋯⋯⋯⋯⋯⋯⋯⋯⋯⋯⋯⋯⋯⋯⋯⋯⋯⋯⋯⋯⋯⋯⋯

❽ **I would really appreciate it if you'd help me ¹（動詞或動詞片語）.**

如果你幫我_____，我會非常感激。

> **1 處可填入**：brainstorm 腦力激盪／make a plan 制訂計畫／edit a report 校訂一份報告

整句可以這樣寫：

I would really appreciate it if you'd help me <u>write a recommendation letter</u>.

如果你幫我<u>寫一封推薦信</u>，我會非常感激。

❶ In closing, I need to tell you to [1] （動詞或動詞片語）**.**

最後，我要請你_____。

> **1 處可填入**：be careful 小心點／remember what I told you 記得我告訴你
> 的話／work harder 更加努力

✋ **整句可以這樣寫：**

In closing, I need to tell you to <u>not worry</u>.

最後，我要請你**別擔心了**。

---

❷ To sum up, I believe that you can [1] （動詞或動詞片語） **if you** [2] （動詞或動詞片語）**.**

結論是，我相信你如果_____，一定可以_____。

> **1 處可填入**：make it 做到／do it 做到／succeed 成功
> **2 處可填入**：work hard 努力／believe in yourself 相信自己／
> have more confidence 更有信心

✋ **整句可以這樣寫：**

To sum up, I believe that you can <u>pull it off</u> if you <u>stay calm</u>.

結論是，我相信你如果**保持冷靜**，一定可以**成功**。

---

❸ Hope to hear from you soon.

希望可以儘快有你的消息。

❹ **Once again, I'm really** [1] （形容詞） **to hear about your** [2] （名詞或名詞片語）**.**

再説一次，我真的很_____聽到你的_____的事。

> **1 處可填入**：glad 開心的／excited 興奮的／sorry 惋惜的
> **2 處可填入**：good news 好消息／promotion 升職／loss 失去親人

🖐 **整句可以這樣寫：**

Once again, I'm really happy to hear about your new baby.

再説一次，我真的很**高興**聽到你的**寶寶**的事。

⸺⸺⸺⸺⸺⸺⸺⸺⸺⸺⸺⸺⸺⸺⸺⸺⸺⸺⸺⸺⸺⸺⸺⸺⸺⸺⸺

❺ **I look forward to** [1] （動詞+ing或名詞）**.**

我很期待_____。

> **1 處可填入**：seeing you 和你見面／your letter 你的來信／tomorrow 明天

🖐 **整句可以這樣寫：**

I look forward to meeting you.

我很期待**和你見面**。

⸺⸺⸺⸺⸺⸺⸺⸺⸺⸺⸺⸺⸺⸺⸺⸺⸺⸺⸺⸺⸺⸺⸺⸺⸺⸺⸺

❻ **It would be great if you could** [1] （動詞或動詞片語） **as soon as possible.**

如果你可以儘快_____那就太好了。

> **1 處可填入**：reply to me 回覆我／call me 打給我／let me know 讓我知道

It would be great if you could <u>give me your answer</u> **as soon as possible.**

如果你可以儘快給我一個答案那就太好了。

· ·

❼ **On the whole, I don't think you'll have any problems if you** [1] <u>（動詞或動詞片語）</u>**.**

整體來説，我覺得如果你_____，就不會有任何問題。

> **1 處可填入：**be careful 小心點／stay positive 保持積極／
> come tomorrow 明天過來

✋ 整句可以這樣寫：

On the whole, I don't think you'll have any problems if you <u>go early</u>**.**

整體來説，我覺得如果你早點過去，就不會有任何問題。

· ·

❽ **If you** [1] <u>（動詞片語）</u>**, you can always** [2] <u>（動詞片語）</u>**.**

如果你_____，你都可以_____。

> **1 處可填入：**have any questions 有什麼問題／
> run into a problem 遇到問題／arrive early 比較早到
> **2 處可填入：**call me 打給我／send me a text 傳個訊息給我／
> ring the bell 按門鈴

✋ 整句可以這樣寫：

If you <u>need someone</u>**, you can always** <u>come to me</u>**.**

如果你需要任何人幫忙，你都可以來找我。

這樣抄就對了！

★別忘了劃底線處可以依自己的
狀況套入別的單字或片語喔！

示範一：勸說的書信

前面我們已經看過了「書信類」題型中超實用的單字片語和句型了！現在就把這些單字與句型組合起來，一篇完整的文章就完成囉！一起來看看幾個例子，都是老師精心為你寫成的高分參考作文喔！注意，裡面套色的地方都是你在前面已經學過的句型。你看，會了這些句型是不是整篇文章就可以完成八成了呢？真的夠實用吧！

以下這篇作文以「勸說」為題材，是以勸說朋友和自己一起去學跳舞為內容。當然，你不見得會想勸你朋友一起去跳舞，但你一定會有想勸說旁人的事情吧！是什麼事情呢？也可以套用模板句型寫寫看喔！

 A Letter to My Friend

Dear Mandy,

I hope you're enjoying your **summer vacation**. I was very happy to learn that you've **begun taking swimming lessons** during the break, but I have another proposal! The community center close to my home is giving dance lessons every Tuesday and Thursday at seven in the evening. Not the boring kind of dance that you hate, but choreography lessons of the newest Kpop music videos! That's why I was thrilled to find out about your **addiction to Korea girl groups**. I'm sure you'd want to come to dance lessons with me, right?

My mom has already agreed to let me go, as long as someone she knows and trusts is with me. And you know how much she likes you! If my mom heard that you would be coming with me, I bet she

給朋友的一封信

親愛的曼蒂：

希望妳正在享受妳的暑假。很高興聽說妳開始在假期中上游泳課了。但我有另一個提議！我家附近的社區中心每個禮拜二和禮拜四晚上七點都有跳舞課，而且不是妳討厭的那種無聊的舞，是最新韓國流行音樂MV的舞步教學喔！所以我知道妳超喜歡韓國女團時，才會這麼興奮。妳一定很想跟我一起來上跳舞課吧，對不對？

我媽媽已經答應讓我去上了，只要有她認識並信任的人和我一起去就

would say yes in a flash. Think about all of the fun we would have together! We could go grab some drinks together after class and relax in an air-conditioned café. I'd be grateful if you could **come with me**, and I look forward to **learning new dance moves with you**, my best friend! It would be great if you could **let me know** as soon as possible. Hope to hear from you soon!

Lots of Love,

Gina

好。妳也知道她超喜歡妳的！如果我媽知道妳會和我一起來，我賭她一定馬上會答應的。想想看，我們會玩得多開心啊！上完課我們還可以一起去買飲料喝，在有冷氣的咖啡店裡休息。如果妳跟我一起去上課，我會感激不盡的，而且我好期待跟我最好的朋友（也就是妳）一起學新的舞步！如果妳儘快給我答覆就太好了。希望能儘快得到妳的消息喔！

愛妳的

吉娜

★別忘了劃底線處可以依自己的
狀況套入別的單字或片語喔！

這樣抄就對了！

示範二：問候的書信

接下來嘗試寫寫看「問候的書信」吧！注意，裡面套色的地方都是你在前面已經學過的句型。你看，會了這些句型是不是整篇文章就可以完成一大部分了呢？真的夠實用吧！

以下的書信以問候許久不見的國小老師為題材，但如果你並不想問候國小老師的話，也可以試試看寫信給其他想要問候的人練習一下。

A Letter to My Elementary School Teacher

Dear Ms. Lin,

I hope this letter finds you well. I haven't written to you in a long time, but today I'm writing to tell you about **something exciting**. I'm getting married! Can you believe it? The little chatterbox in your class is now soon to be a wife and maybe a mother!

I heard from Wendy that your knee condition is getting better, and I was very happy to learn that you've **begun to walk without crutches**. Do you think you can come to my wedding? I understand if moving from place to place is still difficult for you, but I'd be grateful if you could **come**. Lots of elementary school classmates will be here; it will be like a reunion! I've also invited our music teacher, Mrs. Chen, and she agreed to come. I remember that you were very good friends back then! I really love Mrs. Chen, but not as much as I love you, of course!

給國小老師的一封信

親愛的林老師：

希望您收到信時一切安好。我很久沒寫信給您了，但我今天寫信是要跟您報告一件興奮的事！我要結婚了！您相信嗎？您班上那個嘰嘰喳喳的小鬼快要成為人妻了，可能還要當媽媽了！

我聽溫蒂說，您的膝蓋狀況已經逐漸好轉了，我也很開心聽到您開始不用枴杖也能走了。您有可能來參加我的婚禮嗎？我瞭解到處走動對您來說可能還是有點困難，但如果您能來，我會感激不盡的。很多國小同學都會到，就像同學會一樣喔！我也邀請了我們的音樂老

Once again, I'm really **excited** to hear about your **recovery**, and I look forward to **seeing you, my favorite teacher, on the wedding.** Hope to hear from you soon. **Here is my number.** If you **can't reach me by phone**, you can always **text**.

Wishing you all the best,

Angie Yu

師陳老師,她已經答應要來參加了。我記得妳們以前是很好的朋友!我很喜歡陳老師,但我當然更喜歡您囉!

再說一次,我很興奮聽到您康復的事情,我也很期待在婚禮上見到我最喜歡的老師(也就是您)。希望可以儘快有您的消息。這是我的電話號碼,如果打電話找不到我,您都可以傳簡訊給我喔。

願您一切順利

余安琪

★別忘了劃底線處可以依自己的
狀況套入別的單字或片語喔！

這樣抄就對了！

示範三：感謝的書信

接下來嘗試寫寫看「感謝的書信」吧！注意，裡面套色的地方都是你在前面已經學過的句型。你看，會了這些句型是不是整篇文章就可以完成一大部分了呢？真的夠實用吧！

以下的書信以感謝外婆帶著作者在鄉下到處玩為主題。你一定也有想要感謝的人，可以試試看以類似的句型，挑戰這篇「感謝的書信」。

A Thank-you Letter

Dear Grandma,

I hope this letter finds you well. This is Erin, your granddaughter. Do you remember me? I hope you do, even though Mom says you're losing your memory. After all, it was only last month when I stayed over at your place for a week! And what an amazing week it was. I don't think I've ever had so much fun in my life. Thank you so much for bringing me to all the fun places in your little village, and cooking me all those amazing meals. I particularly enjoyed going to the market with you. I love how everyone there seemed to know you and you had to stop to talk to every one of them. It almost felt like you were a celebrity! Things like this don't happen here in the city I lived very often; no one ever remembers me when I go to the supermarket, even though I go there so much that I practically live there.

一封感謝信

親愛的外婆：

希望您一切安好。我是愛琳，您的外孫女。您還記得我嗎？我希望您記得，雖然媽媽說您的記憶力不太好了。畢竟我上個月才在您家住過一個禮拜啊！那真是很棒的一個禮拜。我覺得我人生從來沒玩得這麼開心過。謝謝您帶我去您村中各種有趣的地方玩，並煮這麼多好吃的東西給我吃。我特別喜歡和您一起去市場。我很開心那邊的人每個都認識您，而您得停下來和他們一個一個聊天。感覺您好像是明星一樣！在我居住的城市中不常發生這種事。我去超級市場的時候根本沒人記得我，雖然我常去到都快把那裡當自己家了。

Mom told me that you'll be visiting us next month. What would you like to do here? Would you like to go shopping with me? I look forward to **hanging out with you**! Since you've been so kind to me during my stay, I want to do everything I can for you too. If you want to **go to some particular place**, you can always **tell me straightforwardly**!

Once again, I'm really **excited** to hear about your **visit next month**, and so grateful for all you've done for me. I love you, grandma.

Lots of love,

your granddaughter Erin

媽媽說您下個月會來看我們。您想在這裡做些什麼呢？您想和我一起去逛街嗎？我很期待和您一起到處晃晃！因為我在您那裡住時，您對我很好，所以您在我家時我也想為您做很多事情。如果您想去哪個特定的地方，您都可以直接跟我說喔。

再說一次，聽到您下個月要來，我真的超興奮的。我也很感激您為我做的所有事情。我愛您，外婆。

愛您的

外孫女愛琳

★別忘了劃底線處可以依自己的
狀況套入別的單字或片語喔！

這樣抄就對了！

示範四：邀請的書信

接下來嘗試寫寫看「邀請的書信」吧！注意，裡面套色的地方都是你在前面已經學過的句型。你看，會了這些句型是不是整篇文章就可以完成一大部分了呢？真的夠實用吧！

以下的書信以邀請新鄰居到你的新家玩為主題。你或許並沒有搬新家，但也有可能想邀請朋友到家裡玩。試試看用模板句型寫一封邀請的信吧！

A Letter to A New Neighbor

Dear Ms. Chen,

I hope you're doing well. This is your new neighbor, Rita, and I'm writing to tell you about **the housewarming party we're throwing this Friday**. My kids are really excited for the party, and I was thrilled to find out about your **three children**. It would be lovely if your kids and mine could end up becoming friends!

The party starts at six o'clock sharp, and I'd be **grateful** if you could come. I look forward to **getting to know you and your kids**. It would be great if you could **let me know if you could come** as soon as possible, so that we can make sure we have enough seats and eating utensils for everyone. If you **have time**, you can always **swing by before that**; we're very friendly. Just be careful to avoid our golden retriever if you're afraid of dogs; he usually resides in the backyard.

With all good wishes,

Rita

一封給新鄰居的信

親愛的陳女士：

希望您一切安好。我是您的新鄰居麗塔，我寫信來是要跟您說我們這週五要舉辦喬遷派對的事。我的孩子們都很期待這場派對，而我也很興奮地得知您有三個孩子。如果您的孩子和我的孩子可以成為朋友，那就太好了！

派對六點整開始，如果您能來，我會很感激的。我很期待認識您和您的孩子。如果您能儘早讓我知道您會不會來就太好了，這樣我們才能確認我們家的椅子和餐具足夠。如果您有時間，您可以在派對之前就先來我家看看，我們都很歡迎。如果您怕狗，就小心避開我們的黃金獵犬，牠通常都在後院出沒。

祝您好運，

麗塔

自我挑戰試試看：
2012年學測作文題目

有了完整的句型模板，現在的你寫起作文絕對無往不利，大考的題目也難不倒你了！現在我們就來使用模板當武器，挑戰歷屆指考與學測中出現過的「書信類」題型。

2012年學科能力測驗英文作文試題

提示：你最好的朋友最近迷上電玩，因此常常熬夜，疏忽課業，並受到父母的責罵。你（英文名字必須設定為Jack或Jill）打算寫一封信給他／她（英文名字必須假設為Ken或Barbie）適當地給予勸告。

請注意：必須用上述的Jack或Jill在信末署名，不得使用自己的真實中文或英文名字。

Dear Ken,

I hope you're enjoying your **weekend**. I bet you are, actually, since according to what your parents told me, you're most likely shut in your room having the time of your life playing video games!

I'm writing to tell you about **just this**. I'm worried about you, man. You used to be so full of sunshine and energy, but now every time I see you, there are bags under your eyes and your cheekbones are sunken. You look half-dead, and that's because you never get any sleep since late-night gaming takes up all of your time. I'll be blunt and say that I'd be grateful if you could **stop playing**. I understand how fun video games are, but playing so much that it's affecting your health is not okay.

親愛的肯，

希望你正開心地在享受你的週末。我想你應該是很享受啦，至少從你父母的說法聽起來，你現在應該是關在自己房間裡，超開心地在玩電動吧。

我寫信正是要跟你說這件事。我很擔心你啊，老兄。你以前總是充滿了陽光和精力，但現在我每次看到你，你都眼袋超深、臉龐瘦削。你看起來半死不活的，因為你把時間都花在半夜打電動上，幾乎都不睡覺。我必須直白地說，如果你不要再打電動了，我會很感激的。我知道電動很好玩，但玩到你的健康都受到影響，這就不行了。

I'm not the only one who's worried about you. Your parents are too, and you know that. Even Lexi, the girl you have a crush on, commented to me that you look like a walking corpse. You don't want Lexi to think you're a zombie, do you? So put down that headset, come out of your room, and start living in the real world for a while. Virtual reality is great, but not if it makes you sick. If you feel **bored without video games**, you can always **talk to me**, you know? In fact, it would be great if you could **call me** as soon as possible. It seems like we don't talk anymore.

Hope to hear from you soon. I look forward to **hanging out with you again**, bro.

Yours,

Jack

我不是唯一一個擔心你的人。你的父母也很擔心你，你也知道。就連你暗戀的女生萊西，都跟我說你看起來像僵屍一樣。你不想要讓萊西覺得你是僵屍吧？所以放下你的耳麥，從房間裡出來，開始在現實世界中生活一下吧。虛擬實境是很棒，但如果讓你生病就不好了。如果你覺得沒有電動很無聊，你都可以跟我聊天啊，好嗎？其實，如果你能儘快打給我，那就太棒了，不然我們好像都沒怎麼在聊天了。

希望能儘快有你的消息。我很期待再和你一塊消磨時間，老兄。

傑克 敬上

自我挑戰試試看：
2019年學測作文題目

2019年大學學科能力測驗英文作文試題

提示：身為臺灣的一份子，臺灣最讓你感到驕傲的是什麼？請以此為題，寫一篇英文作文，談臺灣最讓你引以為榮的二個面向或事物（例如：人、事、物、文化、制度等）。第一段描述這二個面向或事物，並說明它們為何讓你引以為榮；第二段則說明你認為可以用什麼方式來介紹或行銷這些臺灣特色，讓世人更了解臺灣。

Dear Minister of the Tourism Administration,

We are a group of high school students who care about Taiwan. We're writing to tell you about **a project we've been drafting for months**. We'd be grateful if you could **take a look and consider carrying it out**. As we all live on this beloved land, Taiwan, there are many features we are so proud of that can make a great impression on people all around the world. Firstly, we can say that the night market plays an important role in the memories of most people here. The irresistible street foods like scallion pancakes, sweet potato balls and Taiwanese fried chicken are the must-haves, they provide the authentic flavors of Taiwan. The atmosphere there is filled with the mouth-drooling smell of all kinds, and composed of delighted customers and vigorously peddling vendors. The other characteristic is the hospitality of Taiwanese people. The helping hands showed up in every corner, from showing the way, standing up against

觀光署署長您好：

我們是一群在乎台灣的高中生。來信是為了向您提出一個我們規劃多月的計畫。如果您能參考看看甚至考慮執行它，我們會很感謝的。我們都住在台灣這塊備受喜愛的島上，有著許多我們引以為傲、能讓世人留下深刻印象的特點。首先，夜市可說是大多數台灣人記憶中相當重要的角色。蔥油餅、地瓜球和鹽酥雞這些讓人無法抗拒的小吃都是必須嘗試的，它們有著最道地的台灣口味。夜市中充斥著各種令人垂涎的香味，其中也有愉悅的客人和賣力叫賣的攤販。另一個特色則是台灣人的熱情好客。到處都有願意幫忙的人，從指路、打抱不平到替人急救等等。我們

the injustices, to saving lives with CPR, etc. We're sure good deeds like these can touch the world, and they will be much more impressed when they encounter the good deeds here in person.

To promote these characteristics, we can hold a night market international culture festival. First of all, arrange schedules related to night markets and regional highlights, and design the guidance that combines travel information and culture introductions. The online promotion is indispensable, shooting commercial films is a good option, holding a corresponding short film competition can draw the attention of the creators and the public. Meanwhile, we can also make good use of virtual reality to present the scenes in the night market online. Last but not least, forming partnerships with the b&bs and hostels can combine the hospitality of ours with the local characteristic at the same time. These are the introduction to the project, we look forward to **hearing from you soon**.

Sincerely,

the high school students who love Taiwan

相信這些善舉能夠感動世人,而當他們親身體會到時一定會更印象深刻。

要宣傳這些特色,我們可以舉辦一個國際夜市文化節。首先,安排帶有各地特色的夜市相關行程,並設計結合文化導覽的觀光指南。線上宣傳也是不可或缺的,拍攝形象廣告會是不錯的選擇,舉辦相應的短片競賽也能吸引大眾以及創作者的關注。同時,我們也能利用虛擬實境技術線上呈現夜市中的場景。最後但同樣重要的是,與民宿和青年旅館合作,能同時結合好客形象與地方特色。以上是計畫的介紹,期待不久後得到您的回覆。

愛台灣的高中生們上

你還可以這樣應用：
SAT全真模擬試題09

以下的題目都是專家綜觀先前的SAT試題所整理出的全真模擬試題，題目內容大多以論說為主，別忘了，在論説的同時也可以使用書信的形式表達啊！這裡就帶著大家試試看如何利用模板句型寫出自然又流暢的SAT作文。SAT作文一般建議長度要寫到300～400字左右，趕快來參考一下老師的寫法吧！

SAT全真模擬試題09

Is it more important to do work that one finds fulfilling or work that pays well?

（中譯：做自己有成就感的工作，比做能賺很多錢的工作更重要。你同意嗎？）

Dear Eddie,

I hope this letter finds you well. As your uncle, I was very happy to learn that you've **graduated college** and are now on the hunt for a job. I'm also more than flattered when you asked me for advice on choosing a suitable career. I'm not exactly an expert in this regard, but I'll do my best to answer any questions you have.

One question you asked me was whether you should go for a fulfilling job or a job with a high salary. Well, my first instinct would probably be telling you to go for the one with the good pay. It's obvious that money is important—while money doesn't equal happiness, it can buy you a puppy, and that does equal happiness! But I digress. After a lot of pondering, I think I would have to tell you to

親愛的愛迪：

希望收到這封信時你一切安好。身為你的舅舅，我很開心你已經從大學畢業，開始找工作了。你請我給你一點求職的意見時，我簡直受寵若驚。我在這方面並非專家，但我會盡力回答你所有的問題。

你問過我的其中一個問題，就是你應該選擇一個令你有成就感的工作還是一個高薪的工作。嗯，我的第一個直覺大概會叫你去做高薪的工作。錢顯然很重要，雖然説錢買不到快樂，但可以買到小狗，而小狗會讓你很快樂。唔，離題了。我思考

choose a job that you actually like and makes you feel good about yourself instead of one that pays well. Here's why.

Your uncle used to be a naïve man, Eddie. I had the choice between becoming an engineer in an estimated company, earning piles of cash within each minute, and becoming a simple teacher, who really doesn't earn that much. I chose the one with the piles of cash, of course. I didn't like it, not one bit. The work hours were long, the tasks were repetitive, and I often had to go for days without talking to anyone. My boss was harsh and no matter how hard I tried, I still felt like I was not good enough for him.

By the end of two years I had developed severe chest problems and a devil-may-care attitude. I quit my job for health reasons and found a position in an elementary school after two months of resting, teaching third-graders. The students were little holy terrors, but they could also be the sweetest angels. Watching their progress in various subjects brought me immense satisfaction and happiness. I soon knew that this was my true calling, and the unfortunate salary was not about to deter me.

To this day, I've never regretted my career change. I might not have a lot of money, but on the whole, I don't think you'll have any problems if you **don't splurge on too many things**. To sum up, I believe that you can **find true happiness** if you **get a fulfilling job**, while a job that pays well cannot necessarily give you that.

了很久，最後我想我必須告訴你，還是選一個你喜歡的、而且讓你更喜歡自己的工作比較好，而不是一個高薪的工作。以下是我的理由。

愛迪，你舅舅我以前是個天真的男人。我當時有兩個選擇，一個是在一家著名的公司擔任工程師，每分每秒都賺到翻。另一個則是成為一名普通的老師，賺不了什麼錢。我當然選了賺到翻的工作。結果我一點都不喜歡這個工作。工時很長，工作重複性很高，我有時候好幾天都沒辦法和人說到話。我的老闆很嚴厲，無論我多麼努力，我還是覺得對他來說自己不夠好。

兩年結束後，我得了嚴重的胸部疾病，個性也變得越來越漫不經心。我因為健康的理由辭了工作，休息了兩個月後在一所國小找了工作，教三年級生。這些孩子簡直是小惡魔，但他們有時也是最甜美的天使。看著他們在各方面的進步，都讓我非常滿足、非常開心。我很快地知道，這是我的天職，雖然薪水不高，但這並不會讓我卻步。

直到今天，我都沒有後悔轉職的決定。我也許賺得不多，但整體來說，只要不要亂揮霍，應該不會有什麼問題。總之，我相信如果找到一個令你有

I look forward to **hearing your final decision**. Hope to hear from you soon. If you **have any other career problems**, you can always **hit me up**. I'm a teacher; it's my job to listen!

With kind affection,

your uncle Bob

成就感的工作，你一定能夠得到真正的快樂，而這是高薪的工作不見得能帶給你的。

我很期待聽到你最後的決定。希望可以儘快得到你的消息。如果你有其他求職上的問題，你都可以來找我。我是老師啊，傾聽是我的工作！

由衷地

你舅舅鮑勃

＼老師告訴你／

套上顏色的文字都是你在前面就學過的句型喔！這篇作文並非單純的論說文，不但以書信的形式出現，而且引證了作者自己的經驗。但再度提醒，如果真想要打破傳統用書信題裁寫論說文，要先閱讀題目說明，確定裡面沒有規定一定要寫某個體裁，否則一開始就會因為體裁問題被扣分了。

美國高中升大學的SAT也無往不利！

你還可以這樣應用：
SAT全真模擬試題10

SAT全真模擬試題10

Is it necessary for people to combine their efforts with those of others in order to be most effective?

（中譯：人們一定要合作，做事才會更有效率。你同意嗎？）

Dear Kayla,

I hope you're enjoying **your last year as a student**. I was very happy to learn that you've b**een mapping out future plans far in advance before graduation**. Your mom told me that you hope to work freelance, because you worry that working with others will be too much of a hassle and other people may be too slow and hold you back. Frankly, I'm surprised. I support you doing freelance work as it is a good and profitable career choice if you do it the right way, but I don't quite agree with your opinion that working with others will only hold you back.

I understand your reasoning, I suppose. I bet you've met several slackers in school who are useless when doing group reports, and believe that it will be like that too at work. Let me assure you that it's not true. Most of the time, useless people will get kicked out—no employer wants someone who contributes nothing to the company to sit around and eat up company resources. Also, you

親愛的凱拉，

希望妳正在好好享受身為學生的最後一年。聽說妳遠在畢業前就已經提早開始規劃未來，我很高興。妳媽媽跟我說，妳希望可以當自由工作者，因為妳擔心和其他人一起工作太麻煩了，而且他們可能動作很慢，會拖到妳的進度。說真的，我還滿驚訝的。我支持妳當自由工作者，如果妳做得好，這是個很好也很有利潤的職業選擇。但妳認為和其他人一起工作只會拖累妳的進度，這點我不是很同意。

我想我懂妳的看法。我相信妳在學校一定是遇到了許多懶惰的人，在做小組報告時毫無用處，而妳認為在工作時也會是這樣。別擔心，不會的。大部分的時候，沒用的人都會被踢出去，沒有哪個老

have to remember that no matter how good and efficient you are at your job, it never hurts to have someone to cover for you when the workload gets ridiculous.

Take your cousin Louisa for example. Remember Louisa? You know how fast she works, right? She used to freelance too, but later she decided to go work at a company because her electricity bills are getting outrageous and working in a company means free air conditioning (what a reason!). And she loved every minute of it!

The way she sees it, working in a team brings tons of benefits—for one thing, the more people you have, the more flexible you get. People can adjust their schedules to fit in various tasks to accommodate everyone, while you don't get that luxury when working alone. For another, everyone has different strengths and weaknesses; no one is perfect. While you may be an incredibly fast worker, you may lack in creativity. Or perhaps you can be incredibly creative, but have no idea how to carry your innovative plans out. Here's where others come in! They can do what you cannot for you, and save you tons of time and trouble.

And don't worry that others will become a hassle. Where there are people, there will always be problems, but you can't let that hinder you. Disputes can and will occur, but you will discover that group brainstorming sessions are always much more efficient and fun than staring at a piece of paper, trying to draw up a plan yourself. I promise!

闆會想要一些對公司毫無貢獻的人無所事事地消耗公司資源。而且，妳要知道，無論妳做事多有效率，如果工作負擔太重，有人幫忙總是好的啊！

看看妳表姊露易莎就知道了。妳記得露易莎嗎？妳知道她做事超快的吧！她以前也是自由工作者，但後來決定到公司上班，因為她家的電費太高了，在公司上班就可以吹免費冷氣（這什麼理由啊！），而她非常享受其中。

她覺得，在團隊中工作有很多的好處。舉例來說，人手越多，彈性就越大，大家可以彈性調整時程，分配種種任務，以符合所有人的需求，而一個人工作時則沒有這種餘裕。另外，每個人的強項和弱點都不同，沒有人是完美的。或許妳工作超常地快，但妳沒有創意。或許妳超有創意，但卻不知道如何執行妳的創新點子。這種時候其他人就派上用場啦！他們可以替妳做妳做不了的事，並替妳省下不少時間和麻煩。

別擔心別人會造成妳的麻煩。只要有人，就一定會有麻煩，但別讓這件事阻撓妳。爭執可能會發生，甚至一定會發生，但妳會發現大家一起腦力

In closing, I need to tell you to think it over. Freelancing may be perfect for you, but don't give up on working with other human beings! People are mostly nice; they don't bite. On the whole, I don't think you'll have any problems if you **remain your kind and likeable self**. If you **run into any problems at work**, you can always **talk to me**!

Hope to hear from you soon.

Your cousin, Lynn

激盪，總是比一個人盯著白紙思考來得有效率又好玩。真的！

最後，我希望請妳再想想。自由業當然很好，但別放棄和其他的人類一起工作啊！大部分的人都很好，他們不會咬妳的。整體來說，我覺得只要妳一直如此友善又人見人愛，就不會碰到問題的。如果妳真碰到了問題，妳都可以跟我聊聊喔！

希望可以儘快有妳的消息！

妳的表姊 琳恩

讀完了這麼多的範例作文，現在你一定已經躍躍欲試，想套用模板句型自己寫寫看了吧！請你以「**給十年前的自己的一封信**」（**A Letter to Myself Ten Years Ago**）為題，套用模板句型寫一篇作文。所有的句型都在框框中為你列出來囉！

書信開頭參考句型！

(1) I'm writing to tell you about [1] （名詞片語）.

(2) I hope this letter finds you well.

(3) I hope you're enjoying [1] （名詞片語）.

(4) I was very happy to learn that you've [1] （過去分詞或過去分詞片語）.

(5) I was thrilled to find out about your [1] （名詞或名詞片語）.

(6) I'd be grateful if you could [1] （動詞或動詞片語）.

(7) I hope you're doing well.

(8) I would really appreciate it if you'd help me [1] （動詞或動詞片語）.

書信收尾參考句型

(1) In closing, I need to tell you to [1] （動詞或動詞片語）.

(2) To sum up, I believe that you can [1] （動詞或動詞片語） if you [2] （動詞或動詞片語）.

(3) Hope to hear from you soon.

(4) Once again, I'm really [1] （形容詞） to hear about your [2] （名詞或名詞片語）.

(5) I look forward to [1] （動詞+ing 或名詞）.

(6) It would be great if you could
[1] （動詞或動詞片語） as soon
as possible.

(7) On the whole, I don't think
you'll have any problems if you
[1] （動詞或動詞片語）.

(8) If you [1] （動詞片語）, you
can always [2] （動詞片語）.

Part

7

抄這本就對了！
寫出有想像力的

「假設與
論述類」作文

抄這本就對了！寫出有想像力的「假設與論述類」作文

　　假設與論述類作文是什麼呢？所謂「假設」，就是像「假設你中了一百萬，你會⋯⋯」、「假如你有三個願望，你會⋯⋯」這種問題，多半需要用到假設語氣與「would」（如：If I had a million dollars, I would... 如果我有一百萬，我會⋯⋯）。那麼「論述」類的作文呢？通常是給你一段話（「學生應該懂得利用圖書館」、「學生應該能夠學會創意思考」⋯⋯等等），請你表達你的想法。

　　「假設」的作文中，為了表達自己選擇做某些事的理由，可能會需要使用論述的句子，而「論述」的作文中，為了舉例方便，也可能會需要用到假設的句子。這兩者是相輔相成的，所以就將它們擺在一起看囉！現在就來看看假設類與論述類的作文該怎麼寫。

一定要知道

「假設與論述類」作文的寫作重點

假設與論述 Step 1. 看清題意，選擇發揮方向

　　假設類的題目，通常會給你一個情境，要你延伸想像。以「如果你中了一百萬，你會⋯⋯」為例，你便可以立刻決定一個方向，如「我會捐給孤兒院」、「我會去環遊世界」等等，然後朝此發揮。作文的篇幅有限，考試時寫作的時間更有限，要是同時朝三、四個方向發展，不但每個方向都無法發揮完整，也會帶給閱卷老師這篇作文「草草了事」的感覺，還是選定一個方向發揮比較經濟實惠。

　　論述類的題目，通常會給你一句話或一個觀念，例如「學生不應該帶手機到校」，要你選擇同意或不同意。對於這樣的題目，一開始便請選擇好自己的立場，不要模稜兩可，不肯選擇其一。首先，題目就要你擇一了，所以模稜兩可是會扣分的，

再者,要將兩種論點都一一說清楚,就需要花費更多的時間寫,很可能因此無法寫得完整,這樣也是很划不來的。還是建議一開始就選「同意」或「不同意」,直接朝著這個方向發揮。

假設與論述 Step2. 說服讀者接受你的意見

在假設類題目中,你為何要做「我會把錢捐出來」、「我會去環遊世界」這樣的選擇呢?在論述類題目中,你為何覺得「我不同意學生不能帶手機到校」,而不是「我同意學生不能帶手機到校」呢?你會做出這樣的選擇一定有你的理由,而這樣的理由一定要讓讀者知道,不能只陳述事實,更要有論證。論證的方法有很多,像是以下這些:

舉正面例子

例 **If something big happens in a student's family, he or she would definitely want to know immediately, which is why I believe students should bring cell phones to school.**

如果學生家裡發生大事,他一定希望馬上知道,所以我覺得學生應該帶手機去學校。

舉反面例子

例 **My classmate John's mother got a scam phone call that said John was kidnapped and demanded ransom, and she couldn't contact John because he was at school and didn't bring his phone. She nearly paid the ten million dollars!**

我同學約翰的媽媽接到詐騙電話,説約翰被綁架了,要求支付贖金。約翰在學校,沒有帶手機,他媽媽找不到他,差點就把一千萬元付出去了!

以「⋯⋯固然如此,但⋯⋯」方式,明褒暗貶其他選項

例 **It's true that bringing cell phones to school might cause distractions, but you can always minimize the distraction level by not allowing students to have the phones on in class.**

帶手機到學校可能會造成學生分心,這固然沒錯,但可以請學生在上課時關機,這樣分心程度就會減到最低。

　　你可能覺得「我前面都已經講這麼清楚了，還需要講一次？」但是最後再強調一次自己的論點（我認為學生可以帶手機到學校、如果我中了一百萬我就會捐出去……等等），能夠達成前後呼應的效果。前面可以加上In a nutshell、All in all、In conclusion、To summarize……等等表示「總而言之、總括來說」的片語。

實戰必備

「假設與論述類」作文
必備單字片語

　　假設與論述類的作文中，經常會需要提到自己的「意見」，這裡就提出一些能夠說明自己意見的單字片語供大家參考。其中包括了表達意見時用來強調意見的副詞與形容詞、能夠讓語氣更加生動的動詞，以及加強口氣的名詞。

表達「意見」常用的動詞

❶	估計；估量	estimate
❷	擁護；提倡；主張	advocate
❸	相信	believe
❹	認為	suppose
❺	檢查	examine
❻	考慮；細想	consider
❼	寧願（選擇）；更喜歡	prefer
❽	著手對付；處理（某一議題）	tackle
❾	抓住（機會）；欣然接受（提議）	embrace

⑩	堅稱	claim
⑪	判斷	judge
⑫	認為	deem / reckon
⑬	當作；看做	regard

 表達「人物」常用的名詞

❶	提倡者	advocator
❷	關係者；參與者	participant
❸	相信者	believer
❹	觀察者	observer
❺	目擊者	witness
❻	觀賞者	spectator
❼	支持者	supporter

 表達「可能性」常用的形容詞或副詞

❶	總的；全面的	overall
❷	負有法律責任的；有義務的	liable
❸	潛在的；可能	potential / potentially
❹	確切地；明顯地	decidedly
❺	漸增地；越來越多地	increasingly
❻	明顯地；顯然	evident / evidently
❼	據傳；據宣稱	allegedly
❽	強烈地	strongly
❾	一般而言	general / generally

實戰必備

「假設與論述類」作文 必備實用句型

踏進英文作文考場之前，總得知道寫一篇作文要如何開頭、承接與結尾。以下提供一些「假設與論述類」作文中超好用的句型，依照自己的狀況在劃底線的空格處放入適合的單字（想不出填什麼的話，也可以可參考前面「實用單字」的部分找尋靈感），就能輕鬆寫出考場必備的超實用金句、一口氣加好幾分！

這樣抄就對了 Step1. 文章開頭抄這些句型就對了！

❶ **If I had the chance to** [1] （動詞片語）**, I would most definitely** [2] （動詞片語）**.**

如果我有機會可以_____，我一定會_____。

> **1 處可填入：** travel to another country 到別的國家玩／
> become another person 變成另一個人
> **2 處可填入：** go to France 去法國／
> choose to become the president 變成總統

整句可以這樣寫：

If I had the chance to go back in time, I would most definitely go back to the Tang Dynasty.

如果我有機會可以回到過去，我一定會回去唐朝。

....

❷ **If I could** [1] （動詞片語）**, I think I would probably** [2] （動詞片語）**.**

如果我可以_____，我大概會_____。

210

> **1 處可填入**：have three wishes 有三個願望／win the lottery 中樂透
> **2 處可填入**：wish for some money 許願要錢／
> spend the money on a car 把錢花在買車上

✋ **整句可以這樣寫：**

If I could become invisible, I think I would probably go to the movies in theaters for free.

如果我可以隱形，我大概會去電影院免費看電影。

· ·

❸ **I believe that** [1]（複數名詞） **should/shouldn't** [2]（動詞片語）**.**

我相信_____應該（不應該）_____。

> **1 處可填入**：students 學生／children 兒童／teachers 老師
> **2 處可填入**：use libraries more 更常使用圖書館／
> ask more questions 問更多問題

✋ **整句可以這樣寫：**

I believe that students should not be too obedient.

我相信學生不應該太聽話。

· ·

❹ **I'm a strong advocator of the idea that** [1]（複數名詞） **must/ mustn't** [2]（動詞片語）**.**

我強烈堅持_____應該（不應該）_____。

> **1 處可填入**：students 學生／parents 家長／grandparents 祖父母
> **2 處可填入**：sleep with parents 和父母一起睡／use cell phones 使用手機

✋ 整句可以這樣寫：

I'm a strong advocator of the idea that <u>parents</u> must not <u>use Facebook</u>.
我強烈堅持<u>父母</u>不應該使用臉書。

⑤ **If you ask me, I really don't think** [1] （動詞+ing） **is a good idea.**

如果你問我，我真的不覺得＿＿＿＿＿是個好主意。

> **1 處可填入**：letting sixteen-year-olds vote 讓十六歲的學生投票／
> studying too much 讀太多書

✋ 整句可以這樣寫：

If you ask me, I really don't think <u>letting fifteen-year-olds drive</u> is a good idea.
如果你問我，我真的不覺得<u>讓十五歲的人開車</u>是個好主意。

⑥ **I suppose I'd most likely** [1] <u>（動詞片語）</u> **if given the opportunity to** [2] <u>（動詞片語）</u>.

如果有機會＿＿＿＿＿，我想我應該會＿＿＿＿＿。

> **1 處可填入**：paint a picture 畫一張圖／adopt a dog 收養一隻狗
> **2 處可填入**：give a speech 演講／publish a novel 出版一本小說

✋ 整句可以這樣寫：

I suppose I'd most likely <u>learn to play the ukulele</u> if given the opportunity to <u>pick up a new instrument</u>.
如果有機會<u>學一種新樂器</u>，我想我應該會<u>學烏克麗麗</u>。

❼ The reason I'd choose to [1] （動詞片語） **is that** [2] （句子） **.**

我會選擇_____的原因是_____。

> **1 處可填入**：donate the money 把錢捐出來／get a cat 養一隻貓
> **2 處可填入**：it's good for my resume 對履歷表很有幫助／
> I like it better 我比較喜歡

✋ 整句可以這樣寫：

The reason I'd choose to wish for health **is that** I get sick easily.
我會選擇想要健康的原因是我很容易生病。

這樣抄就對了 **Step2.** 結論收尾抄這些句型就對了！

❶ To conclude, if I could [1] （動詞片語） **, I would always choose to** [2] （動詞片語） **.**

結論是，如果我可以_____，我一定會選擇_____。

> **1 處可填入**：live somewhere else 到其他地方住／
> become a kind of animal 成為一種動物
> **2 處可填入**：live in the country 到鄉下住／become a giraffe 成為長頸鹿

✋ 整句可以這樣寫：

To conclude, if I could visit a planet, **I would always choose to** go to Mars.
結論是，如果我可以到某個星球去玩，我一定會選擇到火星。

❷ All in all, because of the above reasons, I believe that [1]（句子）.

總之，因為以上的理由，我相信＿＿＿＿＿＿。

> **1 處可填入**：art should be taught in school 學校應該教藝術／
> children should learn an instrument 孩子應該要學一種樂器

✋ **整句可以這樣寫：**

All in all, because of the above reasons, I believe that we should be more careful when driving.

總之，因為以上的理由，我相信**我們開車應該更小心**。

---

❸ To summarize, here are the three reasons that I believe that [1]（句子）: **firstly,** [2]（句子）, **secondly,** [3]（句子）, **and lastly,** [4]（句子）.

總之，我相信＿＿＿＿＿＿，是因為以下三個理由：首先，＿＿＿＿＿＿；再者，＿＿＿＿＿＿；最後，＿＿＿＿＿＿。

> **1 處可填入**：children should have their own rooms 孩子應該要有自己的房間
> **2 處可填入**：it makes them more independent 他們會比較獨立
> **3 處可填入**：children need privacy to become more creative 孩子要有自己的空間才能更有創意
> **4 處可填入**：it gives parents some time to themselves 讓父母能有自己的時間

✋ **整句可以這樣寫：**

To summarize, here are the three reasons that I believe that children should go to school: **firstly,** they can learn to interact with peers, **secondly,** it's less trouble for parents, **and lastly,** they can make friends.

總之，我相信**孩子應該要去上學**，是因為以下三個理由：首先，**他們可以學著與同儕相處**；再者，**這對父母來說比較不麻煩**；最後，**他們可以交到朋友**。

4 You can see from the above example(s) that we really should/ shouldn't [1] （動詞片語）.

你可以從以上的例子看出，我們真的應該（不該）＿＿＿＿＿。

> **1 處可填入：** eat too much junk food 吃太多垃圾食物／believe everything
> books tell us 相信書上寫的所有事／trust strangers 相信陌生人

🖐 **整句可以這樣寫：**

You can see from the above examples that we really should be nice to stray animals.

你可以從以上的例子看出，我們真的應該<u>善待流浪動物</u>。

- -

5 While it may sound [1] （形容詞） to some, I believe that this is a decision that I would not regret.

雖然這對某些人來說可能很＿＿＿＿＿，但我相信這是個我不會後悔的決定。

> **1 處可填入：** frivolous 輕浮的／strange 奇怪的／unbelievable 難以相信的

🖐 **整句可以這樣寫：**

While it may sound <u>crazy</u> to some, I believe that this is a decision that I would not regret.

雖然這對某些人來說可能很<u>瘋狂</u>，但我相信這是個我不會後悔的決定。

- -

❻ Overall, I would definitely call myself a supporter of the idea that [1] （句子）**.**

整體來說，我認為自己絕對是_____的支持者。

> **1 處可填入：** children need more exercise 孩子們需要更常運動／
> people should not be addicted to television 人們不可以沉於
> 看電視

✋ **整句可以這樣寫：**

Overall, I would definitely call myself a supporter of the idea that <u>parents should not force their children to go to cram school</u>**.**

整體來說，我認為自己絕對是「<u>父母不該強迫孩子去補習班</u>」的支持者。

⋯⋯⋯⋯⋯⋯⋯⋯⋯⋯⋯⋯⋯⋯⋯⋯⋯⋯⋯⋯⋯⋯⋯⋯⋯⋯⋯⋯⋯

❼ Personally, if I get to [1] （動詞片語）**, I would** [2] （動詞片語） **every time.**

我個人覺得，如果我能夠_____，我一定會_____。

> **1 處可填入：** choose a new pet 選擇一種新寵物／make a wish 許一個願望
> **2 處可填入：** pick a rabbit 選擇一隻兔子／wish for a pony 許願要一匹小馬

✋ **整句可以這樣寫：**

Personally, if I get to <u>learn a new skill</u>**, I would** <u>learn to make apps</u> **every time.**

我個人覺得，如果我能夠<u>學一種新的能力</u>，我一定會<u>學做應用程式</u>。

★別忘了劃底線處可以依自己的
狀況套入別的單字或片語喔！

這樣抄就對了！

示範一：假設未來的事

前面我們已經看過了「假設與論述」題型中超實用的單字片語和的句型了！現在就把這些單字與句型組合起來，一篇完整的文章就完成囉！一起來看看幾個例子，都是老師精心為你寫成的高分參考作文喔！注意，裡面套色的地方都是你在前面已經學過的句型。你看，會了這些句型是不是整篇文章就可以完成八成了呢？真的夠實用吧！

If I Became an Inventor

If I had the chance to **invent something**, I would most definitely **try to put together a flying skateboard that is powered by heat**. The reason I'd choose to **invent this kind of object** is that **boards like this not only look cool but are also very convenient**. They wouldn't consume gas and are able to move as long as they feel the heat your body generates, and therefore they wouldn't cause pollution. If you ask me, I really don't think **inventing something that would further harm our environment** is a good idea!

An inventor, in my opinion, is someone who possesses at his or her fingertips the ability to create something that can change the world for the better. A skateboard that flies would definitely improve people's lives: the disabled would be able to get around by riding it very easily; performers would find ways of using it to do much more fascinating tricks. I would make it programmable so that no traffic accidents would happen because of it. And think of

如果我成為發明家

如果我有機會發明某個東西，我肯定會試著做一台會飛的滑板，是靠著熱能發電的。我會選擇發明這種東西的理由是，像這樣的滑板不但看起來很酷，而且還很方便。它們不會消耗汽油，只要感應到你身體的熱，就能夠移動，所以也不會造成污染。如果你問我，我真的不覺得發明一個會傷害環境的東西是個好主意！

對我而言，發明家就是一個擁有改變世界能力的人。會飛的滑板一定可以改善人們的生活，像是身障人士能夠輕鬆地騎著它到處移動，表演者可以想辦法利用它做一些很吸引人的演出。我會把它做成能夠以程式編碼，這樣就不會因為它而發生交通

all the time we can save because of it! If I live on the 20th floor and want to get the 20th floor of another building nearby, I don't have to go all the way down to the first floor, walk to the other building, and then go 20 floors up. Instead, all I have to do is open the window and soar to my destination on my flying skateboard! To conclude, if I could **invent something**, I would always choose to **start with making a flying skateboard**. And then I would use the money I made from it to make the world an even better place!

事故。想想看,這樣我們可以省多少時間啊!如果我住在二十樓,想到旁邊一棟大樓的二十樓,我就不用下到一樓,走到那棟大樓,然後又一路爬二十樓上去。我只需要打開窗戶,就能踩著我的飛行滑板飛到我的目的地了。結論是,如果我能夠發明某個東西,我一定會選擇從做會飛的滑板開始。接下來,我會再用我從中賺到的錢讓世界變成一個更好的地方!

★別忘了劃底線處可以依自己的
狀況套入別的單字或片語喔！

這樣抄就對了！

示範二：假設過去的事

接下來嘗試寫寫看「假設過去的事」吧！注意，裡面套色的地方都是你在前面已經學過的句型。你看，會了這些句型是不是整篇文章就可以完成八成了呢？真的夠實用吧！

If I Could Change Something in My Past

If I could **change something in my past**, I think I would probably **relive my elementary school life**. You see, I'm a strong advocator of the idea that **children** must not **study all day without doing anything fun**. However, my elementary school days consisted of school, cram school, tests, and more tests! Doesn't that sound unhealthy? If you ask me, I really don't think **doing that** is a good idea.

That's why if I could go back and change my past, I would try to become a happier elementary school student. I would still study, of course, because my parents would cry if I didn't! But I would also have fun. I would hang out with my classmates more and relax on weekends. While it may sound **strange** to some, I believe that this is a decision that I would not regret.

如果我能改變過去的一件事

如果我能改變過去的一件事，我想我應該會重新過一次國小生活。事情是這樣的，我強烈堅持兒童不應該整天讀書，一點好玩的事都不做。然而，我的國小生活卻都在學校、補習班、考試和更多的考試中度過。聽起來不是很不健康嗎？如果你問我的話，我真的不覺得這樣做是個好主意。

因此，如果我可以改變過去，我會試著當個比較開心的國小學生。我還是會讀書，這是當然的，因為如果我不讀書的話我父母會哭的。但我也會做些有趣的事。我會更常和同學們一起玩，週末也會放鬆一點。雖然這對一些人來說聽起來可能有點奇怪，但我相信這是個我不會後悔的決定。

這樣抄就對了！

示範三：贊成的論述

接下來嘗試寫寫看「贊成的論述」吧！注意，裡面套色的地方都是你在前面已經學過的句型。你看，會了這些句型是不是整篇文章就可以完成八成了呢？真的夠實用吧！

I Agree that "Students Shouldn't be Allowed to Use the Internet Every Day"

I'm a strong advocator of the idea that **students** must not **be allowed to use the Internet every day**. It's students' duty to study and learn as much as they can, and I doubt playing mindless online games can help them much in terms of learning. It will also take away precious time they have each day to review their subjects and refresh their memory on things they learned in class. If you ask me, I really don't think **spending all that time on pointless things** is a good idea.

Of course, studying all day can be quite tiring, but there are many other ways to relax without using the Internet. You can play sports, play an instrument, or maybe cook something. There are many things you can do with your time that don't concern curling up in a corner staring at a tiny screen that is most likely not good for your eyesight. Overall, I would definitely call myself a supporter of the idea that **curbing students' Internet usage is helpful for their improvement and growth**.

我同意「學生不該被允許天天使用網路」

我強烈堅持學生不應該被允許天天使用網路。學生的職務就是讀書、盡可能學習，而我覺得玩一些無腦的網路遊戲實在對學習沒什麼幫助。網路也會減少他們每天可以複習課業、重溫上課內容的時間。如果你問我，我真的不覺得把這麼多時間花在無用的事情上是個好主意。

當然，每天唸書是很累的，但還是有很多方法可以放鬆，不一定要用到網路。可以運動、練習樂器、煮煮東西。有很多方法可以利用時間，不需要蜷縮在角落，盯著對眼睛不太好的小小的螢幕。整體來說，我認為自己絕對是「減少學生的網路使用，對他們的成長與進步有幫助」這個觀點的支持者。

★別忘了劃底線處可以依自己的
狀況套入別的單字或片語喔！

這樣抄就對了！

示範四：反對的論述

接下來嘗試寫寫看「反對的論述」吧！注意，裡面套色的地方都是你在前面已經學過的句型。你看，會了這些句型是不是整篇文章就可以完成八成了呢？真的夠實用吧！

I Disagree that "Students Shouldn't be Allowed to Use the Internet Every Day"

If you ask me, I really don't think **limiting students' Internet usage** is a good idea. In fact, I'll go as far as to say the concept of "limiting Internet usage" is stupid. You think students don't study because they spend time on the Internet? Think again. Students need the Internet to do research (gone are the days when research has to be done in stuffy libraries), to turn in reports (gone are the days when reports have to be handwritten), to rewatch videos of their teachers' lessons to make sure that they didn't miss anything! Surprising, isn't it? The Internet is just as useful (if not even more useful) a tool as boring textbooks are.

It's also quite foolish to think that as long as students study hard they're going to succeed in the future. Please! It's the 21st century! If a student isn't Internet savvy enough, he's not going to be able to keep up with the times, and if one can't keep up with the times, it's sure going to be hard for him to nail a job. It's much better to let your child start honing his

我不同意「學生不該被允許天天使用網路」

如果你問我的話，我真的不覺得限制學生使用網路是個好主意。事實上，我甚至要說「限制網路使用」這個概念根本就很蠢。你覺得學生不唸書是因為他們把時間花在網路上嗎？請你再想想。學生需要網路查資料（以前那種在悶悶的圖書館裡面查資料的時代已經過去了）、交報告（以前那種報告都用手寫的時代也已經過去了）、重看他們老師上課的影片以確認他們沒有漏聽什麼重點。很驚訝吧？網路和無聊的課本一樣有用喔（可能還更有用）。

還有，覺得學生認真唸書未來就會成功，這想

skills of using the Internet to accomplish various tasks (search for important data, contact people, make advertisements) sooner than later. We no longer live in the stone age; every boss wants an employee who knows how to get him what he wants, and said employee needs the Internet for that.

To summarize, here are the three reasons that I believe that students need to use the Internet: firstly, **they need it for schoolwork**, secondly, **they need it to keep up with the ever-changing world**, lastly, **they need it to get a job**. All in all, because of the above reasons, I believe that **students should be allowed to use the Internet every day**.

法也有點傻。拜託喔！現在是二十一世紀耶！如果一個學生不懂網路，他就跟不上時代了。而如果他跟不上時代，就找不到工作了。最好還是盡早讓你的孩子開始練習使用網路完成一些事情（例如搜尋重要的資料、與人聯絡、做廣告）。我們又不是活在石器時代，每個老闆都想要一個能幫他弄到所需資訊的員工，而員工正需要靠網路來做到這點。

結論是，以下是三個我認為學生需要用網路的原因：首先，他們在學業上需要使用網路；再者，他們需要與世界接軌；最後，他們還需要網路幫助他們找到工作。總之，因為以上的理由，我認為學生必須被允許天天使用網路。

學測指考歷屆試題實戰驗證！

自我挑戰試試看：
2016年指考作文題目

有了完整的句型模板，現在的你寫起作文絕對無往不利，大考的題目也難不倒你了！現在我們就來使用模板當武器，挑戰歷屆指考與學測中出現過的「假設與論述」類題型。

2016年指定科目考試英文作文試題

提示：最近有一則新聞報導，標題為「碩士清潔隊員（waste collectors with a master's degree）滿街跑」，提及某縣市招考清潔隊員，出現50位碩士畢業生報考，引起各界關注。請就這個主題，寫一篇英文作文，文長至少120個單詞。文分兩段，第一段依據你的觀察說明這個現象的成因，第二段則就你如何因應上述現象，具體（舉例）說明你對大學生涯的學習規劃。

I'm a strong advocator of the idea that **professions** must **be chosen with thorough consideration**. Some followed the path that the traditional education indicated, ended up in having a well-paid job lifelessly, not knowing what they truly like. If you ask me, I really don't think **spending eight hours a day on work you don't like** is a good idea. The way to figure out what to pursue, I believe, is through experiencing various things and constant self-reflection. Yet people are forgetful and tend to settle for the safe route, especially when things go well. Some of the graduate students in the news may finally realize their lack of interest in subjects they've studied, and decided to switch tracks. But as long as the thinking starts, it's better late than never.

我強烈主張做出職業選擇前應該要經過審慎的思考。有些人跟從傳統教育指引的道路，最後死氣沉沉地做著高薪的工作，卻不知道自己真正喜歡的是什麼。如果你問我，我真的不認為每天花八小時在自己不喜歡的工作上是個好主意。我相信要弄清楚自己想追求什麼，需要透過體驗多種事物和持續的自我省思。但是人們很健忘又習慣安於安全的道路，特別是當事情進行得很順利時。新聞中一部分的研究生可能也是終於認清他們對自己研究的領域興趣缺缺，而決定轉換跑道。但只要開始思考永遠都不嫌遲。

"The things I learned from school are useless in my workplace." is a statement we usually heard, but the years you spent can always pay back in ways you'll never imagine. Despite the major, there are many activities like competitions and internships on and off-campus, which I would like to participate in. I will also persist in my hobbies of photography, joining the university club is indispensable, and so is assisting in the event photography. To summarize,here are the three reasons that I believe that **we can find our life-pursuing targets in college**: firstly, **it's a place for trying different things you're interested in**, secondly, **the experiences cultivated come in handy wherever you are**, and lastly, **you can reach all kinds of opportunities and people there**.The process takes a lot of time indeed, yet as long as one keeps ordering thoughts, all of the life paths get their meaning.

「學校裡學的東西在職場上都沒什麼用」是我們常聽到的一句話,但是你花的時間永遠會以你意想不到的方式得到回報。除了主修之外,還有許多校內外的競賽與實習活動是我想參與的。我也會持續在我攝影的興趣上努力,參加學校社團是一定要的,還有協助活動的攝影工作。總之,我相信我們能在大學找到人生目標,是因為以下三個理由:首先,這是個讓你嘗試各種有興趣的事的地方;再者,累積起的經驗到哪都能派上用場;最後,你也能在這接觸到各種機會和人們。這個過程肯定需要許多時間,但只要持續梳理思緒,每條走過的路都會有其意義。

\老師告訴你/

套上顏色的文字都是你在前面就學過的句型喔!別忘了要遵照考題的規定,第一段寫導致新聞報導中現象的原因,第二段則是你要如何因應規劃即將迎來的大學生涯。這個題目中涵蓋了「論述」和「假設」兩個重點角度,可以好好發揮模板句型!

學測指考歷屆試題實戰驗證！

自我挑戰試試看：
2018年學測作文題目

2018年大學學科能力測驗英文作文試題

提示：排隊雖是生活中常有的經驗，但我們也常看到民眾因一時好奇或基於嘗鮮心理而出現大排長龍（form a long line）的現象，例如景點初次開放或媒體介紹某家美食餐廳後，人們便蜂擁而至。請以此種一窩蜂式的「排隊現象」為題，寫一篇英文作文。第一段，以個人、親友的經驗或報導所聞為例，試描述這種排隊情形；第二段，說明自己對此現象的心得或感想。

The tendency to get in line has become a well-known habit of Taiwanese people. Where there are people, there are trends. But the rage takes over the subject itself sometimes. I believe that **people** should not **follow trends blindly.** For instance, after being introduced by famous YouTubers, lots of ramen restaurants were crammed. Not quite understanding the regulations and culture of ramen, some of the viewers have only one representative to get in line, which is viewed as queue-jumping there. Such things like wasting food, occupying the seats and review bombing due to all sorts of reasons happened one after another. Some of the ramen restaurants post clear regulations to cope with it, and some turned into opening for regular customers only.

排隊已經成為台灣人廣為人知的習慣。有人的地方就會有潮流。但有時潮流卻大過了事物本身。我認為人們不該盲目地追隨潮流。舉例來說，經過知名網路影片創作者介紹，許多拉麵店開始人滿為患。在不甚了解拉麵文化和規矩的情況下，部分觀眾只派了一名代表去排隊，在那裡被視為是插隊般的行為。諸如浪費食物、佔用座位和基於各種原因洗負評的行為層出不窮。部分店家因而張貼明確規定，也有的店家轉為熟客制。

As a result of the prevalent usage of the internet, the stream on the internet and in real life, become more and more concentrated likewise. People flock into the restaurants, tourist attractions or events being introduced, post thoughts alike on the internet once again, and the cycle continues. You can see from the above examples that we really should not **neglect the phenomenon of trend-chasing**. Let it alone could lead to a decrease in the diversity of culture, as all the spotlight is always centralized on a few targets, and people are always too busy chasing the trends to discover things they truly appreciate. All in all, because of the above reasons, I believe that **forming lines voluntarily is a good custom, but blindly swarming will cause conflicts and misunderstandings instead**.

網路使用盛行的其中一個結果是，人流不分線上線下都越來越集中。人們湧入被介紹的餐廳、景點或活動，又再次在網路上發出類似的心得，就這樣循環下去。你可以從以上的例子看出，我們真的不應該輕忽追隨流行的現象。要是放任下去會因為焦點總是集中在部分對象上，而降低文化的多元性。同時，人們的理解仍舊淺薄，因為總是忙於趕流行而沒空發掘自己真正感興趣的事物。總而言之，基於以上的原因，我相信自發地排隊是個好習慣，但盲目地蜂擁而至反而會造成衝突和誤解。

╲ 老師告訴你 ╱

套上顏色的文字都是你在前面就學過的句型喔！這份考題題目中有規定第一與第二段所需的內容，並沒有提到是否可以寫第三段，一般而言，如果題目中並未規定段落數，有需要可以將第二段分成兩個部分。

美國高中升大學的SAT也無往不利！

你還可以這樣應用：
SAT全真模擬試題11

以下的題目都是專家綜觀先前的SAT試題所整理出的全真模擬試題，題目內容大多以論說為主，正是假設與論述類句型派上用場的時候！這裡就帶著大家試試看如何利用模板句型寫出自然又流暢的SAT作文。SAT作文一般建議長度要寫到300～400字左右，趕快來參考一下老師的寫法吧！

SAT全真模擬試題11

Can people have too much enthusiasm?

（中譯：人們有可能「太熱情」嗎？）

Enthusiasm is something considered "good", "productive", and even "endearing" most of the time. People who work with enthusiasm are typically able to do a better job because they are wholehearted devoted to what they're doing, and people who pursue a certain subject with enthusiasm are usually more knowledgeable in the field because they are excited to know everything about it. However, if you ask me, I really don't think **being too enthusiastic** is a good idea. I believe that **people** should be **enthusiastic**, yes, but not go overboard.

For one thing, while being extremely excited over something may make the person himself incredibly happy, it can cause inconvenience to others. The person in question, being really eager to share his love for a certain subject with other people, may forget that others might not really care about

許多人認為，「熱情」是一種「很好」、「很有效益」、甚至「滿可愛的」的事。懷抱著熱情工作的人，通常都表現得比較好，因為他們全心投入於工作。而對某個主題特別有熱情的人，通常也對這個領域比較瞭解，因為瞭解其中的所有事情都讓他們興奮。然而，如果你問我的話，我實在不覺得太熱情是件好事。我相信人們的確是應該有熱情，但不能太熱情。

舉例來說，雖然為某事感到興奮可能可以讓他覺得非常開心，卻可能為其他人帶來不便。這個人可能因為非常想與他人分享他所熱愛的事物，而忘記其他人不見得對這個主題有興趣。想想你臉書上

227

the subject. Think about the people who spam your Facebook wall with endless posts regarding the same thing, which made you have to sift through thousands of boring pictures every day, just to get to any worthy content hidden underneath.

For another thing, the more passionate you are over something, the more likely you will feel upset if the thing you care about is gone. For example, if you have too much enthusiasm for certain idols who later decide to retire, it's very likely that you would be devastated, because a great foundation of your existence is built on the love for your idol. Also, your passion for your favorite subject may cause you to overlook all of its shortcomings and become irrational. Let's say if you worship a certain basketball player, for example, and someone insults his play. The next thing you know, you're in the car ready to seek the person out and beat him up! No kidding, this is something that actually happened in California. You can see from the above examples that we really shouldn't **be overly enthusiastic in something**.

To summarize, here are the three reasons that I believe that **being too enthusiastic may not be entirely good**: firstly, **it can cause trouble for people around you (especially the pushovers who just don't know how to tell you they don't care about your interests for birds or whatever subject)**, secondly, **it can be devastating if you are too emotionally invested in something**, and lastly, **you may do irrational things when you get too passionate about a topic and tend to get into fights or arguments**. Therefore, overall, I

那些猛貼類似東西的人，讓你必須天天看幾千張無聊照片，只為了能從中看到些想看的內容。

另外，你對一件事物越是熱情，當它消失時你就越容易難過。舉例來說，如果你很熱愛一些偶像，但他們後來退休了，你很可能會一蹶不振，因為你存在的意義有很大一部分建築在對偶像的愛之上。還有，你的熱情可能會讓你忽視這件事物的所有缺點，讓你變得不理性。舉例來說，如果你很愛一個籃球員，然後有人罵他打得不好，你就立刻跳上車，準備要找到這個人揍他一頓。沒騙你，這件事在加州真的發生過。你可以從以上的例子看出，我們真的不能對某件事太熱情。

總之，以下是我覺得太熱情不見得好的三個理由：首先，可能會造成你四周的人的麻煩（尤其是那些不知道怎麼跟你說他們真的對你喜歡的鳥或其他主題毫無興趣的濫好人）；第二，如果你對某事投入太多情感，可能也會傷得很深；最後，如果你對某一主題太熱衷，可能會做出不理性的事，也可能因此打架或

would definitely call myself a supporter of the idea that **it's possible to be "too enthusiastic" and such thing is not exactly a good thing at all**!

吵架。因此,整體來說,我絕對會説我支持「真的有可能太熱情,而且這不見得是好事」這個概念!

\ 老師告訴你 /

套上顏色的文字都是你在前面就學過的句型喔!在SAT的考題中,主要是以論述自己的論點為主。有沒有發現呢?在這篇中並不像前面幾個單元的SAT題型中一樣提出親身例證,而是以見聞為例。

你還可以這樣應用：
SAT全真模擬試題12

SAT全真模擬試題12

Is acting an essential part of everyday life?

（中譯：演戲是日常生活必要的一部分嗎？）

"I'm so worried about the school play! I have a speaking role, and I can't act!" my friend tells me. I laugh, and assure her: "Of course you can act! You do it every day!"

Yep, I'm a strong advocator of the idea that **one must act every single day to survive**. People who are "true to themselves" and can always "be themselves" only exist in myths and fairy tales. And that's not a bad thing! If you ask me, I really don't think **"being yourself"** is a good idea. Think about it. Do you act exactly the same in front of your mom and your best friend? Do you act exactly the same in front of your crush and your math teacher (Unless your crush *is* your math teacher, but such cases are rare)? Of course you don't. And think about when you're alone. Aren't there a lot of things you do alone that you would never do in front of others? I bet there are.

The thing is, acting is a normal part of life. If you said the same things you say to a friend to your grandparents, for example, there would be huge consequences. If you told your least favorite teacher

「我好擔心學校戲劇表演喔！我的角色有台詞耶，我又不會演戲！」我朋友告訴我。我笑了，安慰她：「妳當然會演戲啊！妳天天不都在演戲！」

是的，我強烈堅稱人們必須天天演戲，才能生存。「對自己誠實」、「做自己」的人只活在傳說與童話中。這也不是壞事啊！如果你問我，我真的不覺得「做自己」是個好主意。你想想看啊，你在你媽媽和你最好朋友的面前，會是同一個樣子嗎？你在你暗戀的人跟你數學老師面前會是同一個樣子嗎（除非你暗戀的人就是你的數學老師，但這樣的情形並不多）？當然不會啊。你一個人的時候，是不是也會做很多絕不可能在別人面前做的事呢？我賭會有。

事實上，演戲就是生

what you honestly think about him, you'd probably be in trouble. And do you want trouble? Most of the time, you don't, so you put on an act and pretend to be nice. You act to avoid unnecessary problems, to be liked by others, to get what you want. Everyone does! If we don't, chaos will ensue, war will break out, people will be having fistfights on the streets.

All in all, because of the above reasons, I believe that **acting is indeed an essential part of everyday life**. Personally, if I get to **go a day without acting with no consequences**, I would probably **still act** every time. Acting is so natural to every one of us now that it's pretty much unavoidable!

活常態的一部分。舉例來説，如果你把對朋友説的話拿來對祖父母説，肯定會有很慘的後果。如果你告訴你最討厭的老師對他的真實看法，你大概會惹上麻煩。你想要惹禍上身嗎？大部分的時候，你都不想要，所以就只好演戲，假裝是個好人。你演戲是為了避開不必要的問題、受到其他人喜愛、得到自己想要的東西。大家都是這樣啊！如果不演戲，世界會一片混亂，戰爭會開打，人們會在路上打起架來。

總之，因為以上的理由，我相信演戲是日常生活必要的一部分。我個人覺得，就算我可以無後顧之憂地一天不演戲，我還是會一不小心演起來。演戲對我們來説實在太自然了，根本無法避免嘛！

\ **老師告訴你** /

套上顏色的文字都是你在前面就學過的句型喔！在SAT的考題中，主要是以論述自己的論點為主。這篇中並沒有提出親身例證，而是以反問讀者的方式「逼」出一個結論，也是一個寫論說文時可以使用的方法。

讀完了這麼多的範例作文，現在你一定已經躍躍欲試，想套用模板句型自己寫寫看了吧！請你以**Is the world changing in a positive way?（世界正在朝正面的方向改變嗎？）**為題，寫出自己支持此論點與否，套用模板句型寫一篇作文。所有的句型都在框框中為你列出來囉！

文章開頭參考句型

(1) If I had the chance to [1] （動詞片語）, I would most definitely [2] （動詞片語）.

(2) If I could [1] （動詞片語）, I think I would probably [2] （動詞片語）.

(3) I believe that [1] （複數名詞） should/shouldn't [2] （動詞片語）.

(4) I'm a strong advocator of the idea that [1] （複數名詞） must/mustn't [2] （動詞片語）.

(5) If you ask me, I really don't think [1] （動詞+ing） is a good idea.

(6) I suppose I'd most likely [1] （動詞片語） if given the opportunity to [2] （動詞片語）.

(7) The reason I'd choose to [1] （動詞片語） is that [2] （句子）.

結論收尾參考句型

(1) To conclude, if I could [1] （動詞片語）, I would always choose to [2] （動詞片語）.

(2) All in all, because of the above reasons, I believe that [1] （句子）.

(3) To summarize, here are the three reasons that I believe that [1] （句子）: firstly, [2] （句子）, secondly, [3] （句子）, and lastly, [4] （句子）.

(4) You can see from the above example(s) that we really should/shouldn't [1] （動詞片語）.

(5) While it may sound [1] （形容詞） to some, I believe that this is a decision that I would not regret.

(6) Overall, I would definitely call myself a supporter of the idea that [1] （句子）.

(7) Personally, if I get to [1] （動詞片語）, I would [2] （動詞片語） every time.

Part

8

抄這本就對了！
寫出有說服力的

「二選一類」

作文

抄這本就對了！寫出有說服力的「二選一類」作文

所謂「二選一類作文」就是題目中會給你兩個選項，讓你從中擇一，並說明選擇這一項、不選另一項的理由。舉例來說，題目可能會問你：想要可以隱形的能力，還是可以飛行的能力呢？這時，你就必須在文中說明自己想要的能力是哪一種，不可以兩種都選，也不可以兩種都要。這樣的題目究竟該怎麼寫呢？快點一起來看看！

一定要知道

「二選一類」作文的寫作重點

二選一類 Step **1.** 選擇方便的選項下手

　　作文考的是你的語言表達能力，並不是測謊，所以在兩個選項中，若你比較喜歡A，但想不出怎麼說明A的好處，反而比較知道B的好處怎麼講，那就大膽地選B吧！沒有人會知道你是不是在騙他們，就算知道也不會介意。切記二選一的題目不要兩個都選，然而倒是可以說「Even though both of these sound appealing...」（雖然兩者聽起來都很吸引人……）或「I would love to have both if I could, but...」（如果可以兩個都要那最好，但……）這樣模稜兩可的開頭，再明確說出自己在兩者之間的選擇。

二選一類 Step2.

寫出自己選擇某一項的原因、不選擇另一項的原因

既然是二選一的問題，當然得寫出某一個選項比另一個好（或比較吸引你）的理由。在這個地方可以大量運用和「比較」有關的單字、句型（後面會整理喔！），並善用反義字的比較，更能凸顯其中一項的好處和另一項的不便之處。

如果時間還足夠，也可以嘗試看看寫「不選擇的那一項」的某一些好處，這是為了讓讀者感覺到你確實充分考慮了兩項的優劣。但千萬要記得接下來必須馬上反駁這些好處，或是說明這些好處「還不夠好」的原因，否則要是把另一個選項捧上了天，你卻不選擇它，那就說不過去了。這是時間還充足時可以做的，如果時間並不算充裕，則不需要多此一舉。

二選一類 Step3.　漂亮的收尾讓人印象深刻

最後的收尾可以中規中矩地再度強調自己選擇某一項、不選擇另一項的理由，也可以出人意表地說明自己選擇了某一項後，接下來要做什麼。舉例來說，如果在「隱形」與「飛行」中，你選擇了「飛行」的能力，就可以寫寫你有了這個能力以後要用來幹嘛、飛去哪裡。或是題目問你有兩部電影：一部鬼片和一部浪漫愛情片，你要選擇哪一個，如果你選了鬼片，就可以根據片名預測片中可能會出現的場景，並說明你為何喜歡看這樣場景的電影。

實戰必備

「二選一類」作文必備單字片語

　　二選一類的作文中，首先就是勢必會用到「比較」相關的單字、片語。接下來還可能需要善用「反義詞」，比較出兩者之間的差異。現在就在這裡為大家列出這些可能用到的單字片語！

✏️ 表達「比較、選擇」的單字與片語

①	寧可；比較想要	prefer
②	比較喜歡	favor
③	寧可；比較希望	rather
④	更喜歡	like... better
⑤	比較喜歡	have a preference for...
⑥	選擇	choose
⑦	選項	choice
⑧	挑選	select
⑨	揀選	pick
⑩	選項	option
⑪	另一選擇	alternative
⑫	替代選項	substitute

反義的單字

❶	方便的	**convenient**
❷	不便的	**inconvenient**
❸	有用的	**useful**
❹	無用的	**useless**
❺	有趣的	**interesting**
❻	無趣的	**uninteresting**
❼	吸引人的	**appealing**
❽	不吸引人的	**unappealing**
❾	令人想要的	**desirable**
❿	令人不想要的	**undesirable**
⓫	簡單的	**easy**
⓬	困難的	**difficult**
⓭	實際的	**practical**
⓮	不實際的	**impractical**
⓯	合理的	**sensible**
⓰	不合理的	**insensible**
⓱	令人印象深刻的	**impressive**
⓲	不令人印象深刻的	**unimpressive**
⓳	有利益的	**profitable**
⓴	無利益的	**unprofitable**

實戰必備

「二選一類」作文
必備實用句型

　　踏進英文作文考場之前，總得知道寫一篇作文要如何開頭、承接與結尾。以下提供一些「二選一類」作文中超好用的句型，依照自己的狀況在劃底線的空格處放入適合的單字（想不出填什麼的話，也可以可參考前面「實用單字」的部分找尋靈感），就能輕鬆寫出考場必備的超實用金句、一口氣加好幾分！

這樣抄就對了 Step 1. 文章開頭抄這些句型就對了！

❶ **If given the choice between** ¹ （名詞片語 或 動詞+ing）**and** ² （名詞片語 或 動詞+ing）**, I would without doubt choose the former/latter.**

如果能選擇要＿＿＿＿還是＿＿＿＿，我一定毫無疑問地會選前者／後者。

> **1 處可填入**：a puppy 一隻小狗／reading a book 看一本書／
> eating a banana 吃一根香蕉
> **2 處可填入**：a kitten 一隻小貓／watching the adapted movie 看改編的電影／eating an apple 吃一顆蘋果

✍ 整句可以這樣寫：

If given the choice between <u>being a guy</u> **and** <u>being a girl</u>**, I would without doubt choose the** <u>former</u>**.**

如果能夠選擇要<u>當男生</u>還是<u>當女生</u>，我一定毫無疑問地會選擇<u>前者</u>。

❷ I would most likely prefer [1] <u>（名詞片語 或 動詞+ing）</u> **over** [2] <u>（名詞片語 或 動詞+ing）</u> **if you ask me.**

如果你問我，我應該會選擇＿＿＿＿而不是＿＿＿＿。

> **1 處可填入**：staying home 待在家／visiting the future 探訪未來／
> oranges 橘子
> **2 處可填入**：going out 出門／visiting the past 回到過去／pears 梨子

✍ **整句可以這樣寫：**

I would most likely prefer <u>playing basketball</u> over <u>playing hockey</u> if you ask me.

如果你問我，我應該會選擇**打籃球**而不是**曲棍球**。

- -

❸ I don't know about you, but personally I think [1] <u>（名詞片語 或 動詞+ing）</u> **is vastly better.**

我是不知道你怎麼想，但我個人覺得＿＿＿＿實在好多了。

> **1 處可填入**：a yacht 一艘遊艇／a helicopter 一架直昇機／
> having a robot 擁有一個機器人

✍ **整句可以這樣寫：**

I don't know about you, but personally I think <u>e-mail</u> is vastly better.

我是不知道你怎麼想，但我個人覺得**寫電子郵件**實在好多了。

- -

❹ The reason that I'd prefer [1] （名詞片語 或 動詞+ing）**over** [2] （名詞片語 或 動詞+ing）**is as follows.**

我會選擇_____而不是_____的理由如下。

> **1 處可填入**：being an athlete 成為運動員／becoming a bird 變成一隻鳥／
> visiting Europe 去歐洲
> **2 處可填入**：being a singer 成為歌手／becoming a fish 變成一隻魚／
> visiting Antarctica 去南極

✋ 整句可以這樣寫：

The reason that I'd prefer pizza over fried chicken is as follows.
我會選擇披薩而不是炸雞的理由如下。

❺ There are three reasons for my choice. Firstly, [1] （句子）**. Secondly,** [2] （句子）**. Lastly,** [3] （句子）**.**

我會這麼選擇有三個理由。首先，_____。再者，_____。最後，_____。

> **1~3 處可填入**：it's more convenient 比較方便／I can handle it better 我比
> 較能掌控／it's not too expensive 不會太貴

✋ 整句可以這樣寫：

There are three reasons for my choice. Firstly, going by bus is cheaper. Secondly, there's a stop right in front of my house. Lastly, it's less crowded.
我會這麼選擇有三個理由。首先，搭公車比較便宜。再者，我家門口就有公車站。最後，這樣比較不會人擠人。

❻ I wouldn't want to [1] （動詞片語） **at all, because** [2] （句子）.

我一點都不想要_____，因為_____。

> **1 處可填入**：have too much money 有太多錢／have a snake 養一條蛇／
> go back in time 回到過去
> **2 處可填入**：it's inconvenient 不方便／it feeds on mice 牠以老鼠為食／
> I like the present better 我比較喜歡現在

✍ **整句可以這樣寫：**

I wouldn't want to have a new car **at all, because** my current one is nice enough.

我一點都不想要一台新車，因為我現在這台夠好了。

● ●

❼ I don't think I'd pick [1] （名詞片語 或 動詞+ing） **, since it's too** [2] （形容詞）.

我覺得我不會選擇_____，因為它太_____。

> **1 處可填入**：this hotel 這家旅館／a small dog 小型犬／this book 這本書
> **2 處可填入**：expensive 貴的／nervous 緊張的／boring 無聊的

✍ **整句可以這樣寫：**

I don't think I'd pick this story, **since it's too** long.

我覺得我不會選擇這個故事，因為它太長了。

❶ After choosing [1] （名詞片語 或 to+動詞）**, I'd try to** [2] （動詞片語）.

選擇了_____之後，我會試著_____。

> **1 處可填入：** a new pet 一隻新的寵物／to visit Taipei 去台北玩／
> to go to cram school 去補習班
> **2 處可填入：** take good care of it 好好照顧牠／take many pictures 照很多相
> 片／pay close attention 認真專心

整句可以這樣寫：

After choosing a flying carpet, I'd try to travel the world using it.
選擇了飛毯之後，我會試著用它環遊世界。

....

❷ Though most people may have a different choice, I believe that my choice is the best because of the above reasons.

雖然大部分的人可能會有不同的選擇，但因為以上理由，我相信我的選擇是最好的。

....

❸ The more I think about it, the more I like the idea of [1] （名詞片語 或 動詞+ing）**. If only it could come true now!**

我越想越喜歡_____這個點子。真希望現在就可以成真啊！

> **1 處可填入：** being a millionaire 變成百萬富翁／traveling to Australia 去澳
> 洲玩／becoming famous 變成名人

✋ **整句可以這樣寫：**

The more I think about it, the more I like the idea of <u>becoming a firefighter</u>.
If only it could come true now!

我越想越喜歡<u>「當消防員」</u>這個點子。真希望現在就可以成真啊！

⁎ ⁎

❹ **Though** [1]（複數名詞，人物）**would say that it's better to** [2]（動詞片語）**, I really do think my choice is superior!**

雖然＿＿＿＿可能會說＿＿＿＿比較好，但我還是覺得我的選擇比較好！

> **1 處可填入**：others 其他人／my friends 我朋友們／some adults 有些大人
> **2 處可填入**：buy a house 買房子／get married 結婚／
> invest the money 把錢拿去投資

✋ **整句可以這樣寫：**

Though <u>many others</u> **would say that it's better to** <u>play it safe</u>**, I really do think my choice is superior!**

雖然<u>很多人</u>可能會說<u>保險一點</u>比較好，但我還是覺得我的選擇比較好！

⁎ ⁎

❺ **Even though this is kind of a difficult choice, in the end, my heart will always tell me to pick** [1]（名詞片語 或 動詞+ing）**.**

雖然這是個有點困難的抉擇，最終我心裡還是會選擇＿＿＿＿。

> **1 處可填入**：my family 我的家庭／my friends 我的朋友／
> adopting a dog 收養一隻狗

整句可以這樣寫：

Even though this is kind of a difficult choice, in the end, my heart will always tell me to pick <u>the blue dress</u>**.**

雖然這是個有點困難的抉擇，最終我心裡還是會選擇<u>這件藍色的洋裝</u>。

⸺⸺⸺⸺⸺⸺⸺⸺⸺⸺⸺⸺⸺⸺⸺⸺⸺⸺⸺⸺⸺⸺⸺

❻ Some may say that it's [1] <u>（形容詞）</u> **, but this is a choice that I'll never regret.**

有人可能會說這很＿＿＿＿＿，但這是個我不會後悔的決定。

> **1 處可填入：** stupid 蠢的／crazy 瘋狂的／improper 不合宜的

整句可以這樣寫：

Some may say that it's <u>weird</u>**, but this is a choice that I'll never regret.**

有人可能會說這很**奇怪**，但這是個我不會後悔的決定。

⸺⸺⸺⸺⸺⸺⸺⸺⸺⸺⸺⸺⸺⸺⸺⸺⸺⸺⸺⸺⸺⸺⸺

❼ To conclude, out of the two choices, [1] <u>（名詞片語 或 動詞 +ing）</u> **will unquestionably be my top pick.**

總之，在這兩個選項中，＿＿＿＿＿毫無疑問地會是我的首選。

> **1 處可填入：** a milkshake 奶昔／owning a dragon 擁有一頭龍／
> playing baseball 打棒球

整句可以這樣寫：

To conclude, out of the two choices, <u>teleporting</u> **will unquestionably be my top pick.**

總之，在這兩個選項中，<u>瞬間移動</u>毫無疑問地會是我的首選。

★別忘了劃底線處可以依自己的
狀況套入別的單字或片語喔！

這樣抄就對了！

示範一：物品二選一

　　前面我們已經看過了「二選一」題型中超實用的單字片語和句型了！現在就把這些單字與句型組合起來，一篇完整的文章就完成囉！一起來看看幾個例子，都是老師精心為你寫成的高分參考作文喔！注意，裡面套色的地方都是你在前面已經學過的句型。你看，會了這些句型是不是整篇文章就可以完成八成了呢？真的夠實用吧！

Choose Between: Owning your Dream Car or Owning a Helicopter

　　If given the choice between **owning my dream car** and **owning a helicopter**, I would without doubt choose the **former**. There are three reasons for my choice. Firstly, **a helicopter makes a ton of noise, while my dream car is completely silent**. Secondly, **a helicopter requires a parking space, while my dream car is compact and can be folded to fit in my pocket**. Lastly, **a helicopter attracts a lot of attention, which I hate, while my dream car can turn invisible so it would not bring any problems in that regard**.

　　Though most people may have a different choice, I believe that my choice is the best because of the above reasons. **After all, people prefer a helicopter over a car simply because it can fly, right? Well, my dream car can also fly! That solves the dilemma, doesn't it?** In fact, I want my car to not only fly but also be able to be waterproof, so that it can bring me under the sea like a submarine. What's more, if I could go to space in that car, it would be

二選一：擁有你夢想中的車子 vs. 擁有一架直昇機

　　如果我可以選擇擁有我夢想中的車子或擁有一架直昇機，我毫無疑問地會選擇前者。我會這樣選擇有三個理由。首先，直昇機會製造很多噪音，而我夢想中的車子非常安靜。再者，直昇機需要地方停，而我夢想中的車子很小巧，還可以折起來放進口袋。最後，直昇機會引起大家的注意，我不喜歡這樣，而我夢想中的車子可以隱形，所以也不會有這種問題。

　　雖然大部分的人可能會有不同的選擇，但因為上述理由，我覺得我的選擇是最好的。畢竟人們覺得直昇機勝過車子的理由

amazing! But perhaps that's asking for too much—just a flying car is enough to make me so happy that I even smile while I sleep. The more I think about it, the more I like the idea of **a flying car**. If only it could come true now! To conclude, out of the two choices, **owning my dream car** will unquestionably be my top pick.

就是因為它會飛嘛！我夢想中的車子也會飛啊！這樣就不會左右為難了嘛，對不對？其實我不但想要我的車會飛，還想要它能防水，這樣它就能像潛水艇一樣帶我潛到海裡。還有，如果我可以乘我的車飛到外太空，那就太棒了！但這樣可能要求太多了，只要車子會飛就夠了，我一定開心到作夢也會笑。我越想越覺得「會飛的車」這個點子真是太好了，真希望現在就可以成真啊！總之，在這兩個選擇中，擁有我夢想中的車子毫無疑問地會是我的首選。

這樣抄就對了！

★別忘了劃底線處可以依自己的
狀況套入別的單字或片語喔！

示範二：活動二選一

接下來嘗試寫寫看「活動二選一」吧！注意，裡面套色的地方都是你在前面已經學過的句型。你看，會了這些句型是不是整篇文章就可以完成八成了呢？真的夠實用吧！

Choose Between: A Day on the Moon or a Day on a Luxurious Cruise Ship

If given the choice between **spending a day on the moon** and **spending a day on a luxurious cruise ship**, I would without doubt choose the **latter**. I wouldn't want to **spend a day on the moon** at all, because **it sounds dangerous**! I don't know about you, but personally I think **a day on a luxurious cruise ship** is vastly better. Yes, the ship can sink and whatnot, but it's still much safer than going to the moon, and you don't have to train for it. The moon doesn't seem to be a very comfortable place to be, while an extravagant suite on a cruise ship would most likely be one of the most comfortable places on earth, which I don't plan on leaving any time soon!

Though **adventurous people** would say that it's better to **go to space**, I really do think my choice is superior, **since I'm unfortunately the boring kind that prefers to stay put**. After choosing to **board my lovely ship**, I'd try to **use as many entertainment facilities on it as I can**, such as the swimming pool and buffet.

二選一：在月球上度過一天 vs. 在高級遊輪上度過一天

如果我能選擇在月球上度過一天或在高級遊輪上度過一天，我毫無疑問地會選擇後者。我可不想在月球上度過一天，因為聽起來超危險的！我是不知道你怎想啦，但我個人覺得在高級遊輪上度過一天實在好太多了。是沒錯，船也可能會沉，但還是比去月球來得安全，而且也不用為此訓練。月球感覺不是個很舒服的地方，而遊輪上的豪華套房應該是整個地球最舒服的地方之一吧！我打算還是待在地球上就好了。

雖然有冒險精神的人會說上太空比較好，但我還是覺得我的選擇比較

Or I'd go to the top deck and enjoy the sun and the warm ocean breeze while listening to my favorite music and sipping a cocktail, and maybe even attempt to paint the wonderful scene. Perhaps I'd also have my breakfast in bed since that's something I had always wanted to do! My orange juice and pancakes wouldn't be floating around like they would be in space, that's for sure. Some may say that it's **lazy and materialistic**, but this is a choice that I'll never regret.

棒，因為很不巧地我就是那種寧可不亂跑的無聊的人。選擇搭上那美好的船之後，我會盡我所能地使用各種娛樂設施，像是游泳池和自助餐廳。還有，我可以到頂樓甲板享受陽光和溫暖的海風，聽著我最喜歡的音樂同時啜飲雞尾酒，甚至試著畫下這幅美景。我說不定還可以在床上吃早餐，因為我一直都很想試試看。我的柳橙汁和煎餅肯定不會像在太空中一樣飄來飄去。有些人可能會說我這樣懶惰又物質主義，但這是個我永遠不會後悔的選擇。

這樣抄就對了！

示範三：點子二選一

接下來嘗試寫寫看「點子二選一」吧！注意，裡面套色的地方都是你在前面已經學過的句型。你看，會了這些句型是不是整篇文章就可以完成八成了呢？真的夠實用吧！

Choose Between: Being Able to Control your Dreams or Being Able to See your Dreams on Video

I would most likely prefer **being able to see my dreams on video** over **being able to control my dreams** if you ask me. For one thing, I'm a "lucid dreamer"—I'm already able to control my dreams a little bit. For another, having complete control over one's dreams is not interesting at all! I like to see where my subconscious takes me. Lots of strange new worlds exist in my head, places where I cannot have come up with even in my wildest imaginations. Controlling things requires a conscious effort, and if I exert control over my dreams they will be much less subconscious and therefore be much more boring!

二選一：能夠控制夢境 vs. 能夠在影片中看到夢境的內容

如果你問我的話，比起能夠控制夢境，我大概會比較想要能夠在影片中看到夢境的內容。一方面，我會做「清醒夢」，也就是說我已經可以稍微控制我的夢境了。另一方面，能夠完全控制自己的夢就沒意思了啊！我喜歡看看我的潛意識會帶我到什麼地方去。我的腦中有著許多奇怪的新世界，這些世界是我窮盡所有想像力也無法想出來的。要控制事情就需要有意識的努力，所以如果我想控制我的夢，它們就會脫離潛意識，而變得無聊許多。

Actually, the strange new worlds in my head are the reason I want to see my dreams on video. Just think about it! These worlds are so unique that if I paint them on canvas or even take screenshots (depending on how high-resolution the video is), I can probably become renowned as the world's greatest artist. The more I think about it, the more I like the idea of **painting my dreamscapes**. If only it could come true now!

Though a lot of people would say that it's better to **be able to control their dreams**, I really do think my choice is superior. Since I can already control my dreams somewhat, I would be able to act out my fantasies in my dreams and then view them in video form! I can't imagine anything better than this. To conclude, out of the two choices, **being able to see my dreams on video** will unquestionably be my top pick.

事實上，我腦中那些奇怪的新世界正是我想透過影片看到夢境的理由。想想看，這些世界這麼特別，如果我把它們畫出來或從螢幕上擷取下來（視影片的畫質而定），我大概就可以成為世界最偉大的知名藝術家了。我越想越覺得把夢境畫下來真是個好主意，如果現在可以成真就好了！

雖然很多人應該都會覺得能夠控制夢境比較好，但我真的覺得我的選擇比較棒。因為我已經可以稍微控制我的夢境了，我就可以在夢中演出幻想中的內容，然後以影片形式觀賞它們。我很難想像還有什麼比這更好了。總之，在這兩個選項中，能夠在影片中看到我的夢境毫無疑問地會是我的第一首選。

這樣抄就對了！

示範四：地點二選一

接下來嘗試寫寫看「地點二選一」吧！注意，裡面套色的地方都是你在前面已經學過的句型。你看，會了這些句型是不是整篇文章就可以完成八成了呢？真的夠實用吧！

Choose Between: Going to the Beach or Going to the Mountains

If given the choice between **going to the beach** and **going to the mountains**, I would without doubt choose the **latter**. There are three reasons for my choice. Firstly, **the beach is no fun when it's not sunny, yet I also hate being under the sun. So no matter what the weather is like, it's a lose-lose situation for me**. Secondly, **the beach is usually crowded, and I'm sort of antisocial**. Lastly, **the mountains offer lots of shade, lots of fresh air and lovely scenery**.

Though most people may have a different choice, I believe that my choice is the best because of the above reasons. **The mountains are nice and cool even when the weather is hot, and not usually crowded.** Some may say that it's **more boring than the beach**, but this is a choice that I'll never regret.

二選一：去海邊 vs. 去山上

如果能選擇去海邊還是山上，我毫無疑問地會選擇後者。我的選擇有三個理由。首先，不是晴天的話，海邊就不好玩，可是我又不喜歡曬太陽，所以無論天氣如何，到海邊對我來說都很沒意思。再者，海邊總是很多人，而我又不喜歡和人群接觸。最後，山上有很多遮蔭的地方、空氣新鮮、景色也美麗。

雖然許多人可能有不一樣的選擇，因為以上的理由，我還是覺得我的選擇是最好的。山上總是舒服又涼快，就算天氣很熱也一樣，而且不常人擠人。有人可能會說那裡比海邊更無聊，但這是個我不會後悔的選擇。

自我挑戰試試看：
2013年指考作文題目

有了完整的句型模板，現在的你寫起作文絕對無往不利，大考的題目也難不倒你了！現在我們就來使用模板當武器，挑戰歷屆指考與學測中出現過的「二選一」類題型。

2013年指定科目考試英文作文試題

提示：以下有兩項即將上市之新科技產品：

產品一：隱形披風（invisibility cloak）
→穿上後頓時隱形，旁人看不到你的存在；同時，隱形披風會保護你，讓你水火不侵。

產品二：智慧型眼鏡（smart glasses）
→具有掃描透視功能，戴上後即能看到障礙物後方的生物；同時能完整記錄你所經歷過的場景。

如果你有機會獲贈其中一項產品，你會選擇哪一項？請以此為主題，寫一篇至少120個單詞的英文作文。文分兩段，第一段說明你的選擇及理由，並舉例說明你將如何使用這項產品。第二段說明你不選擇另一項產品的理由及該項產品可能衍生的問題。

If given the choice between **an invisibility cloak that also protects me from harm** and **smart glasses that let me see through walls**, I would without doubt choose the **former**. There are three reasons for my choice. Firstly, **the protection-from-harm function is extremely useful—say, when I get caught in a fire, I'd be able to escape safely**. Secondly, **invisibility can grant me a lot of privileges such as observing wildlife closely**. Lastly, after choosing **the invisibility cloak**, I'd try to **become a spy**—think

如果可以選擇一件能保護我的隱形披風，或一副能讓我有透視眼的智慧型眼鏡，我毫無疑問地會選擇前者。我會這樣選擇有以下三個原因：首先，能夠保護我不受傷害是個很有用的功能，像假如我遇到火災，我就可以安全逃離。再者，如果我能隱形，就會有很多好處，例如可以近距離觀察野生動物。最後，在選擇隱形披

about all the money I can make from that!

Though a lot of people would say that it's better to be able to see living beings hidden behind objects, I really do think my choice is superior. Why would I want to see living beings behind walls? Bugs and spiders can stay hidden for all I care; in fact I'd rather not see them at all. Being able to record everything I see can be useful, but compared to immunity from harm by fire or water, it's still somewhat inferior in my opinion. To conclude, out of the two choices, **the invisibility cloak** would unquestionably be my top pick.

風後，我可以試著成為一名間諜，這可以賺很多錢耶！

雖然很多人都會覺得能看到障礙物後方的生物比較好，我還是真的覺得我的選擇比較好。我為什麼要看到牆壁後面的生物呢？我不在乎蟲子、蜘蛛那些的，事實上眼不見為淨最好。能夠記錄我所經歷的一切可能是滿有用的，但和水火不侵比起來，我覺得還是差了一點。結論是，在兩個選項中，隱形披風一定是我的首選。

╲ 老師告訴你 ╱

套上顏色的文字都是你在前面就學過的句型喔！這份考題中規定了兩段各需要寫的內容，一段寫選擇一項產品的理由，另一段寫不選另一項產品的理由。一定要照著規定的格式發揮，否則會因離題被扣分喔。

學測指考歷屆試題實戰驗證！

自我挑戰試試看：
2015年學測作文題目

2015年學測英文作文試題
提示：下面兩本書是學校建議的暑假閱讀書籍，請依書名想想看該書的內容，
　　　並思考你會選擇哪一本書閱讀，為什麼？請在第一段說明你會選哪一本
　　　書及你認為該書的內容大概會是什麼，第二段提出你選擇該書的理由。

EVERYONE IS BEAUTIFUL:
Respect Others & Be Yourself

Caroline Strong

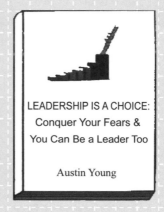

LEADERSHIP IS A CHOICE:
Conquer Your Fears &
You Can Be a Leader Too

Austin Young

If given the choice between **reading a book on how everyone is beautiful** and **reading a book on how to become a leader**, I would without doubt choose the **latter**. The reason is simple: I already think that everyone is beautiful, I already like myself, and I already like just about everyone—I'm known as the overly nice person in class who has no enemies. Therefore, I don't need a book to teach me about beauty in humans. However, I do need a book about leadership, for I might be the most terrible leader you'd ever meet. I imagine that the book

如果能夠選擇閱讀一本關於「大家都很美麗」的書或閱讀一本關於「如何成為領導者」的書，我毫無疑問地會選擇後者。理由很簡單：我已經覺得大家都很美麗了，我喜歡自己也很喜歡所有人，班上大家都覺得我是個不會樹敵的超級好人。因此，我不需要一本告訴我人們有多美麗的書。然而，我倒是很需要一本教我領導能力的書，因為我大概是

would teach me how to build confidence and management skills as well as ways to direct a team, all of these crucial aspects that I lack.

Though some people would say that it's better to **read a book about the beauty in everyone**, I really do think my choice is superior. **You can't learn to respect others just by reading a book, I believe—it's something you have to implement in your everyday life, something that you have to wholeheartedly embrace no matter who you interact with.** Leadership skills, on the other hand, are things you can learn by reading a book, by observing examples the book provides and by following the tips the book lists out for you. To conclude, out of the two choices, **"Leadership is a Choice"** will unquestionably be my top pick for my summer reading.

你見過最差勁的領導者。我預想這本書會教我如何建立信心、增進管理能力以及領導團隊的方法,這些都是我所缺少的關鍵要素。

雖然有些人可能會說讀一本關於每個人的美麗之處的書比較好,我真的還是覺得我的選擇比較棒。我覺得你沒辦法靠著讀一本書就能學會尊重別人,應該要從日常生活中落實,全心全意地接受這個觀念,無論和誰互動都一樣。而領導能力則不同,你可以靠著看書、觀察書中提供的例證、跟隨書中列出的指示學到一些領導能力。總之,在兩個選項中,《領導能力是種選擇》毫無疑問地會是我暑期閱讀的頭號選擇。

\ 老師告訴你 /

套上顏色的文字都是你在前面就學過的句型喔!題目中規定你必須在第一段說明選擇哪本書、以及這本書可能的內容,第二段再說明為何做這個選擇。這篇文章中在第一段便稍微提到了做這個選擇的理由,但只要不佔整段的大宗,且第一、二段還是有描寫到題目中規定的內容,則不會影響到評分。

美國高中升大學的SAT也無往不利！

你還可以這樣應用：
SAT全真模擬試題13

以下的題目都是專家綜觀先前的SAT試題所整理出的全真模擬試題，題目內容大多以論說為主，別忘了，在論說的同時也會需要敘述自己的經驗啊！這裡就帶著大家試試看如何利用模板句型寫出自然又流暢的SAT作文。SAT作文一般建議長度要寫到300～400字左右，趕快來參考一下老師的寫法吧！

SAT全真模擬試題13

Which results in success more often: competition or collaboration?

（中譯：哪種方式更容易成功：競爭或合作？）

Is competition or collaboration more likely to bring about success? I would most likely prefer **collaboration** over **competition** if you ask me. There are three reasons for my choice. Firstly, competition can easily lead to jealousy and malice, which is unhealthy to any environment. There are always winners and losers in any competition, and it goes without saying that no one would want to be the loser. Thus, even though people might not show spiteful attitudes towards their rivals, they certainly aren't going to be all buddy-buddy with them! It's not even on purpose; I've known lots of people who are inherently kind but spout creative insults easily when it comes to their competitors, without realizing that they could have saved the energy they spent coming up with negative words on bettering their own performance, which would more likely lead to their success.

到底是競爭還是合作比較容易成功呢？如果你問我的話，我會選擇合作而不是競爭。我會這麼選擇有三個理由。首先，競爭容易引來嫉妒與惡意，這對任何環境來說都不太健康。在任何競爭中都會有贏家和輸家，想當然，沒人會想輸。因此，就算人們不見得會對競爭對手表現出懷恨在心的態度，他們總不會和對方勾肩搭背的吧！這也不見得是故意的，我認識很多本性善良的人，但一提到競爭對手，各種有創意的罵人方式都冒出來了。他們都沒發現自己可以把那些思索負面言詞的時間省下來，拿來精進自己的表現，這樣才更容易成功。

Secondly, collaboration is a group effort that combines the strengths of many. If any member of the team is lacking in some aspect, the others can cover for them when the problem arises. Lone wolves who would rather demonstrate their superiority over others do not have that luxury. They have to rely on themselves and only themselves. The desire to become better than others can put an unnecessary pressure on themselves and push themselves to unhealthy limits. And since they are not working with others, when they finally break and fall sick or meet other problems that make them unable to continue, there will be no one to finish their job. Working in a team, on the other hand, means that there will always be someone to carry on with the job for you.

Lastly, there's always the problem that, well, competitions can yield really amazing results when both sides are worthy contestants and value each other as respectable enemies. However, such ideal counterparts are not always easy to find. If someone is too weak, they can't be a worthy rival to you because you'd beat them without trying and thus not really improve in the process. If someone is too strong, they would find you an unworthy rival, and that can be frustrating and devastate your self-esteem too. On the other hand, you can collaborate with anyone and everyone; even the weak have something to contribute.

Though most people may have a different choice, I believe that my choice is the best because of the above reasons. Competing is all well and good, but it's impossible to always fight on your own and keep on the winning streak. One day sooner or later you will need to work with someone else, and

再者，合作是團體的事情，綜合了許多人的優勢。如果團隊成員有什麼弱項，在遇到問題時其他人就可以幫上忙。寧願獨身一人，展現自己優越之處的「孤狼」型人就沒有這種好處，他們必須、也只能靠自己。想要勝過別人的慾望可能會帶來不必要的壓力，把自己逼到不健康的極限。而因為他們並未和其他人合作，如果他們終於支撐不下去生病了或遇到其他問題而無法繼續工作，就沒有人幫他們完成工作了。另一方面，如果在團隊中工作，就表示一定會有人替你接手。

最後，還有個問題是，競爭確實可以達成很好的結果，如果雙方都是優秀的競爭者，也把對方視為可敬的敵手的話。然而，如此理想的對手並不容易找到。如果對方太弱了，就不是適合你的對手，因為你根本不用努力就能打敗他們，在整個過程中也不會有什麼進步。如果對方太強了，他們會覺得你不值得當對手，這也會很令人挫折同時重創自尊。另一方面，你和任何人都可以合作，就算是能力很差的人也總有一點貢獻。

雖然許多人可能會有不同的選擇，因為以上的理由，我還是覺得我的選擇是比較好的。競爭是

be pleasantly surprised by what you're able to accomplish with the aid of others.

好事，但總是孤軍奮戰的話，不可能一直保持勝利的。總有一天你必須與他人合作，相信到時候你會驚喜地發現有了其他人的幫助，能夠達成多麼好的成就。

\ 老師告訴你 /

套上顏色的文字都是你在前面就學過的句型喔！論述論點時，可以使用「Firstly、Secondly、Lastly」這樣的句型，讓你的每一個觀點都條理分明。如果覺得用這幾個字太無聊了，也可以試試看「For one example、For another example、The third example is that...」或「My first reason is...、My second reason is...、My last reason is...」等等句型的變化。

美國高中升大學的SAT也無往不利！

你還可以這樣應用：
SAT全真模擬試題14

SAT全真模擬試題14

When is it easier to make friends: now, with lots of new technology? Or in the past?

（中譯：哪個時間比較容易交朋友：科技發達的現在，還是過去？）

It seems to be the common sentiment nowadays that people are too addicted to their various electronic devices to care about forming real relationships. People often advocate that the "new generation" no longer knows how to make friends—I've known several people who said proudly that they've yelled at teenagers who they saw busily typing away on their phones. "Put that damn thing down and start talking to real humans around you," they said. And frankly, the fact that such ignorant people are so abundant in our society is exactly why teenagers would much rather be on their phones! I don't know about you, but personally I think **surfing the Internet** is vastly better than dealing with people like this, **people who wrongly believe that just because teenagers are using electronic devices, it means that they aren't actively making friends.**

The reason that I'd prefer to **say that it's much easier to make friends now than ever** over **claiming that making friends is simpler without electronics** is as follows. The Internet, unlike what

現今大眾似乎普遍認為人們玩電子產品玩上癮了，不再關心在現實中與人交往。人們常說現在的「新世代」不再懂得如何交朋友。我就認識一些人，曾得意地說他們有大罵過一些忙著在手機上打字的青少年。「把那個東西放下來，開始跟你四周的真人說說話好嗎？」他們這麼說。老實說，就是因為現在的社會有這麼多無知的人，青少年才寧可看手機。我是不知道你怎樣啦，但我個人是覺得比起跟這些人打交道，我還寧可上網。這些人錯誤地認為既然青少年在用電子產品，就表示他們沒有主動在交朋友。

我之所以覺得現在比以前更容易交朋友，而不是認為過去沒有電子產品的年代比較容易交朋友，理由如下。和許多人想的不同，網路是個與全世

a lot of people think, is an excellent medium for us to keep in touch with people all around the world. You think a teenager using the phone is "a social recluse who can't make friends"? Well, perhaps she's texting her boyfriend in Canada! You think the young man who keeps staring at his tablet on the subway is "refusing to engage in real life"? Guess what, he may be talking to ten people from different countries all at once. And just because his friends are online, it doesn't mean that they're not real. It's getting increasingly easy for people from around the globe to meet up. Many couples who met online even end up getting married!

For a positive example of the usage of the Internet, let me tell you all about my autistic cousin, Sally. She doesn't have friends in real life because people consider her strange and awkward. She is often depressed over her lack of peeps and had self-harmed many times until she discovered the Internet. She is able to conceal her differences easily online, and has found several like-minded souls who enjoy the same subjects and provide her lots of mental support and courage to face her less-than-bright everyday life. Without the Internet, she claims, she could probably still be completely friendless.

There are lots of people like Sally, much more than you think. Do you still believe that people no longer know how to make friends because of their electronics? These new inventions nowadays don't serve to hinder us from making friends; in fact they are a huge help if you use them the right way.

界的人保持聯絡的良好媒介。你看到一個青少年在使用手機，就認為她是個「不會交朋友的孤僻的人」嗎？可是她說不定正在和她人在加拿大的男朋友傳訊息耶！你在捷運上看到一個一直盯著平板電腦看的年輕人，就覺得他「都不肯好好活在真實世界」嗎？但他現在說不定同時在和十個不同國家的人聊天喔！只因為他的朋友在網路上，不代表他們就不是真人。現在世界各地的人要相遇已經越來越容易了，很多網路上認識的情侶最後還結婚了呢！

我這裡舉一個網路使用的正面例子，和你聊聊我有自閉症的堂妹莎莉的事。莎莉在現實生活中沒有朋友，因為大家都覺得她怪怪的、很笨拙。她常因自己沒有朋友而憂鬱，甚至自殘，直到她發現了網路。在網路上她可以輕易地隱藏自己的不同之處，也找到了許多喜好相近的同好，並給她很多支持與勇氣，讓她可以面對不怎麼開心的日常生活。她說，要是沒有網路，她現在很可能還是完全沒有朋友。

世界上還有很多像莎莉一樣的人，比你想的還要多很多。你現在還覺得人們因為使用電子產品就不會交朋友了嗎？現在的新發明並不會阻撓我們交朋友，事實上如果你用得

To conclude, out of the two choices, **the fact that it's easier to make friends now** will unquestionably be my top pick. I use technological gadgets to keep in touch with my friends every day, both with friends near me and friends on the other side of the globe. My online friends are trustworthy people who have helped me much more than some of the less than likeable people I meet in real life, and I know that they'll always have my back. Obviously, they'll never backstab me when I vent to them about things that happen in my life, because they don't personally know any of the people I'm complaining about and therefore won't be able to spill my secrets to them even if they ever want to! Now, you can't say the same for people who have heaps of mutual friends with you, can you? Some may say that **it's unsafe to make friends online**, but this is a choice that I'll never regret.

好，它們是很有幫助的。

總之，在這兩個選項中，我一定會選擇「現在交朋友更加容易」。我天天都使用電子產品和朋友們保持聯絡，無論是在我附近或遠在地球另一端的朋友。我的網友都是可靠的人，他們給我的幫助比在現實生活中遇到的一些麻煩人物要多得多了，我知道他們永遠會支持我。當然，我跟他們抱怨生活中發生的事時，他們也不會背叛我，因為他們並不認識我在抱怨的那些人，也就不會把我的秘密告訴他們，就算他們想要也辦不到。要是對方是跟你有一堆共同朋友的人，可就不敢這麼篤定了，對不對？有些人會說在網路上交朋友不安全，但這是個我永遠不會後悔的選擇。

讀完了這麼多的範例作文，現在你一定已經躍躍欲試，想套用模板句型自己寫寫看了吧！請你以**Choose one: Meet your Favorite Athlete or Meet your Favorite Singer（二選一：和你最喜歡的運動員見面，或和你最喜歡的歌手見面）**為題，套用模板句型寫一篇作文。所有的句型都在框框中為你列出來囉！

文章開頭參考句型

(1) If given the choice between [1]（名詞片語 或 動詞+ing）and [2]（名詞片語 或 動詞+ing），I would without doubt choose the former/latter.

(2) I would most likely prefer [1]（名詞片語 或 動詞+ing）over [2]（名詞片語 或 動詞+ing）if you ask me.

(3) I don't know about you, but personally I think [1]（名詞片語 或 動詞+ing）is vastly better.

(4) The reason that I'd prefer [1]（名詞片語 或 動詞+ing）over [2]（名詞片語 或 動詞+ing）is as follows.

(5) There are three reasons for my choice. Firstly, [1]（句子）. Secondly, [2]（句子）. Lastly, [3]（句子）.

(6) I wouldn't want to [1]（動詞片語）at all, because [2]（句子）.

(7) I don't think I'd pick [1]（名詞片語 或 動詞+ing），since it's too [2]（形容詞）.

文章收尾參考句型

(1) After choosing [1]（名詞片語 或 動詞+ing），I'd try to [2]（動詞片語）.

(2) Though most people may have a different choice, I believe that my choice is the best because of the above reasons.

(3) The more I think about it, the more I like the idea of [1]（名詞片語 或 動詞+ing）. If only it could come true now!

(4) Though [1]（複數名詞，人物）would say that it's better to [2]（動詞片語）, I really do think my choice is superior!

(5) Even though this is kind of a difficult choice, in the end, my heart will always tell me to pick [1]（名詞片語 或 動詞+ing）.

(6) Some may say that it's [1]（形容詞）, but this is a choice that I'll never regret.

(7) To conclude, out of the two choices, [1]（名詞片語 或 動詞+ing）will unquestionably be my top pick.

分數珍貴，
就讓你一分
都不丟！

一定要注意的
英文作文
常犯錯誤

分數珍貴，就讓你一分都不丟！
一定要注意的
英文作文常犯錯誤

實戰必備

避開21大常犯文法錯誤

在補習班教學這麼多年，也可以稱得上是閱文無數了。在這之中就很容易發現有些錯誤總是一再出現……沒關係！不要怕！這裡就貼心為你歸納出學生英文作文最常犯的21大文法錯誤，上考場前非看不可！寫完作文，如果還有時間，千萬要再檢查幾次，別因為不小心而被扣分了！

寫作技巧 **1.** 搞清楚動詞的被動與主動

錯誤✗ Suddenly, a strong wind was blowed and a big caterpillar was fell into the lunchbox.

正解○ Suddenly, a strong wind blew and a big caterpillar fell into the lunchbox.
突然，強風吹來，一隻巨大的毛毛蟲掉進了餐盒。

錯誤✗ The way it ate was attracted my attention.

正解○ The way it ate attracted my attention.
牠吃東西的方式吸引了我的注意。

錯誤✗ The movie has shown for a while.

正解◯ The movie has been shown for a while.
電影已經被放映一陣子了。

錯誤✗ The villa is belonged to my uncle.

正解◯ The villa belongs to my uncle.
這座別墅屬於我叔叔。

　　使用動詞的時候要仔細想想這個句子的主詞是什麼，到底是誰在做這個動作。例如在第一個例子中，雖然毛毛蟲（caterpillar）掉到便當盒裡基本上也不是自己願意的，但做出「掉進去」這個動作的主詞還是它，所以不應使用被動式。如果這裡是說毛毛蟲被丟進便當盒，那「丟」這個動作就真的不是毛毛蟲自己做的了，這時就要用被動式：A big caterpillar was thrown into the lunchbox.

寫作技巧 2. 除非很確定怎麼用，不然不要濫用倒裝句！

例 It was not until his apartment was filled with smoke that James knew there was a fire.　直到他的套房充滿了煙，詹姆士才知道失火了。

例 No sooner had Mia read the note from Daniel than she burst out crying.
米雅一讀了丹尼爾寫來的字條，就立刻大哭起來。

　　這些都是很漂亮的倒裝句。不過牽一髮動全身，動詞時態和句型的組合都會被影響，沒有完全搞清楚怎麼用的話就不要用，避免被扣分。說「James saw his apartment was filled with smoke, and knew that there was a fire. 詹姆士看到他的套房充滿了煙，就知道失火了」和「Mia read the note from Daniel, and burst out crying immediately. 米雅讀了丹尼爾寫來的字條，就立刻大哭起來」感覺雖然沒那麼帥氣，但減少了一些出錯的機會。

寫作技巧 3.
再檢查一次單複數變化與動詞時態，小錯誤無所遁形！

錯誤✗ doggys and kittys

正解◯ doggies and kitties
小狗和小貓

錯誤✕ He teached me English.

正解○ He taught me English.

他教我英文。

錯誤✕ Writing letter to pen pal is very interesting.

正解○ Writing letters to pen pals is very interesting.

寫信給筆友很有趣。

錯誤✕ Reading English newspaper can enhance your English reading ability.

正解○ Reading English newspapers can enhance your English reading ability.

閱讀英文報紙能夠增進你的英文閱讀能力。

　　複數變化、動詞時態，a跟an等，很容易一不小心就忽略掉了。另外，也要注意不規則的複數和不規則的動詞變化。

・・

寫作技巧 **4.**
盡量不要用but、and和because當一句的開頭或單獨成句

錯誤✕ Whenever I am reminded of this tragic experience, I can't help bursting into tears. Because I realize that my puppy would never come back.

正解○ Whenever I am reminded of this tragic experience, I can't help bursting into tears, because I realize that my puppy would never come back.

每當我想到這次悲慘的經驗，我就忍不住大哭起來，因為我知道我的小狗不會再回來了。

錯誤✕ I am very hungry. But there's no food.

正解○ I am very hungry, but there's no food.

我很餓，但沒有食物了。

錯誤✕ Maria washed the dishes. And Natasha fed the cat.

正解○ Maria washed the dishes, and Natasha fed the cat.

瑪麗亞洗了盤子，而娜塔莎餵了貓。

　　事實上，將but、and、because放在句子的開頭，在許多文學作品中也很容易看到這樣的用法，是一種獨特的語氣與寫作的風格。若你整篇文章的文法無誤，流暢得

宜，則將but、and、because放在句子的開頭，閱卷老師會覺得這是你的寫作風格，不會因此扣分。但若你在其他地方出現了一些文法錯誤，又把but、and、because放在句子開頭，閱卷老師便會覺得這也是文法錯誤的其中之一，因此會給你扣分。所以為了安全起見，除非你對自己的文筆超級有信心，認為不會出現什麼錯誤，否則不要隨便把but、and和because當作句中的第一個字。

寫作技巧 **5.** the next day 和 tomorrow 的差別： 在講「過去的事」的時候，不要用 tomorrow

錯誤✗ When I was a little boy, I brought a puppy home and hid it under my bed. However, my mom found out tomorrow and kicked it out of the house.

正解〇 When I was a little boy, I brought a puppy home and hid it under my bed. However, my mom found out the next day and kicked it out of the house.

我還是個小男孩時，我帶了一隻小狗回家，把牠藏在床下。然而，我媽媽第二天發現了，就把牠踢出家門。

在這段話裡面，雖然狗被踢出家門時的確是狗被撿回家當天的「明天」，但絕對不是你寫下這篇作文當天的「明天」。如果你是在2020年8月1號寫下這篇作文，你作文中的「tomorrow」就會是2020年8月2號，而不是多年前你還在念國小時的某一天。這種時候用the next day或the following day「隔天／第二天」就可以了。

寫作技巧 **6.** 注意相似形容詞的區分： excited / exciting、bored / boring、delightful / delighted、confusing / confused 等

錯誤✗ Thank you for your gift! I'm so delightful!

正解〇 Thank you for your gift! I'm so delighted!

謝謝你的禮物！我好開心！

錯誤✕ This is such a **bored** book.

正解〇 This is such a **boring** book.

這真是一本無聊的書。

前一句子組合：delightful是用來形容一件事情，說這件事情「很令人開心」；而delighted則是形容人的心情，表是這個人「覺得很開心」。這裡講的是這個人的心情（覺得很開心），所以用delighted。I'm so delightful! 雖然文法上無誤，但會變成在說「我真是個令人開心的人！」，這樣稍嫌自我感覺良好，且和收到禮物這件事無關。

後一句子組合：boring用來形容一件事情，說這件事情「令人覺得很無聊」；而bored則是形容人的心情，表示他「覺得很無聊」。這裡是在講這本書令人覺得很無聊，所以用boring。若使用bored，表示這本書有情緒，而且它還覺得很無聊，一般而言應該不會遇到這樣有個性的一本書。

寫作技巧 7. 注意句子的平行結構

錯誤✕ This serious problem came from the technological inventions, such as TV programs, video games and **using computers**.

正解〇 This serious problem came from the technological inventions, such as TV programs, video games and **computers**.

這個嚴重的問題來自於科技發明，如電視節目、電動遊戲與電腦。

錯誤✕ As far as I am concerned, an ideal idol should possess confidence, special talents and **be a humorist**.

正解〇 As far as I am concerned, an ideal idol should possess confidence, special talents and **a sense of humor**.

對我而言，一個理想的偶像應該有自信心、特長與幽默感。

上述的錯誤句不見得文法真的有錯，但同時列舉好幾件事、好幾樣東西的時候，被列舉的每一樣東西、每一件事都統一詞性，會讓文章漂亮許多。

寫作技巧 8. not only A but also B 的句型中，
A和B必須要是相同詞性或結構

錯誤✕ I think that he is similar to Harry Potter. Not only because of his appearance but also his courage.

正解〇 I think that he is similar to Harry Potter because of not only his appearance but also his courage.

I think that he is similar to Harry Potter not only for his appearance but also for his courage.

我覺得他和哈利・波特很類似，不只因為他的外表，也因為他的勇氣。

　　和技巧7的狀況類似，要用常見的「not only A but also B」句型的時候，A與B兩者的詞性或結構必須相同。技巧7的狀況就算詞性不同，也不見得一定是錯的，只是念起來不夠整齊漂亮；但在這裡若詞性結構不同，文法就不對了，要特別小心。

• •

寫作技巧 9. 注意句子的主詞，後面的動詞都要配合它

錯誤✕ Keeping a pet can not only cultivate my sense of responsibility but also accompany me.

正解〇 A pet can not only help me cultivate my sense of responsibility but also accompany me.

寵物不但能培養我的責任感也能陪伴我。

錯誤✕ He always crack a lot of jokes in class.

正解〇 He always cracks a lot of jokes in class.

他總是在上課時開很多玩笑。

錯誤✕ My English teacher not only give me advice but also offer me timely help.

正解〇 My English teacher not only gives me advice but also offers me timely help.

我的英文老師不但提供我建議，也適時給予我幫助。

錯誤✕ The decision of the referees for the soccer match were unjust.

正解〇 The decision of the referees for the soccer match was unjust.
　　　　足球賽裁判的判決不公平。

　　錯誤的例句說「養寵物不但能培養我的責任感，還能陪伴我。」但「養寵物」（keeping a pet）是一件事，它不能陪伴你，陪伴你的是寵物才對。如果改成以「寵物」（a pet）為主詞，就不會有這個問題了。其他例子也是如此，需要讓主詞和動詞維持一致，文法才正確，注意別因為主詞和動詞中間隔得比較遠、插了別的字就因此忘記要保持一致了。

寫作技巧 10. **very 是用來加強形容詞的，不能拿來加強動詞**

錯誤✕ The reason I very admire him is his strong will to win.

正解〇 The reason I admire him very much is his strong will to win.
　　　　我非常欣賞他的理由是他想獲勝的強烈決心。

錯誤✕ Kenny very likes it.

正解〇 Kenny likes it very much.
　　　　肯尼非常喜歡它。

　　中文可以說「很羨慕」、「很喜歡」，但英文則沒辦法，這點要特別注意喔！別和女友說出「I very love you」了！

寫作技巧 11. **注意which、that 搭配逗號「，」的用法**

錯誤✕ When I feel tired, I wash my face which makes me feel better.

正解〇 When I feel tired, I wash my face, which makes me feel better.
　　　　當我累的時候，我會洗臉，讓我感覺好一點。

　　其實這兩句文法上都沒有問題，只是第一句的意思會是「我累的時候，我就洗那讓我感覺比較好的臉」。言下之意就是我還有別的臉，而且洗起來感覺不太好。理論上我是不會有「別的臉」的，所以不會用這一句。第二句的意思就是「我累的時候，我就洗我的臉，感覺會比較好。」這樣就沒有問題了。

在寫這樣的句子時，可以先讀一遍句子，問問自己這個修飾語到底是用來形容什麼的？像上面這個狀況，如果修飾語（makes me feel better「讓我感覺比較好」）是用來形容臉，那就不需要逗號。如果是用來形容洗臉這整件事，那就要加個逗號。

寫作技巧12. **句子的主詞、動詞時態要統一，不要跳來跳去**

只要在寫的時候多留意、多檢查，注意同一句裡面不要有一堆不一樣的時態（前面是過去式，後面又跳回現在式、未來式……）和不一樣的主詞，應該就不會發生這樣的狀況了。

寫作技巧13. **注意斷句（Fragment）的錯誤**

錯誤✗ I was late to school. Because I stayed up late last night.

正解○ I was late to school because I stayed up late last night.
我上課遲到了，因為我昨天晚上熬夜。

錯誤✗ I grew up in Tainan. A small town with beautiful scenery.

正解○ I grew up in Tainan, a small town with beautiful scenery.
我在台南生長，那是個小城市，有著美麗的景色。

即寫出未完成的句子。有些句子雖有主詞及動詞，卻無法獨立成為一個完整的句子。此時，可結合兩個斷句，或是修正原來斷句成為一個完整的子句。

寫作技巧14. **避開連寫句（Run-on Sentence）的錯誤**

錯誤✗ Some students are studying English some are chatting with their classmates.

正解○ Some students are studying English; some are chatting with their classmates.
有些學生在唸英文，有些在和同學聊天。

錯誤✕- The sales are dropping seriously we need to do something about it.

正解〇- The sales are dropping seriously. We need to do something about it.

銷量減少非常多，我們必須做點什麼。

寫作應避免直接連接兩個主要子句，卻未使用任何連接詞。要修正此錯誤，可用句號「.」分開兩個子句，使其成為兩個獨立的主要子句，或用分號「;」來連接兩個子句。但是如果兩個子句太長，則不建議使用分號連結。

寫作技巧 **15.** 逗點謬誤（Comma Splice）

錯誤✕- A home is not just a home, it's more than that.

正解〇- A home is not just a home; it's more than that.

寫作應避免用逗號連接兩個完整的獨立子句。修正此錯誤時，可依照句意，加上對等連接詞、從屬連接詞，或是其他轉折語來連接兩個子句。將逗點改成分號也可以。

寫作技巧 **16.** 中英文的標點不同！

錯誤✕- He said, 「I will come tomorrow。」

正解〇- He said, "I will come tomorrow."

他說：「我明天會來。」

英文的句點是「.」，不是「。」；英文的引號是「" "」，不是「」。要注意喔！接下來的「特別收錄：分數珍貴，就讓你一分都不丟！超容易被扣分的標點符號」篇中，也會非常詳細地跟大家介紹所有的標點符號。

寫作技巧 **17.** 不要直接把中文的諺語照著字面上翻譯成英文

錯誤✗ Three shoemakers are superior to the master strategist, Ju-ger.

正解○ Two heads are better than one.
三個臭皮匠勝過一個諸葛亮。

　　寫英文作文時，要想像讀者是英語母語人士，中文不見得好，對華人文化背景也不見得瞭解。所以，對我們來說耳熟能詳的中文諺語，對老外而言可能根本看不懂意思。像是上面這個「三個臭皮匠勝過一個諸葛亮」，若是直接翻譯了，外國人首先不懂諸葛亮是誰，然後也不曉得為什麼三個臭皮匠會勝過他。因此，如果能夠找到意思類似的英文諺語如Two heads are better than one（兩顆腦比一顆好，意近「三個臭皮匠勝過一個諸葛亮」），就可以改使用這個。

. . . .

寫作技巧 **18.** 不要使用中文式的插入法

　　寫著寫著，忽然發現某個地方漏了一個字，怎麼辦？要像我們寫中文作文時一樣，畫個類似＜的符號插進去嗎？不行喔！要在加插的前後字中間的下方寫出（　　）記號，再把加插的字或片語寫在其上方。

. . . .

寫作技巧 **19.** 檢查單數可數名詞前面是否漏加冠詞

錯誤✗ Teacher has got angry.

正解○ That / My teacher has got angry.
老師生氣了。

錯誤✗ My father is teacher.

正解○ My father is a teacher.
我爸爸是老師。

錯誤✗ Tom is engineer.

正解○ Tom is an engineer. （別忘了an是用在母音開頭的字母前喔）
湯姆是工程師。

在考場作文中，不論主詞或動詞和介系詞的受詞，如果是名詞，就得提高警覺，問自己它是那種名詞？如果是物質和抽象名詞，就不必加冠詞，如果是單數普通名詞，就得加冠詞。若不加保證扣分喔。

寫作技巧20. 仔細檢查，別敗給了小小的拼字錯誤

像是begin寫成bigin、paw寫成pow、giving寫成gaving、embarrassed寫成embrassed、library寫成libery等等，都是常見的拼字錯誤。如果不確定一個單字該怎麼拼，可以試著換一種比較有把握的說法。例如若你想說你這篇作文中的故事發生在二月，但不記得February怎麼拼，那就乾脆把故事的發生月份改到五月，May就好拼多了。

寫作技巧21. 不要使用不確定用法的單字

使用深難單字或許是有加分，但如果硬要用卻用錯，那還不如用簡單的單字把意思表達清楚更好，至少不會被扣分。舉例來說，industrious是「勤勉、努力的」，但長得很像的industrial意思卻是「工業的」。如果誤用此單字寫下：He is an industrial student，句子的意思就會變成「他是個工業的學生」，那可就大錯特錯了！既然這樣，用大家都會的He is a hardworking student（他是個努力的學生）不就簡單又明白嗎？

實戰必備
避開文章開頭與結論常犯錯誤

一篇文章的開頭決定了讀者對整篇文章的印象，而完美的結尾則能讓讀者對此文章留下好感。既然如此，文章的開頭與結論就更不能輕忽，別寫出以下這些句子了，在閱卷老師的心中會扣分的喔！

常犯錯誤 1. 文章開頭拙劣NG句

NG句❶ 自相矛盾：

Although I don't have any pets, I believe no one can live without pets.

雖然我沒有寵物，但我認為沒有人可以沒有寵物。

> **老師告訴你**：別為了滿足用上某一些句型，就硬是寫出了不合邏輯的句子！

✍ **可改為：**

I don't have a pet myself, but if I had one, I would probably treasure it as an important part of my life. 我自己是沒有寵物，但如果我有的話，我一定把牠當作生命中重要的一部分來珍惜。

NG句❷ 連自己都搞不清楚自己的論點是什麼：

Sometimes I think money can buy everything, but sometimes I don't think so. 有時候我覺得錢可以買到一切，但有時候我又不覺得。

> **老師告訴你**：如果要寫出這種模稜兩可的論點，後面要立刻說明自己不確定的理由是什麼。如果後面能夠有條理的說明自己這樣覺得的原因則可以把這裡扣分的印象救回來一點。

✋ 可改為：

I used to think money can buy everything, but lately something happened that made me think otherwise.

我以前認為錢什麼都買得到，但最近發生了一些事，讓我開始有別的想法。

⋯⋯⋯⋯⋯⋯⋯⋯⋯⋯⋯⋯⋯⋯⋯⋯⋯⋯⋯⋯⋯⋯⋯⋯⋯⋯⋯⋯⋯⋯⋯⋯⋯⋯⋯⋯⋯

NG句❸ 毫無意義地向讀者解釋題目單字的意思：

What's the meaning of a house? A house is a building.

房子的意思是什麼呢？房子就是一棟建築。

> **老師告訴你**：解釋題目單字的意思會被視為充字數，老師不會喜歡的。

✋ 可改為：

A house is, to me, not only a building but a safe and cozy place full of love. 房子對我來說，不只是一棟建築，更是個安全、溫馨、充滿愛的地方。

⋯⋯⋯⋯⋯⋯⋯⋯⋯⋯⋯⋯⋯⋯⋯⋯⋯⋯⋯⋯⋯⋯⋯⋯⋯⋯⋯⋯⋯⋯⋯⋯⋯⋯⋯⋯⋯

NG句❹ 對題目提出抗議：

Frankly speaking, I don't keep any pet, so I don't know how to write this composition. 老實說，我沒有寵物，所以我不知道這作文該怎麼寫。

> **老師告訴你**：就算題目出現了不符合你狀況的問題，也不能抗議，畢竟有時候題目也不是閱卷老師出的，向他們抱怨他們也覺得很冤啊。

✋ 可改為：

I don't own a pet, but I have many friends who do. From their interaction with their pets, I observed...

我沒有寵物，但我有很多朋友都有寵物。從他們與寵物的互動中，我觀察到⋯⋯

常犯錯誤 **2.** 文章結論拙劣NG句

NG句❶ 連自己都不知道自己的論點好不好：

Do you think my idea is good? 你覺得我的想法好嗎？

> 老師告訴你：就算對自己的文章沒有自信，也不要説出來。

✋ **可改為：**

Not everyone may have the same opinion, but this is the best choice in my mind. 不見得大家的意見都一樣，但在我心中這是最好的選擇。

● ●

NG句❷ 以老套的方式反問讀者：

My favorite is xxx. How about you?
我最喜歡的是×××。你呢？

> 老師告訴你：反問讀者可以充字數，但同樣的手法太多人用會讓人受不了。

✋ **可改為：**

I don't expect everyone to think in the same way, of course. Perhaps you have some different ideas!
我當然不會預期大家都和我有一樣的想法。説不定你也有不一樣的想法！

● ●

NG句❸ 對自己的論點沒有信心：

To tell the truth, I don't expect everyone to agree with me.
說真的，我不預期大家都會同意我說的話。

> **老師告訴你：**要說這樣的句子的話，後面要有語氣的轉折，說「但……」等句子，表達就算別人不同意，自己也要堅持論點的決心。

✋ **可改為：**

I don't expect everyone to agree with me, but I still believe that this is a choice I will never regret.
我不期待大家都同意我說的話，但我相信這是個我不會後悔的決定。

- -

NG句❹ 指出自己的文章不完整：

I still have many things to say, so tell you next time.
我還有很多其他的事情要說，下次再告訴你吧。

> **老師告訴你：**閱卷老師和你沒有很熟，可能沒有下次了，這樣寫會讓老師覺得一顆心懸在那裡，別這樣讓老師難受啊。

✋ **可改為：**

The above are the most important points concerning this subject in my opinion.
以上這些就是我心目中關於此主題最重要的重點。

特別收錄

2

分數珍貴，
就讓你一分
都不丟！

超容易被扣分的
標點符號

特別收錄 2

分數珍貴，就讓你一分都不丟！
超容易被扣分的
標點符號

雖然標點符號在20分的作文中，只佔兩分的分數，但正因為只有兩分，只要稍微錯一個地方，可能就掉了一分，也就是掉了一半的分數耶！這裡教你怎樣把兩分都拿到手！

一定要知道

使用標點符號有哪些
要注意的地方？

寫作技巧 1. 標點很重要，每句都要有

每句的最後，都一定要有標點符號。

寫作技巧 2. 中英不同要注意

很多英文標點符號用法和中文的不一樣，要注意不要搞混。

寫作技巧 3. 不要把全部的標點都寫得差不多

在寫的時候，一定要把標點符號標清楚。句點、逗點要分清楚，分號、冒號要分清楚，破折號、連字號要分清楚。要很明顯看得出差別，不要腦中想的是一個，寫出來的樣子卻長得像另一個，否則閱卷老師可能會因為眼花看錯而平白無故地扣你分數。

寫作技巧 **4.** 「避頭點」的概念

除了雙引號之外，標點符號不可出現在稿紙每一行最左邊開端的地方。標點符號一定要想辦法塞在每一行的右邊，不然也可以選擇換行。

寫作技巧 **5.** 簡單為上

剛開始練習寫作時，盡量少用破折號、分號、冒號、刪節號等等比較難使用的標點，避免用錯被扣分。

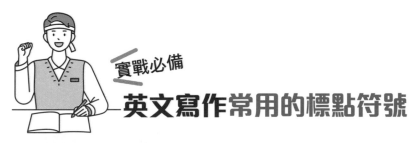

實戰必備

英文寫作常用的標點符號

英文寫作常用的標點符號有十二種。不需要把它們的名字記起來，但一定要認得它們的長相！它們是：

英文名稱	中文名稱	它長這個樣子
Period	句號	.
Comma	逗號	,
Semicolon	分號	;
Colon	冒號	:
Apostrophe	上標點	'
Quotation marks	引號	" "
Hyphen	連字號	-
Dash	破折號	—
Exclamation point 或 Exclamation mark	驚嘆號	!
Question mark	問號	?
Parentheses	括號	( )
Triple dots	刪節號	…

實戰必備

句號「.」的運用

運用技巧 1. 用在直敘句和祈使句的句尾

例 **Necessity is the mother of invention.**（直敘句）
需要為發明之母。

例 **Put on your coat before going out.**（祈使句）
出門前要穿上你的外套。

運用技巧 2. 較長而複雜的句子，最後收尾時當然也要用

例 **I forgot to wash the dishes yesterday, but it was all right because someone else washed them for me.**
我昨天忘記洗盤子，但沒關係，因為有別人幫我洗了。

例 **I wish you would just tell me what it is that's making you so mad, because I won't be happy until I get an answer.**
我希望你可以跟我講到底是什麼讓你那麼生氣，因為我得不到答案的話絕不會高興的。

運用技巧 3. 用來標示單字或片語的縮寫

例 Monday→Mon.（星期一）　　　　January→Jan.（一月）

　　Before Christ→B.C.（西元前）　　Anno Domini→A.D.（西元年）

　　Street→St.（街）　　　　　　　Doctor→Dr.（醫生）

實戰必備

逗點「,」的運用

運用技巧 **1.** 用來隔離由and、but、or、so、for、nor等連接的兩個獨立子句

例 **He is always absent-minded, but never fails to pass exams.**
他總是心不在焉,但從沒考試不及格過。

例 **I really wanted to go surfing, but my mother insisted that I stay at home.**
我真的很想去衝浪,可是我媽媽堅持要我待在家裡。

運用技巧 **2.**
在句中插入獨立的分詞片語時,句子前後要加逗點

例 **He is, so to speak, a walking dictionary.** 他可以說是本活字典。

例 **She is, of course, richer than I am.** 她當然比我有錢。

運用技巧 **3.** 獨立分詞片語放在句首時,則在片語後加逗點

例 **To be honest, I don't think you should try this.**
老實說,我不認為你應該試這個。

例 **Judging from his face, he is probably around fourteen years old.**
從他的臉來看,他大概十四歲左右。

運用技巧 4. 句子中的同位語前後要加逗點，若是在句尾的同位語則在前面加逗點就好

> 例 **Mr. Fan, a friend of mine, came to visit me last night.**
> 范先生，我的一位朋友，昨天晚上來拜訪我。

> 例 **The latest album of Jay, a pop singer in Taiwan, has been released recently.** 台灣流行歌手Jay的最新專輯最近上市。

運用技巧 5.
在句首直接稱呼人或打招呼時，後面通常使用逗點

> 例 **Boys, cheer up!** 男孩們，開心起來！
> 例 **Hey, I'm over here!** 嘿，我在這裡！

運用技巧 6. 附加問句前加逗點，以和主要子句隔開

> 例 **Let's go swimming, shall we?** 我們去游泳吧，好不好？
> 例 **You love me, don't you?** 你愛我，對不對？

運用技巧 7.
在疑問句中要對方做出選擇，在提供選項前使用逗點

> 例 **Which do you prefer, tennis or badminton?**
> 你喜歡哪種，網球還是羽球？
> 例 **When should we leave, today or tomorrow?**
> 我們該哪天走，今天還明天？

運用技巧 **8.** 口語或感嘆語後使用逗點

例 **Well, I guess you're right.** 嗯，我想你是對的啦。

例 **Oops, I'm lost again.** 糟糕，我又迷路了。

運用技巧 **9.** 書信中，稱呼語或結尾語後使用逗點

例 **Sincerely, James** 詹姆士敬上

例 **Yours, Amy** 愛咪敬上

運用技巧 **10.** 一系列等級相同的字或子句可用逗點分開

例 **We sang, danced and chatted all night.**
我們整晚唱歌、跳舞、聊天。

例 **We have to postpone the meeting because John is sick, Jane's flight is delayed and Judy has mysteriously disappeared.** 我們必須延後開會，因為約翰病了，珍妮的飛機誤點，茱蒂又莫名其妙地消失了。

運用技巧 **11.** 以逗點由小而大分隔地方和時間

例 **I live at No. 155, 3rd Sec, Roosevelt Rd., Taipei, Taiwan.**
我住在台灣台北市羅斯福路3段155號。

例 **I was born on February 26th, 1980.**
我在1980年2月26日出生。

分號「；」的運用

運用技巧 1. 分號常用於隔開兩個相關的主要子句，或是放在轉折語之間來連結兩個主要子句（若是三個以上，那就要用逗點而不用分號）。它可以代替and、or、but、because這樣的連接詞

例 He is very diligent; she is very lazy. = He is very diligent but she is very lazy. 他很認真（但）她很懶。

例 I regretted having dinner at that restaurant; the food there was awful.
= I regretted having dinner at that restaurant because the food there was awful. 我真後悔去那間餐廳吃飯（因為）那裡的菜真難吃。

運用技巧 2. 兩個獨立子句若用下列的連接副詞來連接：besides（此外）、consequently（因此）、nevertheless（然而）、otherwise（否則）、still（仍然）、then（那麼）、therefore（因此）、thus（因此），那就在這些連接副詞前用分號，後面用逗點

例 He did not pass the examination; therefore, he was unhappy.
他考試沒過；所以心情不好。

例 She worked and worked from morning till night; consequently, she fell sick. 她從早到晚工作又工作；因此，她病倒了。

例 I really want to go with you; however, I have to finish my assignment.
我真的很想跟你去；可是我必須完成我的作業。

例 We plan to take a trip to Germany; however, it's canceled because of the bad weather. 我們計劃到德國旅遊；可是因為天候不佳而取消了。

實戰必備
冒號「：」的運用

運用技巧 1. 在舉例或是表明理由時，可以用冒號來表達「就是……」的意思

例 **The students who join the competition share the same goal: they want to win the championship.** 參加競賽的同學都有一個相同的目標：贏得冠軍。

例 **The squad consists of five people: James, Mia, Sean, Jasmine, and Max.** 這個小隊共有五個人：詹姆、米雅、尚、潔絲敏和麥斯。

運用技巧 2.

用於信箋開頭的客套語，會比使用逗點更莊重正式

例 **Dear Sir:** 親愛的先生：

例 **Dear Professor:** 親愛的教授：

運用技巧 3. 用來分隔「時」與「分」

例 **3:45 P.M.** 下午三點四十五分

例 **2:00 A.M.** 凌晨兩點整

省略符號「'」的運用

運用技巧 1. 表示字母的省略

例 **I won't be home tomorrow. = I will not be home tomorrow.**
我明天不會在家。

例 **You shouldn't kick your dog. = You should not kick your dog.**
你不應該踢你的狗。

運用技巧 2. 表示數字的省略

例 **Thursday, June 1ˢᵗ, '89. = Thursday, June 1ˢᵗ, 1989.**
1989年6月1日星期四。

例 **I was born in the '90s. = I was born in the 1990s.**
我在90年代出生的。

運用技巧 3. 平時替名詞加複數時，不需要加省略符號，而直接加s就好，但表示字母、單字、數字的複數時就要

例 **There are five s's in "sleeplessness."**
在sleeplessness（睡不著的狀態）這個字裡面有五個s。

例 **Our teacher told us not to use so many so's.**
我們的老師告訴我們不要用那麼多次「so」這個字。

例 **Her 7's and 9's look alike.** 她的7和9寫得都好像。

運用技巧 4. 用來當名詞的所有格使用。如果名詞的字尾不是[s]或[z]，就用's來表示所有格。如果是[s]或[z]，那就直接加上'。要注意的是，如果前面的名詞是專有名詞（人名等），而且還是單音節，那就要加's

例 **my mother's earrings** 我母親的耳環

例 **my friends' opinions** 我朋友們的意見

例 **Chris's house** 克里斯他家

運用技巧 5. 職業或人物等後面，可使用's，再把其後面的名詞省略，以表示場所、地點

例 **I'm going to the dentist's today. = I'm going to the dentist's office today.**
我今天要去牙醫診所。

例 **I think my dad is probably at my uncle's. = I think my dad is probably at my uncle's house.** 我想我爸大概在我叔叔家。

實戰必備

引號「" "」的運用

運用技巧 1. 用在引用句的前後

例 **"I don't like her," she explained, "because she is far too proud."**
「我不喜歡她，」她解釋，「因為她實在太驕傲了。」

例 **My teacher always says, "Where there is a will, there is a way."**
老師總是說：「有志者，事竟成。」

運用技巧 2. 如果引用句本身是敘述句，但整個句子是問句，那就必須先用引號，再用問號。如果引用句本身是問句，則必須先用問號，再用引號

例 Did he say, "I am going to college next year"?
他有說「我明年要去上大學」嗎？

例 Did he say, "Are you going to college next year?"
他有沒有說「你明年要去上大學嗎？」

- -

運用技巧 3. 引用句中另有引用句時，用單引號表示。但要注意：美式英文中，雙引號在外，單引號在內，英式英文中則恰好相反。

例 She said, "I quite agree to the saying 'To love and to be loved is the greatest happiness on earth'." 她說：「我很同意『愛與被愛是世界上最快樂的事』的說法。」（此例為美式英文）

例 I thought, "Wow, did he really say 'I'm the most handsome guy ever'?"
我心想：「哇，他真的說了『我是有史以來最帥的男子』這種話嗎？」（此例為美式英文）

實戰必備

連字符號「－」的運用

運用技巧 1.
分數用英文表示的時候，分子與分母之間要用連字符號。

例 one-fourth 四分之一　　例 five-ninths 九分之五

- -

運用技巧 2. 21到99之間的數字用英文表示時，十位數與個位數之間要用連字符號

例 **twenty-one** 二十一　　例 **ninety-eight** 九十八

運用技巧 3. 名詞與字首字合用時，使用連字符號

例 **Anti-American** 反美的　　例 **non-drinker** 不飲酒的人

運用技巧 4.

用兩個或以上單字複合而成的單字，也可以使用連字符號

例 **passer-by** 行人　　　　例 **a heart-to-heart talk** 一場交心的談話
例 **father-in-law** 岳父　　　例 **a strong-willed fighter** 一名意志堅強的鬥士

實戰必備

破折號「──」的運用

運用技巧 1.

用來表示一句話說到一半，主題突然轉變，或整句中斷

例 **I believe that we should try to──oh wait, where did he go?**
我覺得我們應該試著──喔，等一下，他去哪了？

例 **I thought we would be fine, but──** 我以為我們不會有事，可是……

運用技巧 2. 兩個破折號互相配合，可以代替圓括弧使用，特別是一次要舉很多個例子的時候

例 **Your friends—Emma, Karen and Lisa—all told me to say hi.**
你的朋友艾瑪、凱倫和莉莎都要我跟你打個招呼。

例 **These presents——the book, the doll, and the puppy—are all from your aunt.** 這些禮物，書、娃娃和小狗，都是你阿姨給的。

運用技巧 3. 可以代替逗點來介紹特別重要，需要強調的事物

例 **This book will teach you one important thing—how to speak in public.**
這本書將教你一件重要的事——如何在公開場合說話。

例 **She has only one interest—food.** 她只對一件事有興趣—食物。

實戰必備

驚嘆號「！」的運用

運用技巧 1. 在感嘆句的結尾使用

例 **What a beautiful lady she is!** 她是位多美麗的女士啊！

例 **What a wonderful experience!** 多棒的經驗啊！

運用技巧 2. 表達命令語氣時也可以使用

例 **Go home now!** 現在就回家！　　例 **Finish your dinner!** 把你的晚餐吃完！

實戰必備
問號「？」的運用

運用技巧 **1.** 用在直接問句之後

例 **Do you find English difficult?** 你覺得英文難嗎？

例 **Would you please do me a favor?** 你可以幫我一個忙嗎？

運用技巧 **2.** 用在附加問句之後

例 **You don't have a pet, do you?** 你沒有寵物，對嗎？

例 **I can't turn back now, can I?** 我不能回頭了，對吧？

運用技巧 **3.** 用在選擇疑問句之後

例 **Which do you like better, coffee or tea?** 你喜歡哪個，咖啡還是茶？

例 **What do you want for dinner, noodles or rice?**
你晚餐要吃什麼，飯還是麵？

括號「( )」的運用

運用技巧 1. 括號可以用來在句中補充一些其他的資訊。一般而言，如果是拿掉以後對句子的文法不會有任何影響的東西，都可以放在括號裡面

例 **For the last five years (some say longer), the house on the hill has been haunted.** 最近這五年（有人說還要更久），這間山丘上的房子一直在鬧鬼。

例 **We read *Hansel and Gretel* (one of my favorite stories) this semester in class.** 我們這學期在課堂上讀了《糖果屋》（我最喜歡的故事之一）。

運用技巧 2. 在搞不清楚你想要講的名詞確切的數量到底是多少時，可以用括號把複數的s括起來

例 **If anyone has any information about the person(s) who committed this crime, please call the police.**
如果有人知道關於犯了這個罪行的人（們）的資訊，請打電話到警察局。

例 **In the following section of the exam, circle the grammatical error(s) in each of the sentences.**
在這個測驗接下來的部分，把每個句子內的文法錯誤（們）圈起來。

實戰必備

刪節號「...」的運用

運用技巧 1. 用以表示引用句中省略的文字。如刪節號用在句尾，另加原句句尾的標點符號

🔹 Stephen King once said, "Fiction writers... don't understand very much about what they do".

史蒂芬・金曾說：「小説家……不太懂他們到底在做什麼。」

（這裡就表示史蒂芬・金講的這句話，在fiction writers和don't understand之間還有一些別的字，但引用的人可能覺得太長或是不適用，就把那些字拿掉，用刪節號代替。）

運用技巧 2. 刪節號也可以拿來表示講話時語氣中的停頓、或是被打斷的地方

🔹 "Well, I... uh... don't know," she said.
「嗯，我……呃……不知道。」她説。

🔹 "I think we should..." she said, but didn't get to finish because she saw a giant spider and ran out screaming.
「我覺得我們應該……」她説，但她沒説完，因為她看到一隻巨大的蜘蛛，就尖叫著跑出去了。

🔹 "If you insist, then okay..." he mutters as he walks away.
「如果你堅持的話，那好吧……」他喃喃唸著走掉了。

🔹 "Sorry if I'm bothering you, but I noticed that..." Sonia began.
"Shut up and leave," Jenna barked.
「我打擾了妳的話很不好意思，可是我注意到……」索妮雅開始説。
「閉嘴，走開啦。」珍娜大罵。

🔹 "I really want to go home..." she whispered as she shed tears.
「我好想回家……」她邊哭邊説。

NOTE

....
....
....
....
....
....
....
....
....
....
....
....
....
....
....

原來如此 系列 *E271*

英文作文，抄這本就夠了：
實用句型＋學測例題＋豐富範文，
輕鬆擺平英文寫作

跟著英文名師學習套用實用句型，大考英文作文手到擒來！

作　　者	李宇凡
顧　　問	曾文旭
社　　長	王毓芳
編輯統籌	耿文國、黃璽宇
主　　編	吳靜宜
執行主編	楊雲慶
執行編輯	詹雲翔
美術編輯	王桂芳、陳竹姈
法律顧問	北辰著作權事務所　蕭雄淋律師、幸秋妙律師

初　　版	2024年03月
	2024年初版2刷
出　　版	捷徑文化出版事業有限公司
電　　話	（02）2752-5618
傳　　真	（02）2752-5619

定　　價	新台幣380元／港幣127元
產品內容	一書

總 經 銷	采舍國際有限公司
地　　址	235新北市中和區中山路二段366巷10號3樓
電　　話	（02）8245-8786
傳　　真	（02）8245-8718

港澳地區經銷商	和平圖書有限公司
地　　址	香港柴灣嘉業街12號百樂門大廈17樓
電　　話	（852）2804-6687
傳　　真	（852）2804-6409

▶書中圖片由Freepik網站提供

捷徑 **Book**站

國家圖書館出版品預行編目資料

英文作文，抄這本就夠了：實用句型＋學測例題＋
豐富範文，輕鬆擺平英文寫作 / 李宇凡著. -- 初版.
-- 臺北市：捷徑文化出版事業有限公司, 2024.03
　面；　公分. --（原來如此：E271）

ISBN 978-626-7116-48-7(平裝)

1.CST: 英語教學　2.CST: 作文　3.CST: 中等教育

524.38　　　　　　　　　　　　　113001159

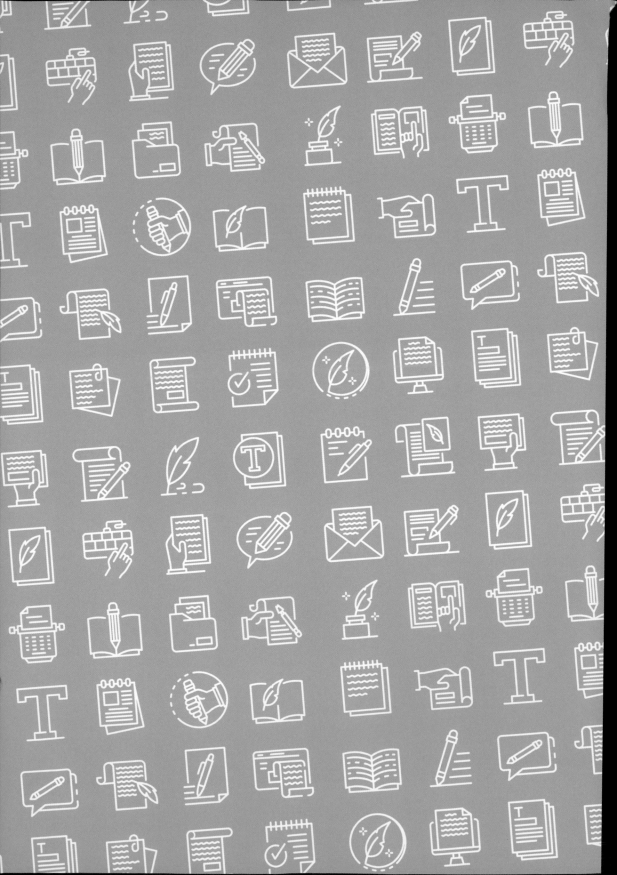